C000118984

Love as human virtue and human need and its role in the lives of long-term prisoners

A multidisciplinary exploration

by
Christina Valeska Straub

Critical Perspectives on Social Science

VERNON PRESS

Copyright © 2021 Vernon Press, an imprint of Vernon Art and Science Inc, on behalf of the author.

All rights reserved. No part of this publication may be reproduced, stored in a retrieval system, or transmitted in any form or by any means, electronic, mechanical, photocopying, recording, or otherwise, without the prior permission of the copyright holder and Vernon Art and Science Inc.

www.vernonpress.com

In the Americas:	*In the rest of the world:*
Vernon Press	Vernon Press
1000 N West Street,	C/Sancti Espiritu 17,
Suite 1200, Wilmington,	Malaga, 29006
Delaware 19801	Spain
United States	

Critical Perspectives on Social Science

Library of Congress Control Number: 2020949857

ISBN: 978-1-62273-966-0

Product and company names mentioned in this work are the trademarks of their respective owners. While every care has been taken in preparing this work, neither the authors nor Vernon Art and Science Inc. may be held responsible for any loss or damage caused or alleged to be caused directly or indirectly by the information contained in it.

Every effort has been made to trace all copyright holders, but if any have been inadvertently overlooked the publisher will be pleased to include any necessary credits in any subsequent reprint or edition.

Cover design by Vernon Press.

Cover image by the author.

What do the undeserving deserve?

(Robert Johnson & Hans Toch — *The Pains of Imprisonment,* 1982)

Table of Contents

List of Figures and Tables

Figures

Tables

Acknowledgments

This exploration would have not been possible without the steadfast, wise and level-headed support of my supervisors Emma Wincup and Adam Crawford at the School of Law, University of Leeds. Their invaluable knowledge and expertise have guided me as a moral compass through stormy seas and deep waters. Without the generous funding of the Economic and Social Research Council (ESRC), this ship of enquiry would have never even left the harbour, and I am deeply grateful for this opportunity and the trust my sponsors have invested in me.

Two of my indispensable light-buoys were Helen Arnold and Alison Liebling. They have illuminated my path into the unknown territories of prison research. It has changed my life forever. I also want to thank Deborah Drake (Open University) for sharing her knowledge and critical thinking, and for being my fellow traveller.

Lucky is the adventurer who has a safe haven to return to after being battered by the storms of doubt and uncertainty. I have been very lucky indeed to have been surrounded and supported by my loving parents, as well as a circle of friends who never lost faith in me, no matter how far-fetched my ideas.

I would also like to thank Barbecue Coffee Shop and Tea Hive in Chorlton, Manchester for keeping me caffeinated, hydrated, and (relatively) sane. Shouts go out to Will Smith whose unconventional YouTube-leadership has enlightened me to the fact that self-love is self-discipline.

Abstract

As a contribution to the literature on the effects and pains of imprisonment, this book examines one influencing variable in the lives of prisoners serving long sentences in an English low-security prison: the absence and presence of love. Based on empirical findings, it seeks to provide a deeper insight into the meaning and role of love in the social-ecology (i.e. relationships between people and their environment) of human existence, human development and well-being. A multidisciplinary analysis of psychological, moral philosophical, neuroscientific and sociological literature helps to shine a light on love as an elusive concept that seems impossible to ever fully grasp.

This book follows love's lead through the past and present lives of 16 long-term prisoners. In semi-structured interviews, they provide a vivid insight into the pains and effects of love deprivation in early experiences of violence, abuse and trauma as well as in their current prison environment. At the same time, the presence of love features as motivational power and resilience factor for getting them through their long sentences and for investing in positive identities. Viewing their narratives through a multidisciplinary lens brings love's significance as a twofold concept of human need and human virtue into focus. It plays a major role in matters of deprivation and nurturance, dysfunction and resilience, sickness and health throughout the human life course.

Given love's essential importance in human existence, this book would like to inspire the reader to critically consider what is at stake if we leave love out of consideration in our dealings with human beings in state institutions such as prison? What could be gained if these environments – predominantly devoid of love – included this human need and human virtue into its set-up and purpose?

1. "There's no love in the concrete" — Introduction

The inspiration for this book first found me more than 10 years ago, in a high-security prison in a rural area of England. As a total prison research novice, I was finding (or rather meandering) my way through a puzzling environment. As part of a team, I was looking into dynamics of staff-prisoner relationships together with Alison Liebling and Helen Arnold (Liebling et al. 2011). Writing up our findings, I found myself working on chapters like "Identity Change and Self-Improvement" or "Sources of Hope, Recognition and Humanity" in prison (Liebling et al. 2011) which were and are close to my heart until this day.

As a "naïve" outsider, it struck me how little topics like love and emotions seemed to be part of the conversation in and about the prison environment, the prison experience and the purpose of prison. On the contrary, talking about love had developed into a no-go-area in this high-security environment. Its denial amplified the awareness of its absence even more. The longing for fulfilment of this basic human need ran like an undercurrent through various prisoner (and some staff) interviews, while it was mostly missing in the public and political discourse about prison at the time. Stating there was "no love in the concrete" and that "even the walls despise you" one prisoner referred to the perceived structural and symbolical qualities of this high-security prison as a loveless place (Liebling et al. 2011). Although one might not find it particularly surprising that love seems to have disappeared from an environment primarily designed around punishment, I could not help but ask myself: Why? If love plays a major role in human existence, why is its absence so readily accepted in this context?

This first experience in the field of prison research sparked a burning interest to further examine the background and implications of the (perceived) absence of love in the prison environment. Was there *really* no love in the concrete? This interest expanded into researching the effects of imprisonment, but soon enough, I had to realise that I did not know enough. I was looking at a complex web of meanings, (popular) opinions, cultural and moral values, political and economic constraints, as well as at practical institutional struggles on the daily "front-line" of offender management. I did not know enough about these issues and their interrelations. Their exploration became one of the main aims of an evolving research proposal which developed into an ESRC-funded PhD in Criminology/Sociology at the School of Law (University of Leeds, UK). My research journey and my findings form the basis of the pages to follow.

I will be asking "inconvenient" questions, such as "Who deserves love?" – "Do prisoners deserve love?" – "Under which circumstances and for which reasons is it deemed acceptable to exclude prisoners from the human experience of love?" Ultimately, these are questions of moral concern. They impact my work as a researcher. I want to be as transparent as possible and therefore lay out my normative and moral stance right from the beginning. For want of better or clearer words - which I have not been able to find - I would like to use those of Norwegian criminologist and sociologist Christie. Calling for *Limits to Pain* (1981) of imprisonment he decided to take a distinct moral stance:

> Let it ... be completely clear that I am also a moralist ... One of my basic premises will be that it is right to strive for a reduction of man-inflicted pain on earth. I can very well see objections to this position. Pain makes people grow. They become more mature ... receive deeper insights ... But we have also experienced the opposite: Pain which brings growth to a stop, pain which retards, pain which makes people evil. (Christie 1981: 3)

Above normative orientation and motivation towards critically (re-)considering limits to the pains of imprisonment have left their mark throughout this book. They played a crucial role in my decisions on what I wanted to look at, how and with what motivations and aims.

In this book, I want to revisit the pains and effects of imprisonment, this time with special regards to the absence and presence of love as the deprivation and provision of a basic human need. I postulate that love matters in the lives of long-term prisoners (why these have become the focus of this study will be discussed at a later point) because it matters as a human need. According to Maslow's classic hierarchy of needs theory it matters, in fact, greatly. Human behaviour and well-being are influenced by (if not dependent on) the satisfaction of certain basic needs. They "stand in a special psychological and biological status" (Maslow 1987: 53). The belongingness and love needs occupy a relatively high rank, emerging after the physiological and safety needs have been gratified. Those basic human needs "must be satisfied or else we get sick" (Maslow 1987: 53) mentally and physically.

On the other hand, love as the very factor that can induce mental and physical struggle when missing, also seems to be the most effective antidote to these effects. As much as the absence of love can induce distress, its presence seems to exert positive and strengthening effects. This book will therefore also consider the effects that the opposite of love deprivation, i.e. the presence (or provision) of love can have on human life. The exploration of love as human virtue (Peterson and Seligman 2004) and its role in fostering resilience and well-being in individuals will form a substantial part of this research journey.

Just as love reaches beyond prison walls, so do prisoners occupy more than the temporal space of prison during the course of their lives. It will therefore also be a purpose of this book to follow love's traces throughout the human life span, examining the role it plays neurologically, psychologically, socially and morally at different times and in different social-ecological spheres of human existence (which will be encountered in greater detail in Chapter 3). Ultimately this approach leads us to the underlying critical question: Does love matter (or indeed *should* it matter) in the set-up of the (long-term) prison experience? This question is posed from the vantage point of critical theory, which shall be used here and throughout this book in its non-capitalised spelling, thus to be regarded as different from *Critical Theory.* The latter specifically refers to a theoretical approach within the Frankfurt School. As a novel orientation toward social sciences, *Critical Theory* claimed that social inquiry ought to combine the disciplines of philosophy and social sciences in order to be practical in a moral sense (Bohman 2005). Approaches with similar practical aims which do not strictly follow the Frankfurt School, are commonly referred to as *critical theory* (Bohman 2005).

The critical theory approach, which will be applied here, uses empirical data as basis for a moral and philosophical questioning of current conditions of long-term imprisonment and penal practices. This will be done with a view to exploring alternative approaches to the current set-up of the prison environment. Ideally, it will deliver suggestions for policy considerations in line with critical theory's practical purpose to act as a "liberating … influence … to create a world which satisfies the needs and powers of human beings" (Horkheimer 1972: 246). The superordinate scope of this book lies in providing a theoretical resource not only for academic purposes as a contribution to prison research but also one that can be used to inform practical and policy decisions about the set-up and purpose of prison. Although Bloor points out rather discouragingly that "policy influence for social researchers is quite possibly a chimera" (Bloor 2011: 309), this book would like to make its findings accessible and useful for academics and practitioners alike. As a qualitative exploration, it follows a meandering path between multidisciplinary, academic theory and its empirical manifestation whilst keeping its main focus – *love* – firmly in view.

Accordingly, Chapter 2 sets out to prepare the theoretical ground for the empirical explorer, revisiting classic and contemporary UK (and some US) prison research, tracing the absence and presence of love within it.

Chapter 3 represents the second theoretical pillar on which this book's empirical research and analysis rests. It illustrates how the abstract concept of love has been operationalised into thematic building blocks guiding empirical enquiry by deploying two theoretical approaches. Walker and Avant's (1994) concept analysis and Bronfenbrenner's (1974) social-ecological theory of human development were combined into a multidisciplinary literature review, discussing findings on love in neuroscience, psychology, sociology and moral philosophy.

Chapter 4 reflects on methods and conditions under which empirical data underlying this book's analysis has been collected. It paints a picture of fieldwork difficulties which have become representative not only of a deteriorating prison estate but also of the increasingly precarious and difficult work of a prison researcher in England.

After preparing the theoretical ground in the first three chapters of this book, four extensive chapters are dedicated to presenting and analysing empirical data with regards to the absence and presence of love in long-term prisoners' past and present lives.

Chapter 5 introduces participants' perceptions, feelings and associations connected to the concept of love. Talking about past and present experiences with the absence and presence of love, their narratives revolve around the "light" and the "dark" side of love as a dual concept.

Chapter 6 and 7 explore the effects of the absence and presence of love in prisoners' current outside and inside connections. It enquires into reasons for maintaining certain relationships and cutting off others whilst also considering what the prison is or is not doing to provide opportunities for love.

Chapter 8 shifts the focus from interpersonal engagement towards a broader perspective of the effects that prison as an emotionally structured social environment exudes on its population. The topic of emotion management guides the analytical discussion before considering its gendered elements. It leaves the reader with the suggestion for critical consideration of an alternative culture and set-up of the prison's emotional environment: What could it look like and what could be gained, if the benchmarks of love were included in a potential reformulation?

Chapter 9 recapitulates this book's main empirical and theoretical findings. It aims to integrate those with a consideration of love in broader social-ecological terms, ultimately arguing for alternative outlooks on the role of prison as state institution. In doing so, it revisits critical theory and feminist approaches regarding love as a necessary element for humane institutions and societies. Taking these approaches further, the concluding discussion of this book suggests nothing less than a paradigm shift, resulting in recommendations for penal policy- and prison-design that bring love (back) into the picture.

Before we can fully embark on our exploration of the life-worlds of long-term prisoners, it is important to take a step back, however: to remember what it means to be incarcerated and why a close examination of the effects of long-term imprisonment (still) matters.

2. Affective dimensions of prison effects research

An extensive body of international prison research literature has been collated over decades, providing insights into the fundamental characteristics of the prison experience. This specific field of interest developed out of a broader orientation of research on prisons and their role in the criminal justice system. In its beginnings, prison research predominantly focused on the sociology of prison life, encompassing "the systematic study of prisoner societies, of prison staff culture and/or of prisons-as-organisations" (Drake et al. 2015: 925). Some of its earliest contributions were made by sociological scholars from the United States, such as Clemmer on the effects of a dominating prison environment as an atomised world (Clemmer 1940) or Jacobs' (1977) socio-historical study of a US maximum-security prison and its interdependence with social and political developments and mechanisms of mass society.

Works such as Sykes' (1958) study of a US maximum-security prison, Goffman's (1961) participant-observation study of a mental institution, or Cohen and Taylor's (1972) research into psychological survival of long-term imprisonment in the UK have by now become "staple items" of the criminological prison research canon. Although they focussed primarily on the adaptational effects of a total institution onto those subjected to it, critical attention was also paid to formal and informal power-relations and trade-offs between institutional staff and prisoners that enable an undisturbed running of the prison establishment. Subsequent and contemporary studies of prison life have developed over time into a body of work examining the prison world through a diversity of concepts, such as "space, place, architecture, gender, ethnicity, law, political economy and national and global governance" (Drake et al. 2015: 925), deploying qualitative, quantitative as well as mixed-method research approaches.

According to King and Liebling (2008: 432) "it was in the UK that the strongest tradition of academic prison research has developed." Since this book is based on a study centred around prisoners' experiences within the English penal system, the remainder of this review will thus mainly consider literary contributions by prison researchers based in the English jurisdiction.[1] It is fair to say that my research trajectory was and is heavily inspired by prison research conducted at the Prisons Research Centre at the Institute of Criminology (University of Cambridge). As a founding member (in 2000) and present director, Alison Liebling has contributed to the establishment of a diverse research community there. Her and her team conducted extensive qualitative (for example on prisoner suicide (1992), self-harm and safer custody (Liebling et al. 2005), staff-prisoner relationships (Liebling et al. 2011), the moral performance of prisons (Liebling and Arnold 2004)) as well as large scale quantitative survey research (e.g. Measuring the Quality of Prison Life (MQPL) in UK prisons).

This work has been and is continuously expanded by English scholars such as Crewe on the social structures of *The Prisoner Society* (2009 inter alia); Jewkes on carceral geography and architecture (2018 inter alia); Arnold (2005) on prison officer work; Crawley (2004) on the emotional performance of prison officers; Drake (2012) on the effects of high-security imprisonment; Scott (2015) contributing an abolitionist perspective on prison; Meek exploring physical and mental health issues of prisoners and young offenders (e.g. Meek 2008); or Sparks critically examining the *Politics of Imprisonment* (2007). The list is extensive and continuously expanding. Scholarly work mentioned here can only be regarded as a first insight into the diverse and ever-evolving field of prison research in the UK (and more specifically English) jurisdiction. It is above work - its continuous examination and critical challenge of how the prison environment affects those under its influence - that has mainly influenced my research interest in the effects of imprisonment.

Insights into prison life delivered by academic scholars are complimented by a wide range of practice-oriented research and reports by organisations such as the Prison Reform Trust and its annually published Bromley Briefings Prison Factfiles. These keep a close eye on social and political developments within the criminal justice system. They critically examine how different factors such as sentencing numbers or prison staffing and resource levels interrelate with certain "prison climate" indicators such as suicide and self-harm cases or intra-prisoner and prisoner-staff violence. Additionally, the Howard League of Penal Reform sustains their engagement with largely underexplored issues such as sexual experiences in prison (e.g. 2016) or the concept of justice and its role and implementation in the prison environment (2020).

---

[1] Contributing to the second edition of *Doing Research on Crime and Justice* (King and Wincup 2008), King and Liebling produced a chapter on "Doing Research in Prisons" (2008) that offers an extensive list of past and contemporary UK prison research covering a vast area of academic enquiry. At this point, the interested reader shall be pointed towards this source for further reference.

While most of the prison research literature reviewed so far is conducted by "outsiders" - i.e. external academic researchers and organisations – the number of "insider" research, carried out by those formerly or at present associated directly with the prison system is growing. Examples include ex-prison staff (e.g. Bennett et al. 2008; Bennett 2015) and ex-prisoners (e.g. Earle 2014). The development of "convict criminology" takes Cohen and Taylor's approach in their seminal work on *Psychological Survival* (1972) one step further. At the time it represented one of the first studies to take prisoner accounts of their lived prison experience as a starting point to critically explore the long-term prison experience. It deployed a new and unconventional – regarded by some critics as controversial – approach of not only taking prisoners' oral and written testimonies at face value but also to involve them actively as reviewers of their analytical work. However, the ultimate authority to compile and publish findings remained in the hand of academic researchers with no "first-hand experience" of prison life.

This changed significantly with the emergence of research conducted by former prisoners. It "draws on direct experience of penal confinement," exploring, for example, "whether, and how, 'spending time' is different from 'serving time'" (Earle 2014: 429). Although ethnographic prison research aims at creating an in-depth and "truthful" account of the prison experience, it has been acknowledged by scholars such as Stevens (2012) that it remains "impossible for any 'free-world' researcher to become completely immersed in, or truly experience the realities of, the prison" (Stevens 2012: 530). The immediate custodial experience remains accessible only to those serving time. More recently, academic contributions focusing on the role of convict autoethnography (e.g. Newbold et al. 2014) or Crewe and Bennett's (2012) collection of prisoners' voices embedded in an academic discussion of research practice and policy, have started to "populate the void of scholarly accounts by prisoners on prison" (Earle 2014: 432). Although depth and perspective of outsiders' and insiders' accounts on prison life may vary, themes of institutional organisation, adaptation and structures of interdependence feature in both. There exists, in fact, a whole body of literature that has dedicated itself specifically to the social and psychological interplay between the prison environment and those exposed to it.

2.1 (Re-)Examining the effects and pains of imprisonment

As a subcategory of prison research, studies on the effects of imprisonment have captured academic interest for more than 60 years now. Accompanied by and reflecting social, organisational and political changes, theories and findings in the field of prison effects research have undergone various developmental stages.

Regarded as one of prison research's seminal studies, Sykes' (1958) juxtaposition of the extent of state power – exemplified in the total institution of prison – and the extent to which its subjects define, create and defend their own identities and needs, paved the way for later academic explorations of prison effects and dynamics. Extending this focus to include mental hospitals, monasteries and boarding schools into the sociological analysis of the closed world of total institutions, Goffman (1961) put forward his theory that the roles and ideologies imposed on inmates exerted an overpowering influence on reactions and adjustments to their respective environment. According to him, this could lead to an institutionalisation of the individual. Similarly, Cohen and Taylor stated in their classic study of *Psychological Survival* (1972: 53) that imprisonment represents an "extreme situation in which an individual is forcibly removed from his or her community and placed in a total environment ... enforced and manipulated by others for punitive reasons." In this capacity, prison entails specific structures, conditions and deprivations that influence prisoners' experiences and behaviours.

Sykes and Goffman, for example, followed a paradigm that "presupposed the primacy of the institution in structuring the world within it" (Crewe 2009: 4). Prisoners' behaviour, prisoner culture and social organisation are thus predominantly linked to the specific influences the environment exudes on them. They find themselves in a world that is not theirs, a world that is artificially created to serve certain purposes which they are now exposed to and forced to cooperate with. Prison demands physical and psychological adaptation and change from its inmates. Building on that, Liebling et al. (2011), for example, found that one common form of psychological adaptation to life in a high-security prison was represented by prisoners' "self-censorship." Their interviewees described this as a process "that fundamentally changes who you are as a person" (Liebling et al. 2011: 28); a change initiated by high levels of enforced compliance with institutional rules and values. This theoretical framework, whereby prisoners adapt to their surroundings, represents an example of the so-called "indigenous" or "deprivation" theory deployed in prison research. It regards the prison environment as a "virtually self-contained system" (Crewe 2009: 4) that moulds those within it. Later studies would question the perceived unidirectional interrelation whereby the prison environment's deprivations and regulations are predominantly responsible for prisoners' behavioural and psychological performance.

An alternative model derived from Irwin and Cressey (1962) and exemplified in Jacobs' organisational ethnography *Stateville* (1977) "suggests prison identities are less discrete to the prison itself and draw more from external ... identities" (Earle 2014: 431). This "importation framework" implies that (sub-)cultural and social norms imported from prisoners' outside community are constitutional to prisoner culture and behaviour (e.g. Crewe 2009). Not long after the development of these two frameworks, prison research scholars started arguing that both importation and deprivation frameworks, were potentially connected. Prisoner culture and behaviour could therefore be regarded as "related to *individual adaptations* to imprisonment as well as the prison's *culture and social structure*" (Crewe 2009: 5 [emphasis in original]). Hans Toch's monograph on *Living in Prison* (1992) as well as aforementioned *Pains of Imprisonment* (Johnson and Toch 1982), for example, examined this interrelation and interplay of individual and the environment. As such, they addressed not only the impact of the prison environment, but also "the issue of significant variations in the environmental requirements of different people" (Toch 1992: 7) depending on imported characteristics. In regard to the prison experience and its effects, Toch's work, for example, points towards a realisation that the demarcation lines between importation and deprivation approaches can sometimes be blurry and not as clear cut as some of the literature suggests. Although seemingly subjected to complete compliance with prison rules and regulations, prisoners can still find ways to cater to individual needs and preferences. Trying to reconcile institutional pressures with maintaining individual identity, prisoners can, for example, resort to wearing their own clothes, cooking their own food, or listening to their favourite music in their cells (Liebling et al. 2011) when and if given the opportunity.

Although it could be taken from the previous discussion that prisoners do not entirely capitulate to processes of enforced adaptation (Goffman 1961), most prison effects theories veer towards adopting a deprivation approach. After all, being exposed to the prison environment means finding oneself as "subordinate to ... social and institutional forces" (Crewe 2009: 5) exerted by a total institution. Especially those adaptations to prison rules which prisoners experience as being oppressive and incongruent with their "true selves," can have negative effects on the individual's sense of who he or she is. Liebling et al. (2011) for example, described a process whereby "prisoners lost touch with their identities ... and the feeling of not knowing themselves anymore was disturbing and constituted one of the deep pains of imprisonment" (Liebling et al. 2011: 32). This and other pains have been established by prison effects research as an intrinsic part of the prison experience. They can have lasting and detrimental effects on incarcerated individuals over time.

Even though one of the main purposes of prison is to deprive "offenders of their liberty and certain freedoms enjoyed by the rest of society" (Gauke, MoJ 2018). Along with this deprivation go others, however, which have been found to go far beyond the loss of freedom. They reach deeper levels of the individual's psyche and sense of self. In his classic study on life in an American maximum-security prison, Sykes, for example, identifies "five basic deprivations – of liberty, goods and services, heterosexual relations, autonomy, and personal security" (Sykes 1958: 79). Studying stress in a prison setting, Toch puts forward findings that qualify some prison deprivations as stressors. Certain "features of the prison environment deprive – that is, adversely affect – inmates" (Toch 1982: 28). Johnson and Toch (1982) likewise consider the prison environment as highly stressful. Potential responses to deprivations as stressors "include physiological reactions (high blood pressure, ulcers) ... indicators of psychosocial malfunction (alcoholism)" (Toch 1982: 29), self-harm, suicide, or feelings of anxiety, rage and a sense of impotence. These may in turn lead to psychological coping strategies defending against negative feelings which are generally regarded as maladjustments and may be diagnosed as mental health problems. To avoid over-generalisation, it must be mentioned at this point that different personal needs may well "produce different reactions to imprisonment ... Pressing problems for some are tangential or irrelevant to others" (Johnson and Toch 1982: 18).

More than 30 years after Toch and Johnson's ethnographic study on *The Pains of Imprisonment* (1982) prison effects researchers still concede that psychological scales have so far failed to reflect the degree of harm caused by prison deprivations (e.g. Drake and Crewe 2008; Drake 2012). "Damage may be immediate, or cumulative, and independent of time spent in custody" (Liebling and Maruna 2005: 12). An investigation of the UK Department of Health into the mental well-being of the general population including prisoners stated that "some 90% of all prisoners are estimated to have a diagnosable mental health problem (including personality disorder) and/or a substance misuse problem" (Mental Health and Disability Department of Health 2011: 8). It remains to be clarified, however, whether these mental health problems have been imported into prison or have arisen due to the detrimental effects of the environment. There is some evidence that it may likely be the latter case, since "clinicians ... have long suspected that correctional institutions ... contribute directly to the emergence of major psychiatric disturbances" (Wiehn 1982: 228). Especially long periods spent in custody, extensive cell-confinement with limited social interactions and a lack of meaningful activities can have destructive psychological effects. These include, but are "not limited to, worsening mental disorders and extraordinarily high rates of suicide" (Kupers 2006: 11).

Further studies have confirmed that themes of deprivation, mental distress and pain continue to be relevant over time, although prison structures and regimes may have changed to provide a less restrictive environment. A recent study of the experience of long-term imprisonment (Crewe et al. 2020) has found, for example, that there are certain features of prison life that seem to remain somewhat unaltered over time regarding their negative impact on prisoners. The life-sentenced prisoners of their interview sample across all ages and sentence stages were "most concerned with external issues; specifically, those related to the health and well-being of family and friends" (Crewe et al. 2020). The study found that the most important problems are similar to the problems of long-term imprisonment identified by Richards (1978) 40 years ago, as well as those found by Flanagan (1980) in his replication of Richards' study. Richards' UK-study of *The Experience of long-term Imprisonment* (1978) was set up as an "exploration of some aspects of long-term prisoners' own experience of the psychological stresses in their situation, and their methods of coping with them" (Richards 1978: 162). Richards developed a set of "problem statements" to measure the perceived severity of the difficulties long-term prisoners face. It included such issues as "Being bored," "Wishing that time would go faster," "Losing your self-confidence" and "Feeling suicidal" (Richards 1978). "He found that all of the five 'most severe problems' were related to deprivation of relationships with and in the outside" (Flanagan 1980: 151).

Two years later, Flanagan took up the problem-ranking exercise developed by Richards (1978) and administered it to a group of American long-term prisoners in order to compare British and American perspectives. "The problem-ranking task was included as part of an interview schedule in a larger study of … self-perceived problems, needs and perspectives" (Flanagan 1980: 148). Testing for correlation, his findings implied that the most frequently experienced problems were also perceived by inmates "as being the most serious (intense) problems to deal with" (Flanagan 1980: 150). Among his sample of 49 American long-term prisoners "'missing somebody' was ranked as the most severe problem … followed by 'missing social life' and 'worrying about how you will cope when you get out'" (Flanagan 1980: 150). These findings indicated a high level of correlation with Richard's UK respondents. In both studies, the "loss of relationships with family and friends outside the prison was consistently mentioned as the most serious deprivation" (Flanagan 1980: 155) with time as an exacerbating factor. Especially for long-term prisoners, the combination of both can develop "into major problems of survival over the duration of a long prison sentence" (Flanagan 1980: 155).

Comparing Richards' (1978) and Flanagan's (1980) previous findings with their own, Crewe et al. (2020) conclude that the top-ranking problem of long-term prisoners across all three studies was "Missing somebody" (Crewe et al. 2020). "Missing somebody," i.e. feeling incomplete and being separated from someone significant on the outside was experienced as most stress- and painful during long-term imprisonment.

2.2 The absence of outside relationships as one of the pains of long-term imprisonment

As established by Richards (1978), Flanagan (1980), Crewe et al. (2020) and others (e.g. Sampson and Laub 1993; Giordano 2002; Brunton-Smith and McCarthy

2016b with more authors to be discussed in due course), outside relationships play an important role in the lives of long-term prisoners. The loss of family or romantic relationships can contribute to immense emotional pain. Physical separation and emotional trauma go along with incarceration and can place significant strain on relationships, often heightening the risks of relational breakdown (Lynch and Sabol 2001; Lopoo and Western 2005). Concerns "about how long it will last" (Cohen and Taylor 1972: 67) can cause fears of abandonment and loss. Especially for long-term prisoners, these concerns do not seem exaggerated, since the strain on outside partners and families is considerable, and the demand to hold out faithfully for an incarcerated partner's uncertain release can seem insurmountable. To decrease or eliminate these fears, prisoners might resort to strategies of withdrawing from outside relationships. As found by Flanagan (1980) as well as Cohen and Taylor, this can feel like an almost "fatalistic relief in reducing the emotional reliance upon outsiders" (Cohen and Taylor 1972: 67). Copious research has highlighted that relationships between prisoners and their family before, during and after their prison sentences are often strained (e.g. Hairston 1991; Visher and Travis 2003; Niven and Stewart 2005; Travis 2005; Brunton-Smith and McCarthy 2016b).

However, losing or cutting close relationships to the outside can have negative consequences on prisoners' mental well-being and sense of identity. Relationships with children, for example, have been found to act as a protective factor. Losing those can lead to a potential "deterioration of the emotional security of prisoners during their sentence, as well as limiting the extent of social ties on release" (Brunton-Smith and McCarthy 2016b: 2). Especially parent-child relationships can have an important impact on re-entry outcomes such as employment, mental health, and refraining from substance use (Visher and Travis 2003). They often represent a means to retain a "sense of connection with … preprison identities" (Datchi 2017: 64). These mechanisms in turn have been found to play a role in offender rehabilitation by offering an alternative identity to that of a prisoner (Paterline and Petersen 1999; Roy and Dyson 2005). Research such as Mills and Codd's (2008) into *Families' Role in Desistance* has also shown that stable family ties can have very practical implications. They have been linked to "a greater chance of having housing on release and … a decreased risk of reoffending" (Scott and Codd 2010: 145). Keeping the focus on a home and a life to return to after prison can serve as a major motivator for prisoners to take care of their physical and mental well-being (as will be shown in Chapter 6). This, in turn, helps to manage the pressures of prison life (Naser and La Vigne 2006; Rocque et al. 2013) and plays an important role in reducing reoffending (Laub et al. 1998; Brunton-Smith and McCarthy 2016b).

The role of relationships as rehabilitative turning points in (male) criminal offending behaviour was likewise established by Sampson and Laub (1993).

Researchers came to understand that long-term stable relationships, particularly marriage can promote "informal social control (and thus desistance)" (Wyse et al. 2014: 373). At this point, it is important to distinguish, however, between the effects of beneficial and non-beneficial relationships. Although marriage can deliver a range of benefits, those trajectories depict an "ideal scenario," a relationship with a "desirable," i.e. non-criminal partner, a stable relationship, free from economic, social and emotional deprivation or strain. Although the loss of close outside relationships can be experienced as painful, the continuation of difficult or even abusive relationships can be detrimental to prisoners' well-being (and to that of those outside for that matter).

That being said, relevant literature reviewed in this section still identifies the loss of close relationships as one of the most severely experienced pains of imprisonment. This discussion would be incomplete, however, without considering the ripple effects of prison's disruptive and separating qualities on those outside of its walls. Scott and Codd (2010), for example, argue that the disruption of families and partnerships likewise harms those left behind on the outside. Prisoners' families and loved ones often feel punished by a sentence that is not intended to punish them, but the offender (Scott and Codd 2010). The "collateral damage" caused by the secondary effects of long-term imprisonment represents an issue not to be underestimated.

2.2.1 The secondary effects and pains of imprisonment

Research by Murray (2005), Light and Campbell (2007) or Scott and Codd (2010) contribute to insights into some of the negative secondary effects of imprisonment. They found that prisoners' partners, children and extended families often find themselves on the receiving end of "social disapproval and hostility due to their affiliation with an offender" (Scott and Codd 2010: 145). They might also experience material struggles connected to the loss of income the incarcerated family member had provided in the past. Also, the costs of prison visits – e.g. travel expenses or paying for refreshments consumed during visits – can put a financial strain on prisoners' families and partners.

Qualitative studies into the gendered secondary pains of imprisonment, experienced by a majority of female partners of a predominantly male prison population (e.g. Condry 2007; Comfort 2008) furthermore showed that the "decision to 'stand by her man' can come with considerable personal costs" (Jardine 2018). "For these women, be they wives, partners or mothers, supporting the person in custody can become their primary occupation" (Jardine 2018: 115). In her account on maintaining family ties in a prison context, Jardine pointed out that especially women feel obliged to "go to great lengths to simultaneously mitigate against the deprivations of the prison environment, and also manage their partner's behaviour within it" (Jardine

2018: 115). Similar studies – e.g. Comfort's *Doing Time Together* (2008) – have enquired into the effects of secondary imprisonment on female loved ones of prisoners and how it affects their sense of love, relationship and justice.

When it comes to the emotional impact of secondary imprisonment, it can "express itself, for example, in depression and anxiety in partners, and behavioural disturbances in children of an incarcerated parent" (Scott and Codd 2010: 147). These are predominantly connected to traumatic experiences of loss and separation (Smith 2014). A joint review on children of offenders conducted in 2007 by the Department for Children, Schools and Families (DCSF) and the Ministry of Justice (MoJ) found that these children were

> three times more likely to have a mental health problem than their peers; have a heightened risk of anti-social behaviour and offending; and experience high levels of social disadvantage … distress … instability … and disruption in housing and schooling. (DCSF and MoJ 2007: 13)

As a recurring theme in this and previous section, the loss or disruption of prisoners' close outside relationships seems to carry with it a range of negative (mental-)health as well as social and economic impacts. These primary and secondary effects have been the focus of prison research for more than half a century. As an underlying theme – as a common denominator defining the relationships that really matter – stands *love*, without explicitly being named as such. Whether it presents itself in the qualities of familial attachment or bonding between romantic partners, its presence is rarely verbalised as such in relevant literature. In fact, the relative absence of the very term itself in the criminological discussion about the effects of long-term imprisonment has contributed to a bafflement that has led me to undertake a more thorough inspection of the relevant body of literature.

2.3 Tracing the absence and presence of love in the prison research literature

Although various classic and contemporary research into the effects of long-term imprisonment acknowledges and expands on prisoners' struggles with "missing somebody" and feeling deprived of (hetero-)sexual relationships, *love* as standalone term seems to remain somewhat obscure. Or so I was led to believe when a first literature review conducted in 2015 brought to the forefront a relative absence of love as direct focus of study and discussion in the field of UK prison (effects) research. At that point, only one article could be allocated that explicitly included love in its title: "What's love got to do with it?" by Maruna (2004). The one time this article touched on love explicitly, was by pointing out its absence and outsider role in the field of resettlement and desistance research stating that

> [t]here is ... a growing body of literature – associated with ... the restorative justice movement – that ... indeed deploys words as foreign to the resettlement literature as "shame," "remorse," "forgiveness" and even "love." (Maruna 2004: 13)

Using love in connection with the term "even" points toward its perceived rarity in the field. However, no follow-up discussion or definition of the concept of love itself has been conducted within the scope of above-cited article. Furthermore, the concept of love was only mentioned in relation to restorative justice literature, not in relation to prison (effects) research. In a similar vein – although related to the significantly broader field of law than to the specific field of prison research – Grossi asserts that "love is not a common subject for law, but it is an important one ... Love is a central discourse in western societies; this ... demands that law interacts with it" (Grossi 2018: 207). Again, the absence of the concept of love was pointed out as a gap in relevant literature and practice.

In his ethnographic account of *The Prisoner Society* (2009), Crewe's study participants referred to outside relationships with partners and families and expressed moral and normative attitudes towards different female figures in their lives, such as mothers or girlfriends. *Love* as a concept of its own, however, was not examined in more depth, but rather alluded to within a framework of attitudes towards romantic relationship partners. One example featuring love as a topic of open discussion could be found in Liebling et al.'s *Exploration of Staff-Prisoner Relationships at HMP Whitemoor* (2011). It mentioned several encounters of the researchers with the longing for love in a highly emotionally regulated high-security prison environment. It was rarely directly or openly addressed but surfaced throughout interviews and informal conversations with prisoners (and some staff). Whenever the topic of love was mentioned, the need for it and the awareness of its absence was "expressed powerfully" (Liebling 2014: 264). Although not explicitly and exclusively identified as love, traces of its presence could be said to be found in criminological literature researching intimate relationships between prisoners containing a sexual element.

2.3.1 Intimate and sexual relationships between prisoners

As will be illuminated in Chapter 7, intimate relationships between prisoners take place and fulfil various purposes. Corresponding literature on sexual and intimate relations between male prisoners point towards a variety of experiences. Mackenzie et al. (2016) for example, endeavour to go beyond research accounts solely highlighting the "ubiquity of prisoner sex and the harms therein to prisoners and innocent women beyond prisons walls" (Mackenzie et al. 2016: 18). Their findings – derived from qualitative interviews with formerly incarcerated bisexual Black men in the US – echo research about intimacy between men conducted by Blackash (2015) in a UK prison. His findings point toward "multiple discursive strategies around intimacies … across a complex spectrum including hetero-flexibility, prison-gay and deep friendships" (Blackash 2015: 56). These intimacies can be expressed, for example, through sexual intimacy, companionship, kinship or caregiving relationships (Blackash 2015). These connections often act as "an integrative framework that captures how power is negotiated by, not merely imposed upon, prisoners through intimate relationships in prison settings" (Mackenzie et al. 2016: 2). Similarly, Donaldson (2001) described a wide range of intra-prisoner relationships, "ranging from ruthless exploitation to romantic love" (Donaldson 2001: 121). Although inquiries into love and intimacy have been conducted in female prison establishments (e.g. Maeve 1999; Einat and Chen 2012) much of the research dedicated to male prisoner relationships seems to focus predominantly on a sexual component.

Portrayed as seemingly ubiquitous by popular culture, research by the Howard League Commission on Sex in Prison (Stevens 2016), for example, asserted, that only a minority of male and female prisoners in England and Wales engage in consensual sex during their sentence (Stevens 2016). Conducting a review of sex inside prisons (Stevens 2016), the commission looked at ramifications of coercive and unprotected sex as well as at dynamics of consensual sexual engagements. Although "Prison Service Instruction 47/2011 confirms that there is no specific rule prohibiting sex between prisoners, … prison staff do 'not allow' prisoners to engage in sexual activity and sexual relationships are 'not encouraged'" (Stevens 2016: 13). This might be one of the reasons why the topic of sexual and romantic relationships between (male) prisoners remains somewhat taboo. In this regard, Stevens alerted to the fact that a lack of academic or institutional engagement with this topic may have consequences "for prisoners' psychological and emotional well-being and, when that sex is unprotected, for sexual health" (Stevens 2016: 14). There is potential – and a need – for a deeper academic exploration of hitherto "underground" topics of prison life, such as close emotional or sexual relationships. Apart from intra-prisoner ties involving a physically intimate component, research into group dynamics in prisons provides accounts of intra-prisoner relationships based on close symbolic allegiances involving the need for attachment, or love.

2.3.2 The search for belonging in prison specific groups

Liebling et al. (2011), for example, found that whilst being separate from close outside relationships, some prisoners were looking to establish a sense of connection and belonging inside. In the prison under study by Liebling et al.

(2011), this appeared to be offered by groups of prisoners who identified or were identified by staff as gangs. Similar to earlier discussed importation approach, the assumption was "that prisoners who felt attracted to gangs on the outside would feel similarly inclined to join an equivalent group inside" (Liebling et al. 2011: 68). Their reasons were said to be similar to those that had brought them into contact with gangs on the outside, namely "a sense of purpose and identity, material comforts, (inmate) relations and safety in a dangerous environment" (Liebling et al. 2011: 68). Similarly, Jacobs had found that apart from a promise of power, protection and economic affluency, gangs would also offer psychological support, contributing to a positive self-image and a sense of belonging (Jacobs 1974). As a surrogate family, these groups offered love and recognition, often not provided in primary family relationships (Albertse 2007). A familial inability to fulfil an individual's love and belonging needs (see Maslow 1987) could therefore motivate an individual to search for these in peer groups such as gangs (Albertse 2007).

Inside as well as outside a prison context, these needs could also be fulfilled by another group – faith communities. In the microcosm of a high-security prison, for example, identifying themselves with the Muslim faith community brought with it the realisation of extrinsic (e.g. protection, better food quality) as well as intrinsic benefits (e.g. recognition, emotional support and social esteem) which were all in short supply in this specific environment (Liebling et al. 2011). This and other accounts (e.g. Guessous et al. 2001; Spalek and El-Hassan 2007) identify faith communities to provide a recognition and fulfilment of emotional needs, such as the need to belong. The specific territory of love is not (explicitly) covered, however, in these studies and requires systematic exploration which this book aims to undertake.

Looking at above efforts to establish a relationship and human connection in prison, it has become somewhat apparent that these often arise out of the need to satisfy love and belonging needs (see Maslow 1987) which are largely left unfulfilled in the prison environment. These effects and pains of prison deprivations have been taken on board by the creators of an alternative approach to imprisonment. The formation of therapeutic communities represents one way of ameliorating some of the most emotionally oppressive effects of the "regular" prison experience. Are these, in fact, places that provide and cater for the love needs?

2.3.3 Therapeutic communities — Space(s) for love?

As an alternative approach to prisoner rehabilitation, the prison-based therapeutic community (TC) was originally established as a treatment modality for substance-using offenders (Hiller et al. 1999; Lurigio 2000; Vandevelde et al. 2004). It was based on two major traditions: "the American drug-free hierarchical

concept-based TC and the British democratic Maxwell Jones-type TC"
(Vandevelde et al. 2004; see also Broekaert et al. 2000; De Leon 2000; Kennard
1998; Lipton 1998; Rawlings 1999). The democratic approach – which has been
mostly implemented in UK-based TCs – has developed "as a professional
groupwork method … using social learning principles" (Vandevelde et al. 2004:
67). Its earliest origins in England can be traced back to two experimental
treatment and hospital units (Hollymoor Hospital, Birmingham and Mill Hill and
Dartford, London) dedicated to the rehabilitation of World War II-soldiers and ex-
prisoners of war using group therapy, founded by Maxwell Jones (see Jones 1952;
Harrison and Clark 1992; Vandevelde et al. 2004). Vandevelde et al. summarised
Jones' (Jones 1968; 1982) principles underlying the design of TCs as follows:

> (1) two-way communication on all levels; (2) decision-making on all
> levels; (3) shared (multiple) leadership; (4) consensus in decision-
> making; and (5) social learning by interaction in the "here and now."
> (Vandevelde et al. 2004: 68)

Based on these principles, HMP Grendon was opened as the first democratic
TC in the UK in 1962. Designed as a category B prison, it predominantly holds
men serving indeterminate sentences for serious violent or sexual offences.
Transfer from a regular prison to HMP Grendon is based on a voluntary
application process (Bennett and Shuker 2017). Compared to other penal
settings – mainly focused on safe containment and punishment – TCs strive to
"offer a unique social climate" promoting "psychological well-being and
improved psychological health" (Bennett and Shuker 2017: 21). Welfarist
"values such as trust, hope, meaning and affirmation … permeate life within a
TC" (Bennett and Shuker 2017: 21) enabling its residents to grow and explore
avenues away from a "primary identity as an offender" (Bennett and Shuker
2017: 21). This includes the practice of "referring to prisoners in TCs
as residents and to prison wings as communities … suggestive of common
purpose and belonging" (Stevens 2012: 533).

Additional focus is put on positive relationships between staff and residents
as well as between residents themselves. These are based on what will later be
established as qualities of love such as intimate knowledge of the other and
overcoming self-interest in favour of an altruistic concern for the other.
According to Stevens (2011: 135) these

> [c]aring relationships become possible when that inherent connection
> and commonality between people results in a recognition and
> acceptance of responsibility for one another and of the perceived
> imperative to react to the expressed or implicit needs of others.

The consideration and respect of each other's needs and shared humanity
takes centre stage in TCs like HMP Grendon and is extended to the institution

itself. One of its core principles is based on expecting TC residents "to work collaboratively for 'the good of the community'" (Stevens 2012: 533). This stands in stark contrast to most regular prison regimes which encourage prisoners' obedience rather than agency. In this sense, TCs incorporate values of love such as morally virtuous agency, self-transcendence for the good of another, forging communal ties and principles of belonging which we will encounter in Chapter 3's concept-analysis as the very qualities of love.

Striving to provide an overview of prison research literature touching on topics related to love – such as outside and inside relationship dynamics as well as efforts made by prisoners and prisons to satisfy the need for love and belonging – it has been shown that there is scope for more research specifically dedicated to love to be conducted. Taking up the issues of love provision and deprivation in prison could furthermore provide a gateway for other emotional dimensions of prison life to be considered academically.

2.4 The role of emotions in prison research

When it comes to the effects that the absence and presence of love (and other emotions) can have within the prison context, there is scope for deeper exploration. Liebling and Maruna (2005), for example, established a lack in contemporary effects literature to sufficiently consider the affective dimension of imprisonment. There still is a lack of research dedicated to unearthing the emotional structures of prison and its effects, although criminologists are starting to place more emphasis on the interplay between *Emotions, Crime and Justice* (Loader et al. 2011), for example.

Especially those who have gained "first-hand experience" of both, incarceration and prison research, point towards and encourage more academic attention to the "struggle for feelings" in "a world officially almost devoid of sensuality" (Earle 2014: 434). Paraphrasing one of the pains of imprisonment as "feeling but not touching," Earle (2014: 434), for example, instigates closer examination of "an existential chill [that] is palpable in prison fieldwork and [which] remains under-theorized and under-examined" (Earle 2014: 434). He furthermore shares Warr's (in Crewe and Bennett 2012) "sense of deep psychic impact that prison has on 'the soul' ... a life inside 'life inside' that largely escapes academic scrutiny" (Earle 2014: 432). A start has been made to extend prison effects research to include affective dimensions by Crewe and Laws, for example. By exploring *Emotion Regulation Among Male Prisoners* (2015) in English prisons, they addressed the fact that so far "little attention has been given ... to the interior emotional worlds of male prisoners" (Crewe 2014: 396) as well as of prisons. This attention could, however, prove crucial for unravelling and exposing the emotional threats of imprisonment on the human psyche and body. The most severe outcomes of emotional strain present as mental breakdowns and a struggle to cope with difficult feelings inside prison.

2.4.1 Prison suicide and self-harm as emotional response to the pains of imprisonment

When academic attention is shifted onto the affective dimensions of prison life, it is often done with a view to describe collective phenomena evolving out of the emotional struggle of individuals, such as prison suicides or prison violence. Liebling, for example, dedicated large parts of her work to the study of suicides and self-harm in male and female prisons (e.g. Liebling 1999) as prisoners' strategies to cope with their environment. More than twenty years ago, Liebling's and others'[2] research already drew attention to relatively high figures of prison suicides in England and Wales (Liebling 1999).

Safety in Custody Statistics on Deaths in Custody published on the 25th of January 2018 painted a similarly alarming picture, stating 70 self-inflicted deaths during 2017 (Ministry of Justice 2018: 1). The same report verified that "self-harm reached a record high of 42,837 incidents in the 12 months to September 2017, up 12% from the previous year ... Quarterly self-harm incidents rose by 10% to a record high of 11,904 incidents" (Ministry of Justice 2018: 1). Then as now, different types and motivations "of prison suicide can be identified, and problems of coping with various aspects of imprisonment take on special significance for some" (Liebling 1999: 311). According to Liebling (1999: 311), "suicide and self-injury may constitute a response (or a 'solution') to painful feelings" such as "uncontrollability, helplessness, and powerlessness" (Liebling 1999: 319). These feelings are all intrinsic to the prison experience and constitute reactions to a critical situation (Giddens 1979). Denominating the disruption of close relationships with families and friends on the outside as one of the pains of imprisonment, Liebling furthermore refers to the work of Grounds (1996) describing prison "as a dislocation, shown to have similarities with those overwhelming dislocations experienced by victims of disaster or trauma, leading to severe problems of relatedness and identity" (Liebling 1999: 321). As will be illuminated further in Chapter 3, the trauma of losing love relations can induce "intense fear and helplessness, sometimes overwhelming an individual's psychological coping mechanisms" (Liebling 1999: 321).

Research into *Self-harm by adult men in prison* (Pope 2018) drew on evidence (Dixon-Gordon et al. 2012; Snow 2002) that differentiated between suicide and self-harm in prisons regarding motivations and functions. Their functions are

---

[2] See for example Lloyd 1990 Home Office Research Study No 115, for an extensive literature review of research on suicides in UK prisons.

distinct with self-harm "conceptualised as a means of surviving or coping with life, as opposed to the ending of one's life" (Pope 2018: 14). Research conducted by Snow (2002) was cited by Pope to identify motivations for self-harm and suicide attempts among imprisoned men:

> 1. men who self-harmed were most likely to be motivated by 'instrumental' reasons ... for example 'being alone/wanted someone to talk to', 'wanted help' ... 2. male young offenders who attempted suicide were more likely to be motivated by factors relating to interpersonal relationships ... 3. adult men who attempted suicide were most likely to be motivated by situational factors that related directly to their imprisonment ... such as 'depression', 'concern over children', or 'homesickness' (Pope 2018: 14).

The absence of close outside relationships as well as missing them, again presented as powerful triggers for emotional distress and related coping behaviour. When it comes to self-harm (non-suicidal) as a form of coping with stressful situations, Dixon-Gordon et al. (2012) suggest that it functions as a form of emotion regulation. However, some studies (e.g. Snow 2002) that draw on the perspectives of staff and prisoners, suggest there may also be an "instrumental element to some ... self-harm ... to achieve a concrete goal ... for example ... a transfer" (Pope 2018: 14). Although this is an important alternative interpretation of the function of self-harm in prisons, therein lies a danger of trivialising the act "and the risk posed by the individual" (Pope 2018: 14). When used to regulate (difficult) emotions, self-harm is but one coping mechanism used by prisoners to adjust to their environment.

2.4.2 Negotiating emotion regulation and expression in the prison environment

As argued by Liebling (1999) as well as Cohen and Taylor (1972), a majority of prisoners find themselves living in a "constant state of anxiety, fearing violence or deterioration ... or more discipline" (Liebling 1999: 323). This is mainly due to their immediate environment, since "violence within prisons is undoubtedly common, in the form of fights, assaults and various forms of aggression and exploitation" (Crewe et al. 2014: 57). Although immediate interpersonal violence may not be experienced by every prisoner, it is, in fact, "the possibility of violence and predation ... which many prisoners find fearful and debilitating" (Crewe et al. 2014: 57). As we will discover throughout Chapter 8, it is "this insidious sense of threat" (Crewe et al. 2014: 57) that dictates most of the repertoire of emotional expression deployed in this environment.

However, not only the threat of violence but also the perceived danger of "making the wrong impression" on staff dictates much of prisoners' emotional expression or suppression. The threat of "more discipline" (Liebling 1999: 323) can lead prisoners to curtail their emotion performance when they feel "on display" in front of staff, mainly on the main prison wings. That emotion performance is often necessarily connected to location and spectators has not only been established by Goffman (1959) in his theory of *frontstage* and *backstage* performance of self (which will be discussed further within the context of Chapter 8). Crewe et al. (2014), for example, have found that emotion regulation and expression varies in relation to the prison's "emotional microclimates" (Crewe et al. 2014: 67). These present as "marginal spaces or intermediate zones ... permitting a broader emotional register than ... main residential and most public areas" (Crewe et al. 2014: 67). There is scope for a deeper exploration by prison research and carceral geography scholars, to map these social and emotional terrains of the prison as truthfully as possible (Crewe et al. 2014).

In order to unearth textures and layers of emotions within prisoners and prisons that help to illuminate related dynamics (such as joining gangs) and behaviours (such as self-harm as emotion management), it is beneficial to broaden the scope of academic inquiry towards the field of sentiment and sensuality. Ultimately, in-depth investigations into the affective dimensions of imprisonment could prove crucial for adequately (re-)evaluating and understanding its effects on the individual. It remains to be critically assessed, whether long-lasting negative effects on long-term prisoners could, in fact, be regarded as incommensurate with a "just punishment" as a means to restore justice.

2.5 Conclusion

It has become apparent that the pain connected to relational deprivation during incarceration already features in the prison effects literature. In fact, this pain has repeatedly emerged as one of the most severe deprivations in studies from the early days of prison effects research. It continues to do so, and its (primarily) negative affective effects warrant further exploration, if we want to gain a deeper and more wholistic insight into the long-term prison experience and its consequences. Although some of the literature examined in this chapter might implicitly include love as an underlying theme, it has so far not been the subject of explicit and exclusive exploration in the relevant literature. The scope and merit for doing so is potentially rich, considering the essential role that emotions, and specifically love, play in human existence. Applying a wholistic lens to the long-term prison experience in relation to love (deprivation and provision) could help to arrive at an increasingly multi-dimensional reflection of its impact.

Before this exploration can begin, however, another theoretical enquiry has to take place, namely, to identify what exactly we are talking about, when we talk about love? Only if its role, meaning and use have been sufficiently clarified beforehand, will it be possible to know what direction and purpose the remainder of this qualitative exploration is going to take. To examine the effects of the absence and presence of love in the lives of long-term prisoners, an abstract and diffuse concept first has to be translated into some common denominators, thus providing the missing link to connect this book's theoretical frameworks with its empirical analysis.

3. Unearthing love's qualities in multidisciplinary concept analysis

This chapter establishes the second of two main theoretical pillars on which my empirical exploration will ultimately be based. After having identified in which way this book is going to contribute to relevant prison effects literature, it is now necessary to discern what is meant by the term *love*, and how it will be used in this book, before I can begin to explore its role in the lives of long-term prisoners. More specifically, it means that my epistemological view on love will have to be circumscribed. It is necessary to be clear about the approach that will be taken when gathering and creating knowledge about love, since this is likely going to stir the analysis in a certain direction. It has to be determined which of love's qualities will be focussed on when examining its empirical manifestation. Of course, an imposition of the researcher's preconceived notion of love on participants' accounts has to be considered carefully, nevertheless it is necessary to apply some operational ground rules approaching this vast and diffuse topic.

This chapter will therefore retrace the thought process undergirding love's operationalisation. The following sections will elucidate, how two theoretical frameworks (concept-analysis and social-ecology) have been combined and embedded within a multidisciplinary literature review in an endeavour to identify love's most prominent features. Once outlined, these will be applied to inform the content and structure of my data analysis approach. Ultimately, this chapter aims to provide a multidisciplinary insight into the role of love with the aim to shed light onto its meanings in human development and human existence.

At first sight, love seems as much of an integral component of human life as it seems a fuzzy, intangible concept. A diffuse awareness of its existence may be omnipresent, but a definition of this phenomenon's distinct traits is difficult. There are manifold perceptions of, beliefs about and experiences with love. Although many schools of thought have examined it over time, love itself seems to remain somewhat elusive in its conceptualisation. Its definition often heavily depends on personal stance, intellectual discipline or "a particular epistemological position of the viewer" (Csikszentmihalyi 1980: 308). Love is meaningful in human existence, but to deliver one universally valid definition of its meaning is difficult due to its ideational quality. Since it represents an intangible idea, love cannot be defined based on empirically observable traits, but on its manifestation through those who claim its existence: human beings.

In most contemporary Western societies, love is reified in a very distinct symbolism: the heart. Lovers give their hearts to each other, Cupid's arrow pierces the heart of the undiscerning lover, and a broken heart symbolises the pain and hurt accompanying the breakdown of love relationships. As a physiological organ, the heart is indispensable for human survival. If love is most commonly represented by the shape of a heart, it points towards its vital importance. It represents a core concept of human existence, a key component of life. Considering the etymology of the term *core* may provide a clue as to why love is symbolised by the heart, since *core* derives from the Latin word *cor,* meaning *heart.* Love touches on and emanates from our very core. This view is echoed by existentialist philosopher Kierkegaard (2009: 26) who contends that "there is a place in a human being's most inward depths; from this place proceeds the life of love." As a first tentative thought, it can therefore be assumed that love operates as "an essential human process that ... remains an ontological foundation of human existence" (Helm 2010: 40).

Although love's heart symbolism might be recognised in many parts of the world, by no means does it imply a culturally unified and historically constant view of the concept of love. In fact, much of the literature argues along the same lines as Armstrong who states that "the variety of relationships and attachments we dignify with the term 'love' don't share a single, common nature" (Armstrong 2002: 10). This intangible and mutable quality of love as a concept presented itself as major theoretical hurdle in the process of deciding on the approach this book was going to take. There was an imminent danger of approaching the topic too broadly. It was necessary to find a suitable way to focus on love and its attributes without imposing too narrow a view onto prisoners' narratives. What do I want (and need) to know about love that meaningfully relates to its role in the lives of long-term prisoners? What is relevant and why? Which questions about love do I want to ask that get to the *core* of its meaning?

Investigating academic approaches towards operationalising abstract ideas in empirical research, an approach borrowed from nursing sciences seemed to provide a viable option to do so. *Concept analysis* as developed by Walker and Avant (1994) finds its main use in helping to clarify meanings of abstract concepts to develop an operational definition. As such it aims at distinguishing between "defining attributes of a concept and its irrelevant attributes" (Walker and Avant 1994: 38) as well as at finding characteristics that appear repeatedly when we talk about the concept under investigation. The underlying question of concept analysis is one about meaning. As Wilson (1963) pointed out, using the concept of fish as an example, "what we want to know is what we normally mean by fish, how one verifies whether something is a fish or not, what counts as a fish" (Wilson 1963: 4). We are asked to scrutinise commonplace uses of a term and "to become aware of the significance of our words" (Wilson 1963: 14).

Given that one of the main aims of this book's underlying research was to identify the presence and absence of love and effects thereof, becoming aware of its presence and absence boiled down to matters of quality. Which qualities does an experience or feeling have to possess in order to be recognised as the presence or absence of love? Since concept analysis aims at verifying whether or not a concept is applicable ("whether something is a fish or not" (Wilson 1963: 14)), I decided to deploy the following modified model of Walker and Avant's original (1994) theoretical framework to explore love's qualities and modalities:

Figure 3.1: Concept analysis after Walker and Avant (1994)

First Stage:
Identification of a suitable concept for analysis
↓
Second Stage:
Determination of purpose
↓
Third Stage:
Review of literature
↓
Fourth Stage:
Clarification of attributes
↓
Omitted stages:
Fifth Stage:
Present a model case
↓
Sixth Stage:
Clarification of antecedents
↓
Seventh Stage:
Clarification of consequences
↓
Eighth Stage:
Defining empirical referents

In its original conception, the above model features eight stages. These are dedicated to transferring a theoretical concept into case-specific manifestations in the field of nursing or other medical sciences. To carry out the theoretical groundwork for this book's empirical analysis, Walker and Avant's (1994) concept analysis model has been applied here in the following manner: After identifying love as a suitable concept for analysis in the first stage, its purpose was determined in the second stage as the translation of an abstract idea into an operational guideline for empirical data analysis. Executing the third (review of literature on love) and fourth stage (clarification of attributes of love) will be the main tasks of the remainder of this chapter. After careful consideration, the remaining four stages of the original model have been omitted because they could not be congruently applied to the present case. After stage one and two had been worked through, commencing on reviewing relevant literature on love in stage three required additional consideration regarding its literary focus and range. Where was one to begin and where to end in a vast field of academic and non-academic literary sources concerning themselves with the topic of love?

3.1 Combining concept analysis with social-ecological systems theory

Since it is one of my aims to contribute to critical theory and to connect micro-social and macro-social levels of enquiry, this has to be reflected in analytical choices, too. Critical theorists such as Honneth point towards systems theory (e.g. Parsons 1951; Luhmann 2012) "to investigate the systemic forms of social ideas' material reproduction in 'life-worldly foundations'" (Honneth 1987: 375). If I want to retrace and understand the manifestation of the individual and the "social idea" of love in the life-worlds of long-term prisoners, deploying systems theory suggests itself as a viable strategy. When it comes to applying a micro- and macro-perspective to the manifestation of factors influencing human life and development, Bronfenbrenner's first (1974) version of his social-ecological application of systems theory presents itself as a fruitful avenue of exploration.

Although originally developed to enrich developmental psychology's approach to child development, Bronfenbrenner's approach can also be applied to human development more generally. It postulates the view that if we want to understand human development and health, the entire ecological system in which it occurs needs to be taken into account. It examines the interrelations between the person and his or her environment in a micro- and macro-context (Bronfenbrenner 1977). In this sense, social-ecology is seen as a continuous "adjustment between organism and environment" (Bronfenbrenner 1974: 439) with any single system being in "a reciprocal relationship of dependency and influence with all the other systems" (Ungar et al. 2013: 356). However, Bronfenbrenner's focus is "not simply on the environment, or context, but on the ecological system that includes the ... individual" (Edinete and Tudge 2013: 246) and his or her distinct characteristics and predispositions. Translated into prison research conceptualisations, the social-ecological approach unites importation and deprivation theories when it comes to prisoners' interrelations with their environment.

In his original theory developed in the mid-1970s (which was refined and redefined several times by him and his colleagues) "Bronfenbrenner conceived of the environment ... as an arrangement of four interconnected structures" (Edinete and Tudge 2013: 246). They represent an ecological system wherein the individual is embedded. It is made up of *microsystem, mesosystem, exosystem* and *macrosystem* (Bronfenbrenner 1976). The microsystem is defined as the environment closest to the individual, e.g. the home, marked by face-to-face interactions with others in dyadic relationships (Bronfenbrenner 1974; 1979). Here, "activities and interpersonal roles and relations ... are the constitutive elements" (Edinete and Tudge 2013: 246). The mesosystem moves beyond dyad or two-party relationships and represents "a system of microsystems" (Bronfenbrenner 1976: 163) which could be a combination of, for example, a person's neighbourhood and church, or – in a prison context – a prisoner's family and his probation officer. The exosystem is perceived as even further away from the individual: "an ecological setting in which the ... person ... does not participate actively within" (Edinete and Tudge 2013: 246). It is represented by institutions such as schools affecting the person without an opportunity to directly influence this relationship.

Lastly, the macrosystem "differs fundamentally from the other levels of context" (Edinete and Tudge 2013: 247). It effectively overarches the institutional systems of a given culture or society and is composed of time- and space-specific cultural values, belief systems, ethics and ideologies (Bronfenbrenner 1979). Macrosystems represent the cultural or social context an individual is part of without actively participating in it. It is important to note that Bronfenbrenner's social-ecology theory does not postulate an "air-tight" and isolated position of the systems, but rather assumes their semi-permeability. Some factors and actors in different spheres of an individual's social-ecological system can overlap and influence each other. What is postulated in the individual's exosystem as institutional rules in school, for example, can clash with and infiltrate personal value systems established in an individual's microsystemic upbringing at home.

Using Bronfenbrenner's social-ecology model (1974) with its focus on the dynamics of different developmental factors on a micro- and macro-level of human existence seemed most suitable for examining how the factor of love operates in an individual's environment. The sections to follow will endeavour to excavate love's essential ontological mode of operation, looking at different categories of love and their relations between them. To adequately limit and define the scope of this ontological exploration, a disciplinary vantage point has to be determined. This is done with a view to circumscribe the vast body of literature on love and to distinguish relevant from non-relevant.

3.2 Establishing a multidisciplinary focal point

A focus on academic disciplines studying human development, behaviour and culture seem most appropriate to achieve this goal. To gain an insight into the influence love has on the individual's physical and psychological set-up and development (the micro-level), neurosciences and psychology can offer relevant perspectives. The first examines the physiological basis of love, while the latter focuses on the effects of love deprivation and provision in human development, behaviour and mental well-being. To examine the role of the love in the context of social and cultural practice over time (i.e. the macro-level), the writings of sociology offer a potential avenue to knowledge acquisition. Approaching questions that relate to the "bigger picture," to universal ideas and to ethical considerations about love, the field of moral philosophy promises to yield manifold insights. These theoretical considerations ultimately contributed to the development of the below, adapted model based on Bronfenbrenner's social-ecology approach (1974; 1979) for carrying out the third (literature review) and fourth stage (clarification of attributes) of a multidisciplinary concept analysis aimed at supporting an operationalisation of love.

Figure 3.2: Operationalisation of love

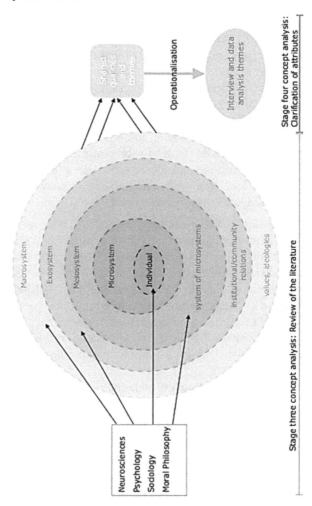

Figure 3.2 illustrates the process of translating love as an abstract concept with manifold and diffuse meanings into fewer, more specific themes representing its main qualities in the third and fourth stage of concept analysis. These themes will be used to structure a later interpretation and presentation of empirical data. The themes of love established in this chapter will be applied throughout Chapters 5 to 8 to evaluate prisoners' accounts of the absence and presence of love in their social-ecological environments. These will then be integrated with literature of the chosen disciplines as well as with criminological research. It will thus be the aim not only of this chapter but of the book per se to follow a social-ecological approach when analysing and evaluating the individual, institutional, social and moral systems love is embedded in. After all, recognising the interplay of these perspectives also supports the endeavour to contribute an original and sociologically imaginative (Mills 2000) piece of research to the relevant field:

> For that imagination is the capacity to shift from one perspective to another – from the political to the psychological; ... It is the capacity to range from the most impersonal and remote transformations to the most intimate features of the human self – and to see the relations between the two. (Mills 2000: 7)

The fact that systemic interrelations have to be considered, even when looking at a problem from a very distinctive disciplinary angle has also been underlined by neurobiologist Hüther (2006). He referred to the benefits, in fact, necessity, of adopting a systemic, multidisciplinary approach looking at human (brain) development, pointing out that

> [t]he complexity of [neuronal] connections ... is shaped by an individual's family relationships, the abilities passed on to him and the guiding ideals and the goals conveyed by the thoughts and aims, by the myths, legends and belief systems of the particular culture in which a person grows up. (Hüther 2006: 1).

The following sections follow this systemic approach when executing the third step of Walker and Avant's (1994) concept analysis. They review and classify a body of multidisciplinary literature, starting with the role of love in the human body as a microsystem itself, before working its way outward to meso-, exo- and macrosystem (Bronfenbrenner 1974).

3.3 Neuroscientific approaches — The physiological origins of love

In their comprehensive work to establish *A general theory of love* (2000), Lewis et al. (2000) utilise findings from evolution theory, neurobiology and neuro-imaging studies to provide insights into the origins and mechanisms of love in the human body, and more specifically in the human brain. Using these findings, they partly dispel the myth that love arises mysteriously out of nowhere stating that it "cannot emerge *ex vacuo*: it must originate in dynamic neural systems" (Lewis et al. 2000: 5) as part of a physical universe. They trace its source back to a part of the brain that had developed when "mammals split off from the reptilian line" (Lewis et al. 2000: 25): the limbic system. This evolutionary new part of the brain played a significant role in the further specialisation of mammals regarding not only their reproductive process, but predominantly their orientation toward their offspring. Compared to a reptilian parental relationship marked by detachment, mammals "take care of their own" (Lewis et al. 2000: 25). This led to the emergence of close-knit, mutually nurturant social relations and groups, such as families (Lewis et al. 2000). Another part of the mammalian brain, the one that evolved last and is the largest of the three brains in humans, is the *neocortex*, derived from the Greek *neo* for "new" and the Latin *cortex* for "rind." It is home to conscious motor control, reasoning, writing and experiencing our senses (Lewis et al. 2000). The limbic system in comparison is where "nurturance, social communion, communication, and play" (Lewis et al. 2000: 32) originate. According to evolution theory and neurobiology, the limbic brain developed additionally to the reptilian brain to enable mammals "to monitor the external world and the internal bodily environment" (Lewis et al. 2000: 52) striving to achieve congruence between the two. Lewis and colleagues (2000: 33) describe a hierarchy of regulation in which "the entire neocortex of humans continues to be regulated by the paralimbic regions from which it evolved." The human mammalian brain is thus divided into competing systems regulating emotions as well as reason.

If we look at love as an emotion in this way, its powerful influence on human motivation and behaviour starts making sense and has been underpinned by neurological clinical studies. Using physiological data gathered from functional magnetic resonance brain imaging (fMRI) one study found, for example, that "when participants gaze at pictures of beloved partners, activation occurs in regions of the brain that are associated with the motivation to obtain rewards" (Bartels and Zeki 2000). Neurologically, love invokes the human brain's imaginative power to activate emotions that can ultimately motivate behaviour. Whether love could be regarded as emotion has been controversially discussed in the fields of neurobiology and psychology. If we followed the definition of emotions "as transient feeling states that manifest themselves in bodily changes related to action or anticipated action" as provided by Plutchik (1994: 72), the above-described experiment would affirm the assumption of love being an emotion. It is connected to the human ability for imagination and the anticipation of rewards which are not rooted in the realistic conditions of the immediate environment. For example, the feeling of love induced by looking at a loved one's photograph referred to above, can transcend physical time and space. It arises as a conditioned response to a previously established connection to the person in the photograph.

3.3.1 Love as interpersonal resonance and mental connection

According to Lewis et al. (2000), the ability to forge mental connections to other mammals is owed to the specialisation of the limbic brain which arose as a "social sense organ," a highly sensitive physical mechanism to detect and analyse "the internal world of other mammals" (Lewis et al. 2000:62). The process by which two mammals forge this connection is one of becoming mutually attuned to each other and which has been termed "limbic resonance" (Lewis et al. 2000: 63) in neuroscience. This mutual attuning to each other's inner processes is achieved mainly by eye contact, enabling two nervous systems to "achieve a palpable and intimate apposition" (Lewis et al. 2000: 63). A similar approach is put forward by Fredrickson. She defines love as "positivity resonance," as a "true sensory and temporal connection with another living being" (Fredrickson 2013: 17). Its main mode is eye contact. According to Fredrickson, in a moment of love, we attune to another person, we mirror each other, and "to some extent ... become the reflection ... of the other" (Fredrickson 2013: 18). It has also been found that engaging in the process of positivity- or limbic resonance repeatedly over time can produce structural changes in the brain (Fredrickson 2013; Lewis et al. 2000). In this sense, love can hold transformative power. Neurobiologist Hüther (2006) echoes these findings, affirming that feeling loved and connected is one of the preconditions for successful (re-)creation of synapses in the brain, thus broadening our neuronal horizon. A prerequisite for such experience-dependent changes is the activation of the emotional centres (limbic system) leading to "the release of trophic, hormone-like substances, which stimulate the growth and the reorganization of nerve cell contacts and connections" (Hüther 2006: 2).

It is worth noting here that love, as defined by Fredrickson (2013), Hüther (2006) and Lewis et al. (2000) is necessarily connected to sharing and mirroring *positive* feelings. This would imply that sharing *negative* feelings with another person would not count as a prerequisite for love. Based on this statement, it stands to reason which outcomes would be produced by connections based on mixed, or purely negative emotions? Departing from the view that limbic systems of human beings are social organs – designed to detect, attune to and mirror each other's respective emotions – it would suggest that this not only applies to (re)producing positive feelings like love, but that negative feelings could also reverberate in two coupled limbic systems. Thus, not only love but hate and other emotional states can spread from one human brain to the other. How this relates to the long-term prisoners' experiences of the *absence* of love in particular, will be discussed in more detail in Chapter 5.

So far, we have gained some insight into how neuroscience perceives love to emerge out of and between mammalian, and especially human brains. How much of an essential role love plays in the maintenance of a healthy mental equilibrium and proper brain functioning will be considered subsequently.

3.3.2 Love as stabilising and regulating factor in the human nervous system

Lewis et al. (2000) not only describe love as a process of interpersonal attunement, but they also go one step further by linking it to neurophysiological stability of the mammalian nervous system – a process coined "limbic regulation" (Lewis et al. 2000). According to this view human beings are necessarily dependent on limbic regulation to feel stable or to even survive as new-borns. Neurosciences trace the original source of consistent limbic regulation back to a satisfactory synchronisation with attachment figures early in human life. The latter can be witnessed primarily in the early attunement process between primary caregiver and child. Since a new-born's physiology and nervous system are maximally open-loop – i.e. dependent on external feedback for its proper development – "without limbic regulation, his vital rhythms collapse, and he will die" (Lewis et al. 2000: 85). It is not only the physical presence of an attachment figure, but "*synchrony* [emphasis in the original] that he requires – … mutually responsive interaction" (Lewis et al. 2000: 62).

Love, therefore, implies a crucially important interpersonal component. Love emerges in human relationships and is based on shared inner processes that promote a balance of the nervous system. In other words, "stability means finding people who regulate you well and staying near them" (Lewis et al. 2000: 85). Without that mental stability, the human organism can suffer grave consequences, as the above example illustrates. Consequently, the meaning and importance of the *presence* of love can be observed very clearly, when it is *absent*. Its dual capacity to influence human well-being, growth and behaviour in positive and negative ways will become increasingly apparent throughout the course of this book. At this point, it will now be necessary to not only consider love's constructive qualities in fostering new neuronal structures and connectivity, but also to examine the destructive effects of its absence.

3.3.3 The role of love's absence in physiological stress responses

As much as "successful" limbic resonance can contribute to changes in the brain due to its neuroplasticity, so can the so-called stress response trigger "adaptive modification and reorganization of neuronal networks at any age" (Hüther 2006: 2). Hüther differentiates between two different reactions to and outcomes of stress: a controllable and an uncontrollable stress response of the brain. Both exhibit the same initial stages, i.e. eliciting "a nonspecific pattern of arousal in the associative cortex and in the limbic structures" (Hüther 2006: 3) as a response to a novel, challenging or threatening stimulus in the individual's environment. However, they can both generate different final outcomes. Whereas a controllable stress response will eventually lead to an enriching learning experience by facilitating the stabilisation of "the neural circuitry involved in the behavioral responding" (Hüther 2006: 4), an uncontrollable stress response can cause irreparable neuronal damage and disintegration. It is "elicited when the activation of the central stress-sensitive systems cannot be terminated by an individual's own efforts" (Hüther 2006: 5). This can be the case if previously acquired coping strategies are ineffective. The worst outcome of an unstoppable activation of the central stress response system is the secretion of adrenal glucocorticoids (a class of steroid hormones). These "have been shown to ... damage ... neurons and their dendrites" as well as affecting "the noradrenergic axons ... which tend to retract and to degenerate" (Hüther 2006: 6). This, in turn, can ultimately lead to the extinction of previously established neuronal connectivity which "may lead to fundamental changes in cognition, emotion and behavior" (Hüther 2006: 6). If these destabilisation processes are repeated, they may contribute to the manifestation of related psychopathologies (Hüther 2006).

Although the plasticity of the brain allows for these processes to take place at any age, their effects can be especially grave, in fact life-changing, during childhood since the brain's basic set-up is established postnatally. As Hüther (2006: 9) points out:

> those neuronal networks and synaptic pathways that have been stabilized
> by virtue of repeated early experience tend to become permanent; the
> synapses that are not used often enough tend to be eliminated.

Love's absence, when experienced as the *absence* of sufficient limbic regulation, resulting in physiological stress responses can impact negatively on the development of the human brain. Simultaneously, the *presence* of love can act as a protective factor or even antidote to stress responses.

3.3.4 Love as resilience factor in mental development

As illustrated earlier, the development and (re)structuring of certain parts of the human brain is necessarily dependent (and therefore vulnerable) to limbic resonance and limbic regulation with other human beings, especially close attachment figures. Much of a person's cognitive and emotional abilities, e.g. coping strategies related to stress, are "determined by the chain of sequential experiences made under the prevailing conditions of a given familial and socio-cultural context" (Hüther 2006: 7). The social-ecological factors of an individual's micro-, meso-, exo- and macrosystem (Bronfenbrenner 1974) therefore play a crucial role in the development of his or her brain and emotional coping strategies. According to Hüther, resilience toward stress is facilitated by attuned, secure emotional relationships which "provide the most potent protection against ... overload and ... act to resilience the stress-system under conditions of massive arousal" (Hüther 2006: 9). At the other end of the child's resilience spectrum lie dysfunctional behavioural adaptations.

As Hüther (2006: 10) goes on to explain, a child that "experiences constant stress and anxiety, risks for its brain structures to become destabilised or to even regress." This could potentially result in an underdevelopment of brain areas responsible for empathy and impulse control, thus potentially leading to the use of "pseudo-autonomous, egocentric ... violent destructive behavior" (Hüther 2006: 12) in an attempt to cope with environmental and personal stressors. Additionally, when it comes to the ability to "feel what others feel, and to experience feelings of connectedness ... and love" (Hüther 2006: 10) the development of the most intricate networks in the frontal cortex is crucially dependent on relationships, since they do not follow a genetically pre-set process. They only develop and are stabilised postnatally by "experience dependent plasticity" (Hüther 2006: 10) provided by the familial, educational, social and cultural environment.

Love, as conveyed relationally through positivity resonance or limbic regulation, can therefore be regarded as a crucial factor in the mental development and health of human beings. In fact, the evaluation of neuroscientific studies and literature on love thus far has unearthed a clear storyline of human interdependency and interconnectedness due to the nature of the mammalian brain. As Lewis et al. (2000) conclude, humans remain social animals, and as such, they continue to require a source of stabilisation outside of themselves. The "open-loop" design of the human nervous system means "that in some important ways, people cannot be stable on their own" (Lewis et al. 2000: 86). In other words, human beings are dependent on each other for some of the most essential emotional and physiological processes of mental well-being and development. One of these processes is facilitated by love as an essential developmental and resilience factor. In this context, it will not only be interesting but necessary to consider a growing field of neuro-biological literature. It concerns itself with the enquiry into the behavioural, anatomical and pharmacological basics of love that go beyond interpersonal dependency but, in fact, resemble patterns of addiction.

3.3.5 Love, attachment, dependency and addiction

Burkett and Young (2012), for example, have found parallels between addictive behaviour, social attachment and love, proposing that love is akin to a behavioural addiction. They suggest that "a deep and systematic concordance exists between the brain regions and neurochemicals involved in both addiction and social attachment" (Burkett and Young 2012: 2). According to their observations, especially romantic attachment features behaviours which are also defined as characteristic addictive behaviours such as "stress-induced relapse, lack of regard for consequences, being unable to quit, and losing track of time" (Burkett and

Young 2012: 3). Various studies – demonstrating, for example, a "mechanism of cross-tolerance between pair bonding and amphetamines" (Burkett and Young 2012: 8) – have contributed further to the assumption of neuroscientists "that the mechanisms that govern both, maintenance of social bonds ... and addiction to drugs of abuse ... are anatomically and functionally overlapping" (Burkett and Young 2012: 8). This brings to mind (pop-cultural) declarations of love, claiming for example, to not being able to live without the partner, or to be *Addicted to Love* (as Robert Palmer famously declared in his 1986 song of the same title).

A similar line of thought had already been introduced by Herman and Panksepp in 1978 with the opioid hypothesis of social attachment. Their neurobiological studies found that "opioid receptors mediate both social reward and social motivation" (Burkett and Young 2012). Their theory suggested that forging social connections could come with feelings of reward and contentment, hence motivating the continuation of related behaviours. This theory chimes with previously discussed findings by Bartels and Zeki (2000) about the activation of reward centres of participants' brains when gazing at pictures of their beloved. Whether the powerful neurological and behavioural influences of love as limbic resonance and limbic regulation, may be called attachment, dependency or addiction, it has become increasingly clear that love is essential to human development and human well-being. Up to this point, recurring themes of love as *connection* and facilitator of *resilience* have been located, and its importance becomes once more apparent, looking at the course of human psychological development.

3.4 Psychological approaches — Love as a factor in human development

Gilligan expresses the significance of love by pointing out that "attachment and separation anchor the cycle of human life, describing the biology of human reproduction and the psychology of human development" (Gilligan 1982: 151). We come into this world after the fusion of sperm and ovum, and after a period of intense connection, nurturance and growth in the motherly womb. The importance of love as connection does not cease postnatally. It continues to play an important role throughout our whole lives. Immediately after birth, the quality of connection with primary caregivers matters most, however, and can have crucial effects on the psychological development of an infant.

Similar to neuroscience, developmental psychology also rates sensory connectors like eye contact and touch as well as attuning and mirroring as crucial factors in the process of infant attachment and subsequent development. Attachment of the child to its caregiver has come to be regarded as "a key component in early life, and a failure to establish or maintain a proper attachment can lead to both psychological and physical problems later which ... may include violent behaviour" (Jones 2000: 65). This has partly to do with the above-discussed development of the prefrontal cortex which assumes a crucial role in inhibiting certain behaviours such as aggression. As has been pointed out already, certain parts of the brain are very dependent on relationships, and especially on "affectionate relationships that will generate ... opiates which will help this part of the brain to grow" (Gerhardt 2004: 180). Human brain development therefore is highly correlated with human relationships and emotions conveyed through them. The development of self-regulation, for example, is largely dependent on "behavioral synchrony between infant and caregiver" (Gerhardt 2004: 34). These findings are partly based on and related to earlier seminal research on infant attachment conducted by British child psychiatrist Bowlby (1973) who showed how temporary separations from mother-figures can evoke distinctive emotions such as separation anxiety and anger.

3.4.1 The effects of love deprivation as human need deprivation in infant development

An infant deprived of physical connection with his or her primary caregiver goes "through a stage of distressed protest, followed by stages of despair and detachment" (Plutchik 1994: 209). The perceived (or real) loss of close contact with the mother is experienced as an existential threat to the child's survival. Similar results have been arrived at by psychologists Harlow and Zimmermann (1958) when observing the harrowingly debilitating effects of varying periods of motherly separation on infant monkeys, as recounted by Plutchik (1994: 210):

> Despite adequate food, cleanliness, and environment, the monkeys became severely dysfunctional, rocking back and forth in a corner, sucking or biting their fingers or skin, screeching or crying, walking on their hind legs while clasping their own body, or curling into a ball. When they were allowed to join other monkeys, their behavior was one of panic, and they were unable to engage in normal social interactions.

The deprivation of motherly care and connection had direct effects on the monkeys' ability to function autonomously or to self-regulate emotional stress responses. This affected their later ability to function socially and engage with their environment. The early development of dysfunctional emotional stress management mechanisms like aggression and antisocial behaviour can have wide-ranging detrimental effects in human life as well. Dysfunctional emotional stress management strategies can become criminogenic risk factors that have been found to be "the most consistent through life, the most linked to adult criminality and drug abuse and marital violence" (Gerhardt 2004: 188).

Criminological longitudinal research such as the Cambridge Delinquency Study (Farrington 1997) likewise confirms a connection between early attachment failures and later offending and mental health problems. For nearly 40 years, it has been following 411 males and identified a number of factors that would influence adult offending behaviour (Ansbro 2008). Although factors interacted on different levels, "the quality of parental care stands out as an important mediating factor in the child's developmental pathway" (Ansbro 2008: 234). In another study looking at the background of 200 serious young offenders in the UK, Boswell (1998) located a pattern showing that all participants had experienced severe loss, neglect or abuse in their childhood.

Deprivation theories like the above point out how the existential importance of love as human connection asserts itself in the effects of its absence. Without its supply "we feel and are endangered" (Parkes 2006: 2). In fact, psychology scholars like Rubin (1973) or Maslow (1987) regarded love as so essential to human life that they classed it as a basic human need. In his classic theory on motivation and personality, Maslow organised those human needs "into a hierarchy of relative prepotency, in which the belongingness and love needs occupy a relatively high rank" (Maslow 1987: 17). They emerge after the physiological and safety needs – for food, shelter and physical integrity – have been gratified, and involve "giving and receiving affection" (Maslow 1987: 20). Although the ranking underlying Maslow's theory of human motivation has been criticised since its establishment (see Neher 1991, for example) theorists like Neef (1991) or Deci and Ryan (2000) likewise endorse the view of love as an essential human need. Deci and Ryan suggest that it functions as innate psychological "nutriment essential for ongoing psychological growth, integrity, and well-being" (Deci and Ryan 2000:29). One main implication of the organisation of basic human needs into a hierarchy is that gratification becomes as important a concept as deprivation. According to Maslow human behaviour and well-being is influenced by the satisfaction of basic needs. Consequently, love as the very factor that can induce severe mental and physical stress as well as dysfunctional coping mechanisms when missing also seems to be the most effective "remedy" or antidote to all of these symptoms.

3.4.2 Love's absence and presence as (mental-)health factor

Harlow and Zimmermann (1958) came to understand the importance of love's absence and presence, when they introduced a so-called "cloth mother" into the set-up of their above deprivation experiment. When the infant monkeys were presented with a choice of either a mother substitute only made of netting wire that provided food, or a soft and comfortable "cloth mother" not providing food, most of them chose to spend considerably more time in close embrace with the latter. Harlow and Zimmermann (1958) hence defined the pivotal factor that was not only most appealing but also able to draw infant monkeys out of severe states of distress as "contact comfort." Loss or prolonged separation from a source of "contact comfort" could lead to a persistent anxiety state which could result in "prolonged negative affect and depressive-like behaviors" (Burkett and Young 2012: 18).

Not only for infants, but also later in life, the thwarting of the love needs and especially sudden and unexpected disconnection from loved ones represents a cause of severe stress to the human organism. Trauma – when defined as the sudden cessation of human interaction (Lindemann 1944) – can affect a person on a physical as well as psychological level. De Zulueta (1993), for example, describes striking similarities found in psychobiological studies between infant-mother separation reactions and bereavement reactions in adults. These presented themselves as

> agitation, crying, aimless activity and inactivity, all of which are attempts to regain the lost "object" ... The adult shows social withdrawal, decreased or variable food intake, sad expressions ... and a depressed mood ... The physiological changes in the adult are those of weight loss, sleep disturbance, muscular weakness and cardiovascular changes (De Zulueta 1993: 56).

As pointed out in above statements, the physiological and psychological effects of the loss of a love "object" can be grave not only for dependent infants but they also severely curtail and disrupt the lives of adults. Lewis et al. explain this phenomenon with the fact that love has to be understood as a "reciprocal physiologic influence" entailing "a deeper and more literal connection than most realize" (Lewis et al. 2000: 207). It is striking how the negative physiological changes occurring after the loss of a love "object" correspond with the changes that limbic regulation affords to lovers who attune to each other, i.e. "the ability to modulate each other's emotions, neurophysiology, hormonal status, immune function, sleep rhythms and stability" (Lewis et al. 2000: 208). Love seems to bestow a certain kind of stability without which the human organism loses its balance.

Exploring *The Art of Loving* (1995) social-psychologist and critical theorist Fromm likewise refers to the pains and mental health risks connected to the failure to sufficiently gratify the love and belonging needs. He points out an almost existential threat emanating from total disconnection:

> The deepest need of man ... is the need to overcome his separateness ... The *absolute* [emphasis in original] failure to achieve this aim means insanity, because the panic of complete isolation can be overcome only by such a radical withdrawal from the world outside that the feeling of separation disappears – because the world outside, from which one is separated, has disappeared (Fromm 1995: 8).

Fromm infers that feeling or even perceiving to be isolated and disconnected from other human beings can induce a fear so intense that the only way out seems to be internal withdrawal. This in turn may exacerbate the initially experienced isolation and the individual is in danger of entering a psychological state of dissociation, disconnecting him or her from his or her own emotions and sometimes bodily sensations also.

It is important to keep in mind, however, that times of solitude can also be invigorating and necessary for an individual to maintain emotional equilibrium. There is a role "in the well-lived life for apartness from others" (Milligan 2011: 49). Too much connection can also become intrusive and engulfing. It is a question of relative measures, of sufficient satisfaction of basic needs to ensure mental well-being. As Milligan (2011: 50) states, "we do not need to be loved ... each and every moment of our lives." This statement entails the notion of satiability, marking a healthy relationship with love. The tipping of the scale either towards an insatiable need for love, or toward a total disconnection from love hence can be taken as an indication that mental equilibrium has been lost. In a similar vein, certain qualities of love may not feel or be equally beneficial for everyone. It is important to consider individual differences at the foundation of how love is experienced. Someone who has struggled for independence whilst growing up with a parental love that felt smothering and intrusive might be sceptical or anxious about closeness and connection, since it came to mean a loss of agency and autonomy.

As Lewis et al. (2000: 116) indicate, "a child enveloped in a particular style of relatedness learns its special intricacies and particular rhythms ... he arrives at an intuitive knowledge of love that forever evades consciousness." This again is owed to how the human brain operates, since it automatically narrows a multitude of felt experiences "into a few regular prototypes" (Lewis et al. 2000: 116) that could otherwise result in overwhelming confusion. Thus, the brain of a child memorises a distilled version of love, depending on the relationship qualities it predominantly witnessed. As likely as love can be associated with protection, care or liberation by one, it can also mean suffocation, abuse or dependence that feels humiliating to another individual (Lewis et al. 2000). This inherent individuality in the interpretation of abstract concepts has to be taken into consideration in the further process of operationalising love.

3.4.3 Love as a dual concept

In the preceding discussion, it has already become clear that love as human need possesses ambiguous characteristics. As Parkes (2006: 270) infers, "love can both cause problems and facilitate their cure." Conceptually, love seems to possess a dual quality described by Perlman (1999: 37) as "akin to a kind of sickness, although also having healing powers." Plutchik likewise points out the essential and dual role that love plays by identifying its counterpart as sadness (with its offshoot depression). In his view, both "represent opposites in that one is based

on receiving ... while the other is based on loss of ... attachment or deprivation"
(Plutchik 1994: 315). Suttie (1935) suggests that love is also interrelated with hate,
another essential human emotion. He claims hate to be an expression either of
frustrated love or an "intensification of separation-anxiety which in turn is *roused*
[emphasis in the original] by a threat against love" (Suttie 1935: 25). Psychiatrist
De Zulueta likewise considers the possibility that "violence and hate, cooperation
and love" might be expressions of "the reciprocal aspects of the same human
needs and behavioural patterns" (De Zulueta 1993: 27).

Love assumes a pivotal role in influencing human growth as well as
deterioration. This quality – together with love's practical expression through
connection and attachment – have been carved out in the discussion so far. After
considering the psychological and neurological factors at play in the human
experience of love, it is now important to consider their "interaction ... with social
experiences, social rules, and social sanctions" (Plutchik 1994: 364), to understand
love not only as a primary feature of individual psychology but also of civilised life
itself (Gilligan 1995). It is necessary to explore love's social, historical and cultural
components, since a mere biological or neurological account could be seen as
"radically ahistorical" (Armstrong 2002: 20) as well as detached from this book's
social-ecological viewpoint. It is paramount not to propose "a universal and
constant human nature," or to imply that "love ought to be always and everywhere
the same" (Armstrong 2002: 20). As in every ecological system, different spheres
are overlapping and interdependent. The same applies to the individual and the
social sphere. As much as perceptions of and attributions to love can be regarded
as highly individual in a micro- and mesosystemic context, as much does it also
represent a cultural practice conditioned by exosystemic institutional and
macrosystemic cultural influences. Embedding and examining the concept of love
within cultural, social and historical meanings will aim to pay tribute to this social-
ecological interplay as well as to the fact that "the experience of love changes as
the surrounding culture of beliefs changes" (Armstrong 2002: 23).

3.5 Sociological approaches — Love as socio-cultural factor

What the following discussion is setting out to do is not only to recount social,
normative stances but to also map their development throughout modern
history. In doing so, it keeps Hirsch and Wardlow's view on *Modern Loves* (2006:
2) in mind that

> [w]hile the forms and idioms of modern love may on the surface appear
> to be similar around the world, those similarities are a product not just
> of cultural globalization but also of specific economic and social
> transformations.

Considering the full breadth of cultural globalisation as well as of economic and social transformations goes beyond the scope of this chapter's aim to carve out love's main qualities. Its focus will therefore be "closer to home" i.e. related to this book's geographical and historical orientation. It will retrace the development of different forms of love in Western societies throughout modernity. In particular, it will examine how love is represented through time- and space-specific social narratives (Lopez-Cantero 2020). Socially shared narratives may be associated with certain attitudes and practices (Lindemann 2014). These can be symbolically charged by and interacting with (pop-)cultural narratives circulating in a given society (Lopez-Cantero 2020). They provide interpretative frameworks, defining what – conventionally – counts as love (Lopez-Cantero 2020), some of which shall be examined hereinafter.

As a prerequisite, however, it is important to differentiate from the very outset between *love* and *relationships*, since it seems all too easy to use both terms interchangeably. Just as previous sections have tried to accumulate knowledge about what love means for the individual's physiological and psychological functioning and well-being, the following passages aim to clarify which role love plays in the individual's relationships with others and his or her environment. Therefore, the focus lies less on a detailed classification of human relationships, but rather on the qualities of love as "a social activity and process" (Restive 1977: 235).

3.5.1 Love as communal connecting element

One of the qualities of love that has been emerging so far is its manifestation as interpersonal connection. The following discussion aims to add a cognitive, intellectual perspective to neuroscience's and developmental psychology's view of love as sensory bridging concept via eye contact or touch. Through focusing our mental attention onto another person, we establish a connection not only physiologically but also inwardly with his or her identity through intimate identification (Helm 2010). The concept of intimate identification can assume an important role in establishing social connections. Love with the ultimate aim to intimately know another's inner self, can contribute to "information exchange and learning" (Restive 1977: 233). At some point, *loving* could in fact come to equate *knowing:*

> [I]f we want to know the truth about another person, the best access to that truth is not through a detached indifference, but through … love for that person (Robbins 2013).

In this sense, love fosters insight. Knowing another intimately can help interpreting his or her – and ultimately human – behaviour better. According to sociologist Restive this could not only be of benefit for the individual but also for society itself, since it raises the aggregate level of knowledge. It allows us to gain "a perspective on the sociocultural, environmental, global ... settings of self and others" (Restive 1977: 241). Knowledge on the microsystemic level of the individual could thus provide insight into more generic predispositions of mankind on a macrosystemic level. Ultimately love can be seen as a critical cooperative factor enhancing the chances of survival and growth of societies through adaptation that has been facilitated by learning about the other (Restive 1977). If seen as the willingness to learn about *an other*, love also inspires the individual to transcend ego-boundaries by focusing on a love object outside of him- or herself. This focus can act collectively as a social "'glue' that enables human beings to form durable connections with ... others" (Rykkje et al. 2015: 2). It is what social critic Ruskin (1985) has come to coin "social affection ... – such affection as one man *owes* [emphasis in original] to another. All right relations ... and all their best interests, ultimately depend on these" (Ruskin 1985: 169).

However, neither Restive (1977), Rykkje et al. (2015), nor Ruskin provide a definition of the qualities this form of love is meant to embody. In an exchange of letters with Einstein – archived in the book *Einstein on Peace* (1960) – regarding potential measures to reduce the risk of war, Freud described a communal form of love as *Eros without sex*, as emotional ties without a sexual component.[1] Its creative force lies in the potential to "create a community of feeling" (Plutchik 1994: 361) by affirming shared interests and identifying with these. In a similar vein, Giddens (1992) suggests introducing *Eros* and its "culture-building capacities" as "pleasurable cooperation" (Giddens 1992: 152) into social relations to strengthen community. It is not clear from the above discussion, however, how this form of love would be represented and implemented in practice. Attempting to specify this process would go beyond the scope of this chapter to identify recurring qualities of love. The qualities seemingly most prominent in a communal form of love present here as its orientation towards sharing common interests and gaining intimate knowledge about the other. Staying with the idea of *Eros* as a form of love, brings into focus its sexual component. It shifts the focus to another idea of love, one that is mainly represented and practiced in microsystemic dyadic relationships most commonly found in contemporary Western society: romantic love.

3.5.2 Love as romantic relationship idea(l)

Love of this kind tends to be based on relationships dominated by *Eros*, marked by elements of physical attraction and close, unified engagement, ideally

---

[1] A more comprehensive introduction of love as *Eros* will be undertaken in Section 3.6 of this chapter. At this point it shall be defined as a form of love that potentially holds creative powers through passionate concern for another excluding sexual interest.

binding partners together "until death do us part." This dyadic relationship ideal has become commonplace in contemporary Western society and its background and principles are rarely questioned today. Romantic love, however, is a prime example for the propensity of cultural concepts to undergo reinterpretation over time, accompanying social and cultural changes. Before the emergence of romantic love in Western and especially European societies from the late 18th century onwards, ideals of love in these societies were closely connected to values of Christianity. Tracking the *Transformation of Intimacy* (1992), Giddens points out, that in pre-romantic societies it was expected that "one should devote oneself to God in order to know him, and ... through this process self-knowledge was achieved" (Giddens 1992: 39). This precondition for knowing yourself through the knowledge of God was then converted into the romantic idea of knowing yourself through the intimate knowledge of the partner and came to form part of a couple's "mystical unity" (Giddens 1992: 39). Its corresponding ideal relationship is one "that establishes a oneness between the lovers" (Grossi 2018: 217).

Another feature of the idea(l) of romantic love was a focus on the element of sublime love predominating sexual ardour (Giddens 1992). With the emergence of romantic love, virtue took centre stage and an emphasis of "qualities of character which pick out the other person as 'special'" (Giddens 1992: 40) predominated bodily passions. It also started to dominate over formerly binding arrangements of marriage according to the borders of class and economic compatibility of partners. Romantic love set out to break with those traditional social and cultural practices, placing loving sentiment before "duties imposed on individuals by ... tradition, class, race, and family" (Grossi 2018: 217). The freedom to pursue individual satisfaction and autonomy in romantic love relationships was held up as an ideal but brought with it also a destabilisation of social structures (Grossi 2018). Ultimately, the emergence of romantic love stood for and was embedded in another, very distinct cultural, social and historical occurrence in Western societies: the rise of modernity.

3.5.3 Modern loves

Sociologist Illouz (2012), for example, firmly places romantic love "within the cultural core of modernity" (Illouz 2012: 11). In modern Western societies, the attainment of this ideal love came to be seen as an "existential goal" and the "ultimate source of meaning and happiness" (Grossi 2018: 219). It also represented a new personal ideal of the "reflexive self that ... defined itself and its identity in primarily emotional terms, centred on the management and affirmation of its feelings" (Illouz 2012: 11). In its wake – and during the further course of modernity – sciences concerned with the inner emotional world of the individual emerged and flourished. Novel findings of psychology, biology, or neurosciences, for example, contributed to the reinterpretation of love from a formerly "ineffable, unique, quasi-mystical experience and selfless sentiment into ... concepts such as 'the unconscious', 'the sex drive', 'species survival', or 'brain chemistry'" (Illouz 2012: 163), as illustrated earlier. However, the achievement of scientific knowledge came at a price for the modern individual and love itself.

Not without a certain melancholy, Illouz asserts a resulting loss of cultural meaning and cultural embeddedness of love because "romantic desire becomes emptied of its mythological content" and loses its "capacity to be experienced as 'enchantment', a surrender of reason and the self" (Illouz 2012: 162). The idea that love cannot be justified, that it does not always make sense, and that it "outstrips our reasons" (Martin 2015: 697) began to fade. In the course of scientific and cultural development, love became the target of increasing rationalisation and commodification. The inexplicable mysticism of love was replaced by disenchantment which is regarded by Illouz (2012: 162) as a pervasive "fundamental cultural, cognitive, and institutional process of modernity." In a modern world, characterised by individualism, capitalism and secularism, love had lost its self-forgetting quality and had developed into a "utilitarian project of the self in which one has to secure maximum pleasure and well-being" (Illouz 2012: 164). According to Illouz, self-interest took centre stage, contributing to a loss of love's sacredness. A very recent example of this and of love's altered role in individual relationships and society can be witnessed in the rise of online dating (respectively dating apps) as part of the digitalisation of modern life.

According to sociologist Kaufmann (2012) the increasing use of online dating, starting in the mid-1990s, has drastically changed the way individuals in large parts of Western society form and maintain dyadic love relationships. Although the need for loving relationships is probably the initial motivator for individuals to engage in online dating, this cultural practice has taken on a life of its own. Increasingly, romantic partners are successfully found through online dating, but a significant proportion of users of this service also describe a disenchantment with love (Kaufmann 2012), echoing Illouz's (2012) criticism of an emerging super-rational, utilitarian consumer culture.

3.5.4 *Using vs. Valuing* — Love as moral choice

A reinterpretation of love in market-economic terms from a "quasi-mystical experience and selfless sentiment" (Illouz 2012: 163) into a calculable commodity and algorithms has taken place in contemporary Western societies. Some sociologists point towards certain disadvantages that can come with it. As Kaufmann states in his studies of *Love online* (2012: 14) "the game can be fun for a while. But all-pervasive ... utilitarianism eventually sickens anyone who has any sense of human decency." His strong normative statement – together with Illouz's overt criticism of modernity's changing love ideal – underpins another important quality of love, namely its apparent resistance to being subjected to rational calculation and economic parameters. Condemning a utilitarian attitude towards love as "sickening," Kaufmann (2012), for example, points towards a moral dimension of love that is distinct from the motivation of personal gain, namely valuing (Martin 2015).

In its value-oriented version, love means ascribing innate worth to the beloved just for his or her uniqueness without guarantees of reciprocation, or as Illouz (2012: 160) put it: "The object of love is ... incommensurable." This perspective refers back to love as selfless sentiment and interest in the other. Love hence becomes a moral choice, an extension beyond self-interest. At this point, we enter the theoretical territory of moral philosophy and the virtues. Below consultation of the discipline of moral philosophy will be dedicated to adding an additional layer of analysis: the enquiry into a greater truth about love as a reality of human existence. A moral philosophical enquiry will engage further with the manifestation of love in its social-ecological macrosystem. It contains myths, ideologies and ethical belief systems pertaining to the "bigger picture."

3.6 Moral philosophical approaches — Love as human virtue

One of moral philosophy's main interests revolves around questions of how to lead the good life, how to do good and which choices a person has to make to reach these goals. Especially the concept of virtue as a distinctively human capability plays an important role in moral philosophy. It entails the capacity for the formation of character and personhood which can be achieved by purposefully integrating a variety of "beliefs and desires, and actions into stable dispositions and habits" (Smith 2010: 52). This is believed by moral philosophers to help fostering happiness and moral goodness (Smith 2010) as well as personhood. In a similar vein, Aristotle's moral philosophy defines a moral agent as someone whose actions are motivated by an inherent knowledge of the good (Schroeder et al. 2010).

In his deliberation on human personhood as hallmarks of *Moral, Believing Animals* (2003) contemporary moral philosopher Smith reminds us, however, to bear all components of the term *moral agent* in mind. Although ancient moral philosophy may depart from an assumption of an intrinsically given ability to recognise the morally good, Smith stresses the fact that personhood and agency also comprise the ability to discriminate, to "judge, embrace, reject, and modify" (Smith 2003: 28) moral beliefs and behaviour. Human moral agents are seen here as "self-conscious animals ... able to 'step back' from and develop alternative ... perspectives on moral orders ... taught by socializers to subjectively embrace" (Smith 2003: 28). It is, thus, also the component of conscious choice and critical reflection that constitutes a moral agent's personhood. The acquisition and performance of virtue rests on the ability to make conscious choices based on morality or, in other words, to "do the right thing."

Screening relevant moral philosophical literature, love is often described as important constitutional factor of human virtue. In fact, one of moral philosophy's fundamental writings – Plato's *Symposium* – declares "love ... with most power when it comes to the acquisition of virtue and happiness by human beings" (Plato cited in Rowe 1998: 31). Etymologically, there are two families of Greek words that could be translated as love in the strictest sense. As Kraut (2008: 286) explains:

> On the one hand, there is the verb *philein* and its cognates (*philia* is the noun, *philos* the adjective) ... On the other hand, 'to love' is also the proper translation of the verb *eran* (*erôs* is the name of this psychological force, *erastês* designates a lover, and *erômenos* is the one who is loved).

Eros most commonly refers to a type of desire driving people to connect sexually, "and also to think obsessively of the person who is loved and to be filled with longing when he or she is absent" (Kraut 2008: 286). *Philia*, in comparison, most likely refers to love between friends. Although it could "be applied to nearly any group of cooperative associates ... *philia* is not necessarily low in affect" (Kraut 2008: 287) and can be the basis of enduring emotional connections between people.

Adding to Kraut's interpretation of love in the teachings of Plato, Greek philosophy encompasses further ideals of love, namely *storge* (familial love) and *agape* (love for humankind or charity). Expanding on these concepts, in his deliberation on *The Four Loves* (1960), Lewis refers to *storge* as "affection, especially between parents and their children" (Lewis 1960: 42). Looking back at previous sections on developmental psychology, this form of love seems to share certain qualities with attachment. In contrast to *storge's* supposedly natural appearance (Lewis 1960), *philia* (friendship) is "the least natural of loves" but seen as "the happiest and most fully human of all loves" (Lewis 1960: 70). It is a love based on shared interests, purposes and truths. It represents a conscious choice to become friends with "the man who agrees with us that some question, little regarded by others, is of great importance" (Lewis 1960: 78). Interpreting section IX 4 of Aristotle's *Nicomachean Ethics* (ca. 350 B.C) Annas (1988: 1) perceives *philia*, to have been invested by Aristotle with the following specific conditions:

> A friend ... is one who (1) wishes and does good ... things to a friend, for the friend's sake, (2) wishes the friend to exist and live, for his own sake, (3) spends time with his friend.

In these specifications, we reencounter the notion of valuing a person "for his own sake," a quality of love that has been established earlier. Under certain circumstances, however, *philia* can become very close and can come to form the basis for another form of love to emerge: *eros*. As indicated above, this concept is most commonly deployed to describe microsystemic dyadic (romantic) relationships, or the state of being in love (Lewis 1960) often involving a sexual element. Its qualities can be partly traced back to Plato's myth of the double people. According to this story – related by Aristophanes in Plato's *Symposium* – the ancient predecessors of human beings were each made up of two persons, with four arms, four legs and constructed as one round whole. Feeling threatened by their power, the Greek god Zeus "cut them all in half, leaving everyone incomplete and yearning to refind his or her other half" (Perlman 1999: 4). This mythical background forms part of the explanation as to why

> *Eros* makes a man really want, not a woman, but one particular woman. In some mysterious ... fashion the lover desires the Beloved herself, not the pleasure she can give. (Lewis 1960: 109)

According to this (hetero-normatively framed) ideal of *eros*, entering such a dyadic relationship inspires the individual to overleap "the massive wall of ... selfhood" and to plant "the interests of another in the centre of his being" (Lewis 1960: 131). It shifts the focus of loving from a self-centred view of gaining benefits and meeting individual needs through another person, onto another's well-being.

3.6.1 Love as self-transcendence and selfless concern for another

According to moral philosophical considerations, human beings in love are able to transcend their ego-boundaries and identify with the beloved, incorporating his or her well-being into their own, and taking his or her identity "to 'heart'" (Helm 2010: 10). This intimate identification "is what distinguishes the kind of concern involved in love proper from other, less intimate forms of personal concern such as compassion" (Helm 2010: 10). The root of the noun intimacy points towards the profound effect love has on our identity. It can be traced back to the Latin verb *intimare*, meaning "impress" or "make familiar" and *intimus*, meaning "inmost." Taking a beloved's identity to heart (Helm 2010) can leave an impression on our innermost self.

Focusing on another's well-being with selfless concern as well as the concept of self-transcendence, moves *eros* closer to *agape*. But unlike *eros*, "*agape* cannot be justified by an appeal to the beloved or her properties" (Helm 2010: 2). It is "a love that does not depend on our own attraction" (Lewis 1960: 150). It is rather an "unconditional ... love toward the neighbour, identifying with his or her needs and recognizing his or her value" (Eriksson 1990). *Agape* is associated with concepts such as compassion, altruism or charity. It does not discriminate but loves "something in each of us that cannot be naturally loved" (Lewis 1960: 151). It contains the idea that individuals forego their own immediate benefit and act instead with a view to consciously benefit someone else. As a virtue, then, love represents the intentional and conscious decision of a moral agent, ideally marked by an "application of individual powers of deliberation, self-monitoring, and self-control" (Nelson 2004: 392).

3.6.2 Love as constituent of personhood and moral agency

Love as a virtuous trait of self-control and deliberation contradicts the previously discussed romantic paradigm of falling in love for no apparent but rather mystical reason. Instead, it establishes the idea that a moral agent is someone consciously choosing *to* as well as *whom* to love. The notion of love as human power of a moral agent also points towards its earlier encountered quality as a factor in realising human potential. Looking back at developmental psychology, for example, love is regarded as a nutrient that can nurture the human propensity of self-transcendence and growth, the "self-fulfilment of one's own potential" (Eriksson et al. 2013: 8). According to Smith this capability "of passing beyond themselves ... to cross a threshold to another place – from the Latin *transcendere*, which means 'to climb over, to surpass' is another constituent of personhood" (Smith 2010: 65). A similar view is conveyed by Csikszentmihalyi (1980: 325) who argues that

> there is no better way of becoming a whole human being than by paying attention to another. Only from an intimate relationship with another person can one learn to use all the hidden potentialities of one's self.

By shifting the focus away from an *I* towards a *Thou* (Buber 1970, emphasis added) a person opens him- or herself up for feedback from the other. He or she re-experiences him- or herself through the other which can potentially lead to an integration of new external information into his or her hitherto existing self-image. It adds to knowledge and awareness of the self. Moral philosopher Williams emphasises love's (re-)creative potential as well, stating that "the attitudes and responses which the self finds in others are powerful factors in moving the self. Being loved creates a new person" (Williams 1968: 120). Love can provide an impulse for re-evaluating self-concepts and possibly alter the individual's outlook on him- or herself. The process of being mirrored by a vis-á-vis holds the opportunity for the other to recognise his or her own human potential through another person.

When it comes to incorporating new ideas into individual self-conception, contemporary philosopher Badiou describes love as "a quest for truth" (2009: 21), an exploration of potential and the unknown. This chimes in with findings of sociology, regarding love as the accumulation of knowledge about the other through intimate identification. Love, in this sense, is necessarily connected to augmentation. It *adds* to knowledge about the self and the other. It creates a connection and cohesion as a constructive human power. When love is present, growth happens – be it the creation of new neural pathways or furthering human potential. When love is absent, the result is decline, manifesting, for example, in the loss of previously established neural connections, or the deterioration in physical and psychological health in humans after the loss of love. Throughout the preceding discussion, it has become apparent that some features of love reappear in different disciplines.

3.7 Recurring themes in the multidisciplinary conceptualisation of love

Exploring the concept of love within a social-ecological framework guided by the disciplines of neuroscience, psychology, sociology and moral philosophy has helped to unearth some of its main features. Besides identifying congruences between disciplines, it is paramount, however, to be aware of discrepancies arising from diverging disciplinary viewpoints. Conclusions about the nature and qualities of love may differ and be owed to a discipline's unique access to the topic. Neuroscience and psychology, for example, postulate a somewhat universal application of love as human need, based on physiological prerequisites. Its absence or presence is said to be affecting human beings generally in a similar, if not the same way. These effects predominantly present on a physiological, psychological and behavioural level of the individual. Love, in that sense, is regarded as developmental and environmental factor, implying a relatively passive stance of those (not) experiencing love. Love deprivation in childhood, for example, or "love-addiction" in adulthood seemingly can only be suffered and endured by the individual, not actively pursued or resisted.

In contrast to neuroscientific and psychological approaches, love is pictured as a mutable concept by sociological and philosophical literature. It is said to be vulnerable to (re-)interpretation on an individual as well as social level. Far from being passively suffered, love is portrayed by moral philosophy as the conscious choice of a moral agent to live virtuously. According to this disciplinary vantage point, love is "what we make it."

Although contrasting in their respective outlooks, the examined disciplines nevertheless work together to bring the qualities of love into sharper focus. In conjunction, they begin to carve out a duality that adds depth and substance to a previously fuzzy concept. In preparation for the design of empirical analysis, it is necessary to move on to an even more substantial view of love. Following the next step of concept analysis (Walker and Avant 1994), I will aim to carve out and summarise love's main qualities as defined by the chosen disciplines. These will ultimately serve as a basis to locate potential overlaps in the last step of the operationalisation process.

3.7.1 Love's themes in neurosciences and psychology

- ○ The source of love can be allocated in the limbic part of the human mammalian brain as an evolutionary adaptation.

- ○ The process of creating feelings of love is anchored in sensory (eye-contact, touch) and mental (mirroring, limbic resonance) connection between individuals. Hence it can only emerge in relationship. It entails the focus on a love object which is the basis of attachment.

- ○ Love as limbic regulation is a necessary prerequisite for the nervous system's equilibrium. As a basic human need and nutrient, it is essential for psychological well-being, development and growth. As a result of prolonged love deprivation an uncontrollable stress response can be induced in the brain, leading to a destabilisation of brain circuitry, as well as dysfunctional or pathological coping mechanisms.

- ○ On the opposite end of the mental health spectrum lies love's ability to promote the creation of new brain synapses, new connections and can thus foster neuronal change. As an emotion, mental power and behavioural addiction love can furthermore motivate behaviour.

3.7.2 Love's themes in sociology

- ○ Love is an experience in relation to others, be it individuals or groups and can promote social coherence and communion through shared interests.

- ○ Love promotes an interest to acquire knowledge about the other. Through intimate identification, this can contribute to knowledge about the self and to aggregate knowledge about a community or society.

- ○ Through focussing on a love object, love inspires the transcendence of ego-boundaries. It defies economic utility thinking. Love is practiced as selfless valuing of the uniqueness of the beloved as a person for his or her own sake.

- ○ As a mental construct of beliefs and ideologies, the concept of love is vulnerable to reinterpretation according to social, historical and cultural changes.

3.7.3 Love's themes in moral philosophy

○   Love is a human virtue said to promote happiness and personhood. It constitutes the conscious choice of a moral agent to live the "good life" guided by virtuous choices.

○   Love has the ability to foster knowledge of self through knowledge and intimate identification with others. The latter can potentially contribute to identity change and personal development by bringing hidden potentialities of the self into view.

○   As a human virtue love implies the transcendence of ego-boundaries and to place the interests of the beloved before self-interest, valuing the beloved as unique and as a person.

After listing its main characteristics derived from a review of multidisciplinary literature in stage three of this chapter's concept analysis, stage four now requires a further thinning out and succinct summary of recurring themes.

3.7.4 Concept analysis step four: Clarification of attributes

Table 3.1 represents the result of a contextual synthesis of the above-outlined multidisciplinary themes. These have been integrated through four interrelating examination criteria: 1) Love as *human need*; 2) Love as *human virtue*; 3) The *presence* of love; 4) The *absence* of love. The former two criteria have been taken as organising principles from psychology's and moral philosophy's definition of love as *human need* and *human virtue*. The latter two criteria pay tribute to this book's focus, namely inquiring into the effects of the *presence* and *absence* of love in human, and more specifically, long-term prisoners' lives. Consequently, Table 3.1 represents a summary of recurring qualities of love that can be assigned to the four chosen criteria.

Table 3.1: Concept analysis step four: Love's recurring attributes

	Love as *human need*	Love as *human virtue*
Mainly represented through	connection, attachment, relationship, (mental) resonance and regulation	Transcending ego-boundaries and valuing of the other
Its *presence* promotes	1) Nurturance, growth, mental well-being 2) Community through intimate identification with another 3) Knowledge and truth about the self and the other	4) Realising human potential, development and growth 5) Creating change in the self 6) Moral agency, personhood, ethical life
Its *absence* can induce	Individual psychological stress responses and pathologies	Lack of mutual valuing, resulting in a loss of communality, social cohesion, and morale; potential (ab-)use of the other

The final implementation of love's operationalisation consists of a translation of the concept of love from the mental image of a phenomenon into a practical representation of its main qualities in the lives of long-term prisoners. It will mainly build on Table 3.2 which itself has been tailored around the same examination criteria as Table 3.1. Its process of operationalisation effectively focuses on how the effects of the presence and absence of love as a human need and human virtue are experienced by prisoners in their respective social-ecological systems throughout their lives. Table 3.2 consequently establishes four related thematic areas on which this book's empirical analysis will predominantly be based:

Table 3.2: Operationalisation of love into data-analysis themes

	Love as human need	**Love as human virtue**
Experienced by prisoners through	1) Outside and inside past and present relationships	3) Perceptions of self, self-development and growth
Effects of presence and absence on prisoners	2) Effects on past and present mental well-being and behaviour	4) Effects on moral agency and personhood

3.8 Conclusion

This chapter set out to operationalise love from an abstract and diffuse concept into analysis themes through the process of multidisciplinary concept analysis. It was not intended to deliver one specific and universally valid definition of love. The literature review conducted in this chapter can only ever be imperfect. The volume of written materials on love is overwhelming, and this chapter might best be regarded as a start of something bigger such as an ongoing multidisciplinary archive, for example. Trying to supply one specific definition of love proved to be unattainable due to the sheer variety of meanings attached to it. Following Armstrong's approach to view the concept of love possessing "rather, a set of themes" (Armstrong 2002:12), it seemed more practical to advance love's operationalisation by identifying constitutive themes. Love is complex, but it is also lawful, just as the human organism is. Excavating love's main qualities can therefore contribute to gaining an insight into its manifestation and meaning in human life.

Another important aim of this chapter has been to establish as much of a wholistic view of the concept of love as possible by adopting a social-ecological approach. Starting from the microsystem of an individual's brain circuitry and psychological attachment, the exploration of love has led to exosystemic insights into cultural and social materialisations of love, until it was able to look at the bigger macrosystemic picture, glimpsing some of the ideas and beliefs around love that have inspired universal human thinking and questioning for centuries.

Ultimately, it has become apparent that love is significant as a core component of human existence on the one hand. On the other hand, a dual nature of love has surfaced. Like a coin with two sides, it is associated with joy and pain, sickness and health, irrationality and conscious moral choice, as well as with selflessness and self-affirmation. As Conn (1998: 326) reminds us, love represents "the two great yearnings of the human person: the desire for separation ... and autonomy on the one hand, and the desire for attachment ... and relationship on the other." Love's ambivalent nature shows in "the desire to be a self ... and the desire to reach beyond, to transcend the self in relationship" (Conn 1998: 326). How this duality of love has come to manifest in the lives of a group of prisoners serving long sentences in an English category C prison shall be the subject of the remainder of this book.

4. Locating the keys to a "no-go-area" — Navigating prison research in uncertain times

Throughout Chapters 2 and 3 the theoretical scope of this book's enquiry has been anchored firstly within the criminological research field of prison effects, and secondly within the multidisciplinary discussion of the social-ecological role and qualities of love. These frameworks provide the theoretical backdrop against which the empirical research methods that generated the data for this book's analysis have been developed and implemented. In the following, I will trace my methodological decision-making process with the aim to provide transparency and insight because

> what matters is … that we are always ready to "show our workings": that we are able to explain … how we arrived at the perspectives we hold; on what terms our perspectives were formed; and on what empirical grounds these perspectives can be challenged. (Gadd et al. 2012: 2)

My "disclosure" will consist of an open discussion of procedural, ethical and organisational limitations involved in the empirical data collection and data analysis process. This process turned out to be riddled with complexities and challenges, not only due to a perceived controversy of *love* as a topic but also due to specifics of the field. The first hurdle presented itself in gaining access to the field, since it included the satisfaction of gatekeeper expectations and regulations.

4.1 *Getting in* — Choice of prison and access to the field

Since my research addresses the issue of prison effects and the lived experience of long-term prisoners, I decided to conduct empirical research in the context of a closed prison environment. For logistical reasons, the aim was to gain access to either a category B or C prison in England. Since access procedures are strict and tend to be proportionately longer, the higher the prison's security category, I decided to not consider high-security category A prisons as fieldwork sites. Due to the more open nature of category D prisons – holding prisoners approaching the end of their sentences already gaining limited outside access – it was decided to not approach these either. Data collection was aimed at enquiring into a prison experience that was still "deep," i.e. ongoing. Category D prisons did not seem to provide much scope to do so.

The issue of prison access had to be considered as the most significant one in potentially limiting work progress. Being permitted to conduct research inside an English or Welsh prison involves several formal steps which could have easily turned into major stumbling blocks. This was due to several reasons: At the time of fieldwork, the political and economic climate surrounding the Prison Service in England and Wales had become increasingly tense. I was looking to study an institution that was in crisis, and it had palpable effects on issues of access and data collection. Due to acute prison staff shortages and increased security and safety risks, stakes were high on both sides. It had to be taken into account that the presence of a civilian researcher on the prison wings would significantly impact on staff resources. Risks of becoming a potential target of violence, conditioning and other personal safeguarding issues had to be considered carefully.

Furthermore, the sensitive and potentially controversial nature of the research topic had to be accounted for when considering which and how prisons should be approached. Some areas of research interest might be surrounded by political controversy, as experienced by Smith and Wincup (2000) during their research projects in criminal justice institutions for women as well as by Liebling et al. (2011) on the topic of radicalisation in a high-security prison. In a political climate marked by controversy around economic austerity, I was aware that my relatively abstract exploratory study of the concept of love might be perceived as too sensitive or as irrelevant in the face of other, more pressing problems. It was thus paramount to address the *getting in* process as swiftly yet carefully as possible, since its complication could have impeded my work significantly.

The first hurdle to overcome presented itself in compiling a thorough and detailed research application for approval by Her Majesty's Prison and Probation Service (HMPPS former National Offender Management Service NOMS). At this point, I became acutely aware that I was first and foremost "dependent upon the state for access to the criminal justice agencies" as realised by Smith and Wincup (2000: 335; King and Liebling 2008) and that a lot of care, diligence and time had to be applied going through the official application process. It required the provision of extensive information about the research's key questions, aims and objectives, methods to be used, reasons for undertaking the study, reasons for the choice of establishment as well as a fairly precise estimation about the length of time and number of staff and prisoners to be involved. After carefully preparing and revising several drafts, the final research application was submitted and approved – without any need for further revision – a few months later. After this (arguably most important) governmental gatekeeper had been satisfied, field access now entirely depended on establishing personal links with the governor of a suitable category B or C prison.

This process turned out to be vulnerable to unforeseen disruptions. I had attempted to establish contact with the governor of a local category B prison fairly early on in the research project. Before any links could be established, however, I learned that he had already been transferred to a different prison. The second category B prison I approached had already granted access to its annually allocated number of researchers and was therefore not able to provide any further research access. Through personal contacts within the UK prison researcher community it was possible to establish links and arrange a meeting with a newly appointed governor of a category C prison in the North of England.[1] During a first meeting, access to the site as well as the number and outline of interviews to be conducted was agreed. A senior manager (Head of Programme Management) was appointed as my dedicated primary contact. Follow up communication via email helped to define and allocate the first potential interviewees in the run-up to fieldwork.

Since the governor decided to equip me with keys, additional security vetting through the Ministry of Justice's official pathway was necessary. Deciding to carry keys was done with a view to relieve access and mobility difficulties during the fieldwork period as well as alleviating potential strain on staff resources. Although drawing keys could be a significant advantage when arranging and conducting interviews, applying and waiting for permission to do so also meant further delay before data collection could commence. This led to continuously changing time schedules, substantially subtracting from my allocated period for data collection, data analysis and project completion. After prison access was finally granted and I had been allocated keys, fieldwork began. Time had by now become the most crucial factor in further fieldwork considerations. It was paramount to press on with data collection as much as possible. To my relief, the overall entry into the field took a smooth course. It was facilitated by a high level of support and helpfulness by senior managers and an experienced personal liaison officer who had served over two decades as a uniformed staff member in the Prison Service. He knew the establishment very well and would soon become a trusted contact, providing practical and personal advice over many shared cups of tea. He supported me in finding my feet in a novel environment, introduced me to staff and prisoners, thus facilitating a growing sense of familiarity and confidence. It was needed to gain a better insight into the workings of the prison and its underbelly.

---

[1] Due to the level of confidentiality and anonymisation agreed with the current governor, the specific institution will not be named in this book. It will only be referred to as "the prison" in the following.

4.2 *Getting on* — Establishing links in a disrupted environment

First informal conversations with prisoners and staff painted a picture of an unpredictable, highly restricted and immensely strained prison environment. Staff and prisoners complained about a high level of drug influx. Especially the prevalence and use of Spice (synthetic cannabinoid) had become a considerable problem. It prompted one prison officer to declare that "This Spice is killing us!" during an informal conversation. It had led to immense organisational strains on staff, since prisoners frequently displayed severe health problems after (over)using Spice and had to receive extra monitoring and care. These ranged from paranoia and hallucinations to increased heart rates, vomiting, loosing faculty to control urination and defecation, panic attacks, aggression and seizures. Prison officers not only had to spend a considerable amount of time dealing with these incidents. If they accidentally inhaled lingering Spice vapours, it furthermore impacted on their own health. Some cases of staff sickness were directly related to the phenomenon of (passive) Spice inhalation. The overall level of disciplined staff on sick leave was reported as the highest ever at the time fieldwork was conducted. Consequently, staff had been ordered to work extra shifts, and prison officers had to be called in from other establishments to help out.

This, in turn, had effects on prison structures. A temporary regime had been implemented, changing weekly. Alternating wings were on complete lockdown either in the mornings or afternoons during the week, which meant that prisoners were unlocked for only two to three hours per day. According to a senior staff member, the amount of lockdown and a constantly alternating regime had contributed to shake-ups in prisoners' routines. Some of them had to change jobs or could not make any phone calls. The prison felt unstable. Violent incidents between prisoners as well as between staff and prisoners were a frequent occurrence. Receiving an emergency "assistance required call" by a prison officer who thought she was going to be taken hostage by a prisoner, a member of staff turned around to me stating "There is not much love in here, I'm afraid. Welcome to [prison name]." During my fieldwork, I heard similar statements on a regular basis. Staff and prisoners seemed frustrated and deflated.

Apart from exerting unsettling and distressing effects on prisoners and staff, above institutional shortcomings also significantly impacted on my fieldwork. I was briefed by senior managers, for example, to not go onto the wings on my own because it was too unsafe at the moment. I was furthermore advised to conduct interviews on a wing only when it was on lockdown and to take an officer with me to unlock the respective interviewee. Strictly following this security advice implied that almost no time could be invested into building rapport with participants before the interview. It also seemed unlikely that I would be able to forge any relationships with prison officers on the wings that would exceed functional interactions. Throughout the fieldwork period, these assumptions turned out to be mostly true. I found myself in several situations when asking staff for help or information was mistimed. Wing officers were so busy that they did not even have the time to acknowledge my presence, let alone enquire about me and my research. On the wings, it was more a matter of being noticed *at all* by staff and prisoners than to not stand out as an outsider or to be seen as taking sides. These problems, as pointed out by Liebling (1992), did not seem to carry as much weight in this environment as they had during my first prison research experience in a high-security prison, where my associations had been closely monitored by staff and prisoners alike (Liebling et al. 2011). Here, the most important skills to have, were decisiveness and persistence in order to be able to set-up and conduct interviews with prisoners. It was largely my responsibility to figure out "the 'dos and don'ts'" (Liebling 1992) of the environment. This also implied waiting for the right moment to approach staff for assistance. When staff were under less pressure, the contact was persistently positive. Prison officers and senior managers were going out of their way to help me locate and approach potential interviewees as well as seeing interviews through.

Suffice it to say that several and ongoing adaptations on my side were required which could raise "fundamental questions about the theoretical and philosophical concessions that might have to be made ... to get the research done" (Smith and Wincup 2000: 337). After spending the first few weeks in the field, I realised that fieldwork would be primarily limited to interviewing. There was not much scope to attain an "insider experience" nor to "get under the skin" of the establishment. Compared to the lengthy period of time that could be dedicated to forming pre-interview "relationships based on trust and rapport" (Smith and Wincup 2000: 342) with prisoners in the high-security establishment of my first prison research experience, I now found myself in a situation where this had to be attempted mostly during interviews. Whereas before I had been able to "hang out" on the wings and socialise – sharing a game of pool or a cup of tea – it now was too risky and there was no time for it during the short periods when prisoners were unlocked. As much as this curtailed approach to interviewing still catered to my methodological choices, it still left me wondering what kind of data could be collected by only briefly dipping in and out of an establishment stretched to its limits? This consideration and a sense of urgency to get interviews done as quickly as possible contributed to certain adjustments and concessions in the participant recruitment and interview process which shall be discussed in the section to follow.

4.3 Participant recruitment and conducting interviews

Determining the number of interviews, considerations of feasibility, time and organisational restraints as well as common research practice presented themselves as decision criteria. It had to be taken into account that time in the field as well as time to write up research findings was curtailed due to a prolonged access procedure to the chosen prison. The final number of interviews to be agreed on was also partly dependent on the governing governor's discretion. After weighing up the strain on staff for supporting me in my tasks, and after several consultations with prison management, I decided to conduct 15-20 interviews with long-term prisoners in the chosen prison. This was mainly due to limiting factors of practicality, thus may have represented more of an opportunistic choice in prison research (Liebling 1992).

Although lower than initially desired, this number was in accordance with general recommendations regarding interviews as a qualitative research method. When it comes to the question of *How many qualitative interviews is enough?* as posed by Baker and Edwards (2012) to 14 social science researchers, "the answer, as with all things qualitative, is 'it depends'" (Baker and Edwards 2012: 3). According to some researchers of their sample, qualitative data would have to be collected "as long as you are getting different answers" (Baker and Edwards 2012: 4). Keeping in mind at all times that frequencies cannot be established from small samples, the qualitative researcher should thus rather aim to locate a range of responses and to report fully how answering the research question was approached.

Deciding on whom to include in the interview sample also brought with it the choice of whom not to. After acquiring initial prison research experience in a maximum-security prison – that by its very nature only housed long-term prisoners – a concern for and research interest in the effects of long-term imprisonment persisted throughout the years between this first experience and the research project this book has grown out of. A tentative decision to focus on long-term prisoners was reinforced considering recent findings of UK prison research regarding the effects and problems of long-term imprisonment, e.g. Crewe et al. (2020) as discussed in Chapter 2. In light of political and legal policy developments, such as the fact that sentence-lengths in the UK had increased considerably in recent years (Crewe et al. 2015), it seemed important, almost pressing, to keep pursuing research exploring the effects of long-term imprisonment on the human self. It resulted in a choice to interview prisoners serving long sentences with minimum tariffs of 10 years or more who had already served a minimum of 4 years in closed conditions. These parameters – determining the basic properties of the sample – were applied after considering that there was no distinct definition of "long-term" incarceration (Crewe et al. 2020), but that indeed definitions vary from four years (Schinkel 2014) to whole life sentences (Johnson and McGunigall-Smith 2008).

Although the participant selection process aimed to be as inclusive as possible within the defined range, I decided to exclude sex offenders from the sample. Since the topic of love could potentially include certain aspects linked to offending behaviour (e.g. relating to intimate relationships), this might have caused complex reactions or dynamics during interviews. After also initially considering the inclusion of prison officers in the interview sample, this thought was dropped before long, since it would have not contributed substantially to my research aims. Although prison officers might have had an insight into how they perceived prisoners to be affected by the presence or absence of love in their lives, this would have been based on their own assumptions or opinions, thus representing second- rather than first-hand knowledge. It is worthwhile and important, however, to consider putting the focus on prison staff in a research project exploring the role of love in staff-prisoner relationships, for example, or its role in the prison officer profession.

Despite being meticulously planned as part of the research design, the sampling process turned out to be highly vulnerable to practical, organisational and environmental factors that could have not been fully calculated before entering the field. In the wake of the implementation of weekly changing provisional prison regimes, access to interviewees was restricted to a maximum of three hours on a weekday. Often this period was shortened due to unforeseen events such as staff shortages or alarms, resulting in a delay of unlocking prisoners. This limitation impacted heavily on the set-up and execution of interviews. Time and security matters restricted my presence on the wings considerably. Informal socialising with prisoners, before recruiting them as interview participants, was hardly ever possible. However, a certain level of trust and rapport had to be built either before or during interviews, considering their deeply private and emotive topic. I therefore decided purposefully to incorporate the following aspects to gain and maintain trust when recruiting and interviewing participants: "introducing the researcher and the research; self-disclosure; and reciprocity" (Beyens et al. 2015: 69).

To introduce myself and the research, posters were put up on-site and also distributed to individual prisoners by my main contact in the senior management team a few months ahead of data collection. Aiming to establish trusted relationships with the prison governor and senior managers, they were continuously informed about relevant developments such as revised interview guidelines or security vetting updates before and during fieldwork. Upon arrival on site, I was informed by my main contact in the senior management team that suitable prisoners had been approached by her with self-made participant request forms and that some had returned a favourable answer. I decided to approach these prisoners first, to introduce myself in person, and to reassure they were still happy to participate in the interview. A majority of this group still was, only two prisoners had changed their minds since and one had been transferred to a different establishment in the meantime. Those that declined either did so because their personal circumstances had put them in a situation where they just did not want to engage with the topic of love (e.g. going through a separation or experiencing estrangement from family members) or they did not want to draw any attention towards themselves. The latter group expressed suspicion towards the interview turning out to be a psychological assessment. In these cases, I had to try to gain trust by explaining my presence (Liebling 1992), my professional background and my motivations as an independent researcher in as much detail as possible. In most cases, this approach was successful, and the first three interviews were set up with prisoners from the above list.

Interviews were preceded by discussing an information sheet and signing a consent form together with the participant. Both documents contained all relevant information about the study, the researcher and the interview procedure. Participants were informed that they were free to withdraw from the interview at any point, and that they were also free to refuse to answer any question(s) without any repercussions. They were also asked if they agreed to their interviews being recorded, since "an accurate record of exactly what was said and how it was said … [was] essential for understanding the meaning of the exchange" (King and Wincup 2008: 31). The (institutionally granted) use of a digital voice recorder also allowed for "a more interactive and natural interview style" as noted by Liebling (1992: 110), since it allowed me to focus on the interviewee and what was said rather than on keeping notes. Furthermore, participants were guaranteed confidentiality during and after the interview. Honouring my duty to comply with prison security policies, however, there were certain limits to confidentiality. If any statements made by prisoners contained a health or safety threat to themselves or anyone else (including but not limited to staff members, other members of the prisoner population, outside family members or associates) or expressed the intention to plan or execute an escape or other criminal offence, confidentiality would have had to be suspended and a member of prison staff had to be informed. However, this situation never arose in interviews.

After conducting the first few interviews with prisoners who had been approached by a senior manager on my behalf, I took full control of the recruitment process. I decided to approach prisoners who fitted the sampling criteria either directly or after enquiring with wing officers whether they recommended approaching certain individuals. On some occasions it turned out to be important to gather additional information from staff beforehand, since some prisoners were not deemed in a good mental state by officers. This was mainly due to personal problems related to family or relationship issues or intricacies of vulnerability due to drug use or mental health conditions. Once a prisoner's availability, willingness and capability for participation had been confirmed, the practical organisation of conducting interviews presented itself as a challenge not to be underestimated.

The implementation of a restricted regime and a shortage of wing staff effectively prevented me from conducting prearranged interviews on two occasions and from setting up interviews on another two occasions because officers could not leave their posts to unlock prisoners. Not only was the time window for conducting interviews narrowed to two to three hours a day, it was also limited to certain days of the week. After two failed attempts to set up or conduct interviews on a Friday, it emerged that this weekday was generally considered "impossible" by staff. This was mainly due to two factors: an even more restricted weekend regime commencing on a Friday afternoon that saw a majority of discipline, managerial and civilian staff leave the premises at 12:30 pm for the weekend on the one hand. On the other hand, Friday mornings were dedicated to issuing ordered canteen items to prisoners. Prison officers and senior managers pointed out that it was the time of the week when assaults were most likely to happen, since prisoners would play up to get themselves off the wings, if they could not pay for their canteen or could not pay off debts to other prisoners.

Apart from *time*, another limiting factor for conducting interviews was represented by *space*. Although all residential prison wings were equipped with a dedicated interview room, on two occasions, it could not be used. Once because it was already in use for a sentence review, another time because it was completely unfurnished. Whenever these unforeseen events occurred, I – sometimes already accompanied by the interviewee – either had to reschedule the interview for another day or to improvise on the spot. On two occasions, the latter resulted in conducting interviews in prisoners' cells with the door ajar. Both interviews had been authorised by a prison officer beforehand. On another occasion, it meant conducting the interview in a wing meeting room bare of furniture. Two chairs had to be brought in from a manager's office. The acoustic of an empty room impacted the audio recording quality so negatively, however, that this solution was dismissed in similar situations later on. Five out of 16 interviews had to be arranged off the wings due to time restrictions. They took place at interviewees' respective workplaces out of earshot of staff and other prisoners, so that confidentiality was maintained.

Taking all limiting factors into consideration, most interviews had to be conducted on an ad-hoc, unplanned basis. The circumstances of the establishment tended to dictate the recruitment process more than my intention to build rapport and trust with potential participants beforehand. I resorted instead to creating a basic level of trust with my interviewees by implementing elements of self-disclosure and reciprocity during the interview as recommended by Beyens et al. (2015). I would like to adopt the definition of self-disclosure here as an "unveiling of commonalities and information about the researcher to the research subjects" (Beyens et al. 2015: 71). This was done within limits of confidentiality and preserved the researcher's personal integrity and safety. Hence no private information such as details about residency was shared, but rather personal preferences such as a shared interest in social sciences or the shared experience of losing a pet. When it came to reciprocity, I occasionally decided to offer time and listening outside of a research context as a reciprocal gesture in exchange for being let into the prisoner's inner world. Giving an interviewee the opportunity to debrief after an interview was offered in the form of time, empathy and acknowledgment. It also represented an ethical choice on behalf of the researcher to "do the right thing" by preserving participants' well-being and mental integrity. A balance crucially had to be struck, however, between "getting the research done" (Smith and Wincup 2000) and adhering to a set of ethical principles without which empirical research becomes vulnerable to professional scrutiny.

4.4 Depth at all costs? — Ethical considerations before, during and after fieldwork

Ethical considerations had to be tailored around the study's highly sensitive and private topic of love and the emotional experience of long-term prisoners. In practical terms, it meant that interviews could infringe upon the privacy of participants and cause psychological distress due to their highly emotive and personal nature. Being asked, for example, to think or talk about the experience of the loss of a loved one, might have been disturbing and distressing to participants. I had to consider setting up safeguarding and debriefing procedures during and after interviews to ensure the psychological integrity of my interviewees. Acting in the participants' best interest, it was especially important to consider the level of vulnerability of prisoners by virtue of mental health problems or private circumstances (e.g. having suffered a recent bereavement). It was paramount to "ensure that the physical, social and psychological well-being of an individual participating in research is not adversely affected by participation in the research" (BSC Code of Ethics 2006: 4.i). Provisions for adhering to these standards were taken by handing out an information leaflet to participants listing all available on-site support services after the interview, as well as explicitly pointing out the voluntary nature of participation.

In general, participants displayed high levels of cooperation in interviews, a willingness to express emotions and to share their stories of love and loss freely. On a few occasions, prisoners cried and expressed distress, desperation and hopelessness, related to certain interview questions. This was a time when I felt it was appropriate to "step outside the research role" (King and Liebling 2008: 446) and to respond with empathy (Watts 2008). On some occasions, I offered a post-interview debrief to prisoners which was taken up by one participant. It took place "off the record" with the voice recorder switched off and consisted of talking through distressing feelings and thoughts for an additional hour. This was an ethical adjustment made more or less spontaneously out of a feeling of responsibility for the participant's well-being. "This adjustment and readjustment ... to ... various individuals ... required some work and emotional management ... and different situations produced quite different research behaviours" (Smith and Wincup 2000: 343).

It could be argued, however, that making those adjustments and concessions during interviews, might have changed the nature of the data. Had I not decided on a few occasions to put a participant's mental integrity before "digging deeper," I might have obtained qualitatively different data. This likely was the case during three specific interviews, when prisoners entered into emotionally very distressing states – recalling past or envisioning impending losses of loved ones – shedding tears and expressing deep hopelessness and desperation. For the sake of "rich data" I could have stayed with or delved into these emotional states further, for example, by asking probing questions about the exact nature of their feelings. However, I became acutely aware of the limits of my role, especially of the fact that I was not acting as a qualified counsellor or psychotherapist. I would have not been able to guarantee professional aftercare for my participants, although I had prepared and distributed information leaflets of available support services on site. My qualms were mainly related to the knowledge of the emotionally harsh reality on the wings which my participants had to return and readapt to, once the interview was finished. Hence, I endeavoured to let participants go as deep as they wished into intense emotions, but I decided to take responsibility to not delve there. This was sometimes done by continuing the interview with a different question instead of staying longer with a high-intensity topic. Ultimately, my ethically and logistically influenced decisions may have exerted effects on the actual depth and length of interviews.

After a total of 28 days had been spent in the field over the course of six months, the decision to leave the prison was eventually made after the 16th interview had been conducted. Although fulfilling the minimum requirement of n = 15, this number fell short of an ideally desired outcome of n = 20. At this point in time, however, it was the most sensible and appropriate measure to terminate fieldwork.

4.5 *Getting out* — Leaving the field

Returning to the prison in the first days of the new year – after taking a few weeks off from fieldwork over Christmas – I found myself coming back to an establishment shaken up by a series of serious incidents. These were all said to be related to the latest influx of Spice. Talking to my liaison officer, I learned that there had been several incidences that morning and two ambulances had to be called in. About ten to twelve prisoners were thought to be under the influence of Spice. On his wing alone three prisoners had overdosed simultaneously on the drug. They were unconscious, had vomited and displayed increased heart rates. One of them was one of my interviewees. I instantaneously felt sorry for him, remembering how hard he had been trying to stay off Spice, when I last spoke to him.

As Smith and Wincup had also experienced first-hand, dealing "with our own emotions in response to our respondents" (2000: 343) comes with the territory of pursuing research in emotional terrain. It also was one of the "side-effects" of engaging with individuals in the field over a prolonged period of time. Forging relationships with staff and prisoners throughout the six months of fieldwork had contributed to human engagement, to caring for the other's well-being and to subjective involvement to a certain degree. As Taylor reminds the qualitative researcher in the field: "The objects of our studies are not objects at all. They are people who may become attached to us and to whom we may become attached" (Taylor 1991: 238). Although I felt this to be the case, it was on a lower level than I had previously experienced during a year of intensive fieldwork in earlier mentioned high-security prison.

I decided to leave the field after managing to conduct enough interviews (n = 16) to fit my target quantity, and after witnessing a mounting level of uncertainty, staff sickness, assaults, drug-related violence as well as harrowing incidents of self-harm (one occasion saw a young prisoner sewing his own mouth shut using fishing hooks). After a self-made explosive device had been found on one of the main wings, I ultimately decided to prioritise my personal safety over any further attempts to recruit interviewees. Although I was acutely aware that the relatively small number of interviews might impact on the quality and transferability of my findings, I prioritised personal and prison safety over the wish to collect more data. Ultimately, my presence on the wings impacted on staff resources that were required more urgently elsewhere to keep prisoners and other staff members safe. I felt it was my responsibility to take myself out of the "line of fire."

Although the above concessions had to be made, a total of 16 prisoners was formally interviewed. Each interview lasted around 55 minutes on average. Interviewees ranged in age from 29 to 70. 11 were serving an indeterminate sentence. Five of these were serving life sentences, whereas the remaining six had all been sentenced to an Indeterminate sentence for Public Protection (IPP)[2]. One prisoner was serving an Extended Determinate Sentence (EDS) and

---

[2] The Indeterminate sentence for Public Protection (IPP) was introduced in 2003 "to provide

the remaining four prisoners of the sample were serving determinate sentences. Tariff length ranged from 18 months to 19 years. At the time of the interview, all participants had served at least four years in closed conditions, and each one of them was looking at a different trajectory that had ultimately brought him to this specific prison.

4.6 Encountering the interview sample — Pen pictures

In the following, I will introduce the 16 men I have talked to. Their pen pictures will provide an insight into their individual stories, elucidating those parts of prisoners' lives and identities that were shared in interviews. Their self-portrayals are reproduced in conformance with the chronology of interviews. In line with confidentiality arrangements, interviewees' real names have been changed into non-related, fictional pseudonyms. Personal details giving clues to real-life identities have been excluded. The aim of each pen picture is to reflect participants' personal trajectories as well as attitudes towards their prison experience and its effects on their identity. These were gathered from responses to interview prompts such as picking three words describing their current life at the prison as well as three words to describe their overall prison experience so far. Some of the personal summaries are augmented by brief interview excerpts (in quotation marks) representing the interviewee's experiential representations.

1) Adam

Adam was in his mid-60s, worked as an outside cleaner and had been in the prison for about nine months when the interview was conducted. He was

---

an answer to a … public and political concern over offenders thought to be dangerous but whose offences existed outside of the mandatory life sentence for murder" (Taylor and Williams 2014: 5). It "allowed the courts to impose a minimum time in prison before the offender goes before the Parole Board. The Parole Board must then be convinced that the offender no longer poses a risk to the public" (Taylor and Williams 2014: 5). After expiration of the tariff, an indeterminate period of imprisonment lasts until – and only if - the Parole Board decides on release (or another form of sentence progression). Accordingly, risk assessments endeavour to calculate the likely risk of an IPP prisoner to commit offences in the future. To prove that this risk has lowered, (s)he has to successfully complete accredited programs and interventions. Compared to determinate sentences, IPP-sentences have no fixed release date which has led to significant levels of stress and anxiety for those serving them. A person serving an IPP-sentence will be on licence indefinitely after release from custody but can apply to the Parole Board to have his or her licence removed after ten years. The IPP-sentence was formally abolished in 2012 by the Legal Aid, Sentencing and Punishment of Offenders Act, yet there were 2,134 IPP-prisoners still in custody, and 93% of IPP-prisoners were post-tariff as of 31 December 2019 (Ministry of Justice 2020).

serving a life sentence and had served 40 years in closed conditions up to that point. He identified himself as a member of the travelling community and had lived most of his life in mobile homes, before he was sentenced. According to him, he never got registered at birth and grew up "feral" in the countryside. He described his childhood as being dominated by guns, theft, economic deprivation, hunger and "a violent drunk for a father." His father would regularly beat him and his mother. After his father was killed by fellow travellers during a row, Adam took over the role of provider and head of the family. He perceived prison to be "a bone idle, poverty stricken, unwell life" and chose the words "time" and "pressure" to describe his prison experience over the years. He felt this pressure was arising from feeling powerless and having his manhood and agency taken away by the institution. For Adam, prison was all about survival. His survival strategy was isolation and putting up a (psychological) shield towards other people as a means of self-preservation.

2) Tom

Tom was serving a life sentence with a tariff of 17 years. At the time of the interview, he was 51 years old and had already served ten years in category A and category B prisons, before he came to this category C prison. He hoped to use the remaining seven years of his sentence to rebuild bridges with his children and grandchildren. For him, it was harder to serve his sentence in this kind of establishment because he felt prisoners here were not "like proper criminals," since they were only doing short sentences. Intra-prisoner respect levels were low, and the prison felt unsettled in his view. He described it as "boring" with "no regime" and "loads of bang up." He also put that down to the mix of prisoners that seemed to be dominated by drug users in general but Spice users in particular. In his view, this impacted greatly on the regime. Tom's preferred coping mechanism for serving his life sentence was to refrain from thinking too much, especially about family, friends and loved ones on the outside. He had chosen to put mental barriers up to protect himself from "bad news" and from missing people on the outside. Instead, he focussed on his life inside.

3) Bo

Bo was 29 years at the time of the interview. He was serving an IPP-sentence with a tariff of four years but had done 10 years in closed conditions altogether. He had been transferred to the prison 25 months ago and described his current prison experience as "interesting, hectic and boring." He identified as mixed race and had been raised by foster parents from the age of three. He had three foster brothers and three brothers of his own blood but was not in touch with any of them. He had no problem with the seemingly ever-changing prison regime. On the contrary, he liked to be kept on his toes and being on edge. In his view, the atmosphere was "ready to boil over" after it had gotten progressively worse over the past two years. Serving an IPP-sentence had been the most stressful part of his overall prison experience because time was passing relentlessly, and there seemed to be no progress. Additionally, he found it hard to accept the fact that the sentence itself had been abolished in 2012 but he was still serving it. A vital part of coping with prison life was maintaining self-respect and valuing himself by being clean, keeping his cell tidy and being polite to other people.

4) Paul

Paul was a 48-year old IPP-prisoner with a tariff of 3.5 years. He had served 12 years altogether, and it was his third time in this category C prison after several moves to and from category D prisons. He had a hard time dealing with conditions in category D prisons which he claimed were not clear and reasonable enough for him and left him feeling like "walking on eggshells." He described his five-year experience in this prison as "hell, just hell" and felt that every day of his overall prison experience had been "constant torture." He had developed mental health problems such as depression, anxiety and high levels of stress whilst incarcerated. He was harbouring suicidal thoughts and had been on suicide watch previously. At the time of the interview, he had given up showing any positivity or prosocial behaviour because he felt it was not recognised by the prison or Probation Service. He felt deeply mistrusting towards institutions and people working for them, stemming from experiences of staff abuse and violence going through the care system as a child and adolescent. Paul described himself in predominantly negative terms. He would resort to putting up a mask as his coping mechanism for everyday life inside. He felt he could not express any emotion and that prison had broken him.

5) Frank

Frank was serving an IPP-sentence with a tariff of 18 months but had been in custody for 12 years on that charge. He was in his mid-40s and had spent most of his life in prison. It was his fourth time in this prison, after having been moved between prisons for security reasons. To describe his current life inside, he chose the words "nightmarish," "disgusting" and stated that morale and empathy of prison officers were low. He traced this back to severe understaffing and a high influx of drugs, especially Spice. He felt he could best cope with being in prison by being locked behind his door. It gave him an opportunity to escape "from all the bullshit and all this crazy talk" around him. In his current environment and situation, he felt "fearful" and "lost." He had been "battling drugs over twenty years" and was now engaged in an Narcotics Anonymous 12-step program. He was suffering from anxiety and severe depression and felt hopeless and uncertain about how much more he could take in terms of uncertainty related to his IPP-sentence and release date.

6) Theo

At the time of the interview, Theo had served 10 years on a 3.5-year IPP-sentence and was on his second recall from a category D prison. He had served a total of four years in this prison and he described its current atmosphere as "crazy," "chaotic" and staff losing the battle against a huge Spice influx. It left him feeling vulnerable. He had been smoking Spice for seven years but was currently on a drug rehabilitation wing to recover from his addiction. He grew up with a violent father and later a violent stepfather. From the age of three, he had been witnessing severe levels of domestic violence and remembered spending periods of time in child refuges. He left his parents' home at the age of 12 and moved in with a friend's family. Since drug and alcohol use was a regular occurrence in this surrogate family, he started smoking cannabis as a form of escapism when he started secondary school. He described a snowball effect in drug use and drug-related crime that escalated in stabbing himself in the stomach whilst overdosing on alcohol and crack-cocaine. His main motivation to get better and to get out of prison was his son who had been born at the beginning of his sentence.

7) George

George had been sentenced to life imprisonment with a minimum tariff of 15 years. At the time of the interview, he was in his early 50s. He had served nine years of his sentence, four of which were spent at this category C prison. He chose to describe the current atmosphere at the prison as a "nightmare," "turbulent" and "devastating." His nightmarish feelings were related to having been convicted for a crime he claimed he had not committed, being separated from his family and losing out on the best years of his and his family's life. He was appealing his sentence and saw himself as the victim of a miscarriage of justice.

8) Phil

Phil had been given a life sentence with a minimum tariff of 19 years. He had already served 15 years and had been at this category C prison for five years. He was ready to move on and described the atmosphere in the prison as unsettled and "dominated by a Spice epidemic." He had now reached the stage of his sentence where he was starting to mentally prepare himself for release and to return to his family. In his view, keeping the family together had saved him from becoming institutionalised because his "head was outside" most of the time.

9) Tony

Tony was serving an eight-year determinate sentence. He had been in prison for seven years altogether and had come to this category C prison two years ago. He was working as a Listener and gym instructor. He described the prison as "a nightmare" and one of the worst prisons in the country to get anything done or from which to progress. This was due to understaffing that resulted in staff not having sufficient time to prepare paperwork which was vital for prisoners' progressive moves. He had experienced his overall time in prison as "horrible" and described his survival strategy as "keeping your head down and being polite."

10) Oliver

Oliver was serving a determinate sentence of four years. He worked as a gardener and loved his job. He described life on the main prison wings as madness and the regime as "terrible" and "unpredictable" due to staff shortages. He had been to the same prison before in 2002, when it was specifically catering for long-term prisoners. He found it to be a lot better then and thought it had changed for the worse. He kept in touch with family and friends throughout his sentence but tried to avoid any involvement in romantic relationships, since it could "mess with your head."

11) Peter

At the time of the interview, Peter had been serving nine years on a 4.5-year IPP-sentence. He was a very well-read, highly educated and politically interested man in his 60s, and had spent 3.5 years at this category C prison which he described as "grim," "unsuited" and "very restrictive." He perceived the prison system to be run by psychology and saw his IPP-sentence as a "never ending treadmill." His overall prison experience had been one of "neglect after neglect after neglect" which had led to a deterioration of his physical and mental health. He had suffered a stroke in another prison a few years ago. At the time of the interview, he was wheelchair-bound and his range of movement was restricted. This left him dependent on fellow prisoners taking over the roles of carers and contributed to his overall feeling of physical and psychological vulnerability.

12) Will

Will was in his late 30s and serving an IPP-sentence with a minimum tariff of two years. At the time of the interview, he had served 10 years on this sentence. He had been at this category C prison for 11 months and was one of the few people who described it in positive terms. To him, it was a good local prison. He had good relationships with the staff whom he saw almost as friends. This was partly due to the fact that he had known some prison officers from the outside since he was a child. He identified as a member of the traveller community, and he felt that him, his friends, and family had been scrutinised and supervised by the police for most of his life. He thought the police had arrested him "to life him off" on behalf of his criminal family and to break up the traveller community in his hometown. Will had been struggling throughout most of this sentence and nearly lost his life on two occasions being assaulted by other prisoners. He was expecting more violence to happen at any point and always felt on edge.

13) Lewis

Lewis was 29 and had been sentenced to a 10-year Extended Determinate Sentence (EDS). This meant he had to serve two-thirds of his tariff, i.e. six years and nine months in closed conditions. At the time of the interview, he had already served 4.5 years and had been in this category C prison for two years. He described his current experience as "horrible, just horrible" with no rehabilitation and extended periods of being locked up. Lewis had been in and out of prison since he was 13, making his journey through the system from children's homes to Young Offender Institutions into the adult prison establishment. According to him, he had been put into childcare by the Probation Service because his father was serving a lengthy prison sentence and his mother was overwhelmed with raising him and his seven siblings. He had been exposed to drug use, drug dealing and crime since he was a child, with both parents being drug dealers. At the time of the interview, Lewis was actively looking to associate with people who would model a good and prosperous life, away from crime.

14) Arthur

Arthur had served 35 years on a life sentence and had been in this prison for ten years. He was in his mid-60s at the time of the interview. He preferred to keep himself to himself and to not get involved in any events on the wing. He was working as a cleaner in a textile workshop and approached his sentence "just day by day." Prison had become normal to him and he was aware that he had become institutionalised. He was very apprehensive about being released and had developed anxiety and panic attacks related to this topic. He had no one on the outside he felt connected to. All family members were dead, and the only people he still knew outside were his solicitor and his probation officer. Arthur felt there was more pressure outside than inside prison and that his life happened inside.

15) Ryan

Ryan was serving a recall sentence of four years and six months, and he had been at this prison for about six weeks. He was 37 years old and identified himself as mixed race, his mother being half-Jamaican and his father being white. He had previously served sentences of four years, 3.5 years and five years. He had spent over 14 years in prison and described this time as "insidious," "soul destroying" and "good training." He had come to perceive himself as "surprisingly resilient" after facing bullying, violent assaults as well as being robbed and abused in custody from the age of 15. Growing up as one of the only white(-looking) kids in a predominantly black minority ethnic urban neighbourhood proved to be taxing. He was singled out and bullied by other kids on a regular basis. Additionally, he had witnessed a high level of domestic violence at home, watching his stepfather "absolutely annihilating" his mother. His biological father had been involved in international thievery and drug-trafficking, before he ultimately went to prison for several years. His stepfather used to deal with cannabis on a large scale and had introduced Ryan's mother to drugs. He also got sentenced to imprisonment. From the age of 12, Ryan had to take over the role of the provider and head of the family. He consequently left school and started selling drugs for a gang to make money, his two younger brothers following his example. He described his whole life as a living nightmare.

16) Bruce

Bruce was serving two consecutive determinate sentences of four years each. At the time of the interview, he had served four years and was looking to be released in a few months. He identified as born-again Christian and placed a lot of importance on studying the Bible and developing his spiritual life. His mother had died whilst he was imprisoned, and he was estranged from his father. Whilst being incarcerated he wanted to "keep the two worlds separate" and had decided to not have any visits of family members but instead to (re)build relationships with his children and his father once he had been released. Bruce thought he had changed positively since he had come to prison. After feeling suicidal and smoking heroin on the outside, he now explicitly focused on personal development.

In the chapters to follow, I endeavour to tell my participants' stories as I found them, to make sense of their narratives and to integrate them with what we already know about love and the long-term prison experience. I will do so with the ultimate aim to understand whether love matters, and whether it should matter more in the set-up of prison. Delivering recommendations for penal policy and penal practice is one of the desired outcomes of this endeavour. This desire may have influenced the storyline as it emerges, but it ultimately is my goal to depict the truths of individual inner life-worlds (Crotty 1998) as related to me by my interviewees.

I would like to embed individual stories within a *critical research paradigm*, thus also discussing their accounts as socially constructed realities influenced by structures and power relations of the prison environment (Crotty 1998). In doing so, it is important to frame data interpretation with theory, if it is to be perceived as reliable.

4.7 Inferring theory — Validity, reliability and the question of truth

According to Coffey and Atkinson (1996: 141) "the kinds of ideas that can be generated as the outcome of qualitative research are various, and ... what counts as theory in this context is open to a variety of understandings." Although this might be the case, there are nevertheless criteria that can be applied to evaluate these ideas concerning their credibility, validity and generalisability. These are largely related to the trustworthiness (Lincoln and Guba 1985) of statements and theories inferred from data, to a question of truth. The definition of these criteria is in itself largely dependent on the epistemological view of the researcher. A qualitative researcher working within the tradition of positivism, for example, may "pursue conceptions of reliability and replicability that are rooted in a realist view of a single external reality knowable through language" (Seale 1999: 41).

Since I have chosen to adopt an interpretive, exploratory strategy, the search for "absolute truth" is not the ultimate goal of theory development here. My research rather aims at charting a "relative," individual truth, aiming to deliver a qualitative "snapshot" of a specific social environment, at a specific point in time, informed by a limited and specific sample of viewpoints. Data analysis and theory induction are embedded within a critical research paradigm as well as in a critical theory approach aimed at identifying normative idea(l)s through social analysis of prison as an institution. A critical research paradigm underpins my data analysis by means of pointing out and reviewing ideologies that present themselves in interview themes (e.g. fatherhood or motherhood ideologies in Chapter 5). Departing from individual accounts and points of views, these point towards the emergence of a bigger picture.

This already implies a certain researcher position towards the validity of inferred theories, namely that individual perspectives potentially reflect and point toward more general (ideological) views or social conditions. To avoid over-generalisations or snap judgments, it has to be kept in mind, however, that only one fieldwork site was chosen for data collection, that the number of interviews was relatively low, and that this implies certain specifics regarding validity and generalisability of theoretical claims. The choice to follow an interpretive data-analysis process caters towards these specifics. As recommended by King and Wincup (2008), theoretical conclusions were arrived at by first drawing inferences from particular cases, then developing more general theoretical propositions, i.e. grounding theory in data. It is "an important element in achieving the ... aim of supporting claims with credible evidence" and in "constructing a theoretical language grounded in instances of data" (Seale 1999: 88). If carried out well and with diligence, this strategy of data analysis and representation produces "an evocative meta-story ... that is potentially generalizable because it is able to highlight common experiences" (Seale 1999: 88). It is my aim to stay true to the data as much as possible when developing ideas about and describing the life-world of long-term prisoners in relation to love. I strive to deliver a fair and data-based representation of participants' views. However, it also has to be taken into consideration that analysis and development of theoretical assumptions are often largely anchored in a researcher's personal value system, thus potentially "staining" data interpretation.

I aim to make any personal normative, ideological or philosophical orientation as transparent as possible from the outset (see Chapter 1.) and throughout this book. Although necessary to provide a research focus and theoretical framework, taking a specific ethical and moral position can have implications regarding research(er) objectivity and bias. This represents an ongoing discussion and criticism in social sciences, of which criminology is not exempt. Reflecting on the question of *Whose side are we on?* Liebling (2001) ponders an academic dilemma observed by Becker (1967) in his article of the same title:

> To have values or not to have values: the question is always with us. When sociologists undertake to study problems that have relevance to the world we live in, they find themselves caught in a crossfire. Some urge them not to take sides, to be neutral and do research that is technically correct and value free. Others tell them their work is shallow and useless if it does not express a deep commitment to a value position (Becker 1967: 239).

Reflecting on this further, Liebling goes on to conclude that it is not about whether to take sides, since it is difficult, if not impossible, to be neutral. "Personal and political sympathies contaminate (or less judgmental, inform) our research" (Liebling 2001: 472). It is necessary to acknowledge personal value orientations that inform the research perspective, and to continuously question them as a potential source of bias and distortion of findings (Liebling 2001).

It is important, therefore, to critically examine my findings and analysis as to whether I have tailored them around what I wanted to find in order to draw a moral conclusion catering toward personal value orientations and research interests. I have endeavoured to address this issue by letting interview excerpts speak for themselves as much as possible. This was done with a view to let prisoners tell their stories first, before assigning and "subordinating" them to theoretical findings in relevant scientific fields. However, I want to recognise my personal perspective as an integral part of the research process, a part that may give a distinctive shape to this book's narrative. It should therefore be stressed again that my study has been conducted under a certain presupposition, resulting from my initial bafflement described in the introductory sections of Chapter 1. It is the assumption that love indeed *is* absent from the long-term prison experience and that its presence would have beneficial effects on those affected by its deprivation. In this sense, my research is framed around the notion that love matters in human existence and that it therefore would likely matter in the lives of prisoners serving long sentences. This represents a certain moral and ethical position of myself as a researcher. I aimed at not letting it "contaminate" the framing of empirical enquiry by designing an interview guideline, for example, that was as neutral as possible and that did not implicitly or overtly lead interviewees into a certain (ideological) direction. I chose to structure not only interviews but also their analysis around three main topics:

I. How does love feature in prisoners' individual views?
II. What role do love, connection and relationships play in prisoners' lives?
III. What role do love and other emotions play in the prison environment?

These categories of enquiry provided a guideline for this book's thematic organisation, wherein topic I. is explored in Chapter 5, topic II. in Chapters 6 and 7 and topic III. in Chapter 8. It will be the task of the following chapters to incorporate not only prisoners' individual life-stories but also shared characteristics of the sample into data analysis. The first step into this exploration will be taken by examining interviewees' views on love in correlation with individual life-trajectories and collective representations. In doing so, it will work its way from the micro- to the macro-levels of experience. It will obtain its theoretical depth by linking the analysis of interview excerpts with relevant multidisciplinary literature from the fields of neurosciences, psychology, sociology and moral philosophy as chosen disciplines guiding this exploratory journey.

5. Prisoners' perceptions of love
— Two sides of the same coin?

5.1 Synonyms of love

> Love's fantastic [smiles], love's a labour … love's pain, love's … every emotion … Love's fear, negative, fuck everything and run … Love's letting them go … You know, it hurts me … Love's face everything and recover. Love's … crazy. Love's belonging …. But I don't belong in jail … I belong out there. It's frustrating, it's hard [cries]. I got a love … but I don't love that person doing drugs. (Theo)

Love could mean a plethora of things, as represented by Theo's spontaneous associative monologue. In line with this book's structural approach, this chapter will juxtapose the effects of love's *presence* as *human virtue* and love's *absence* as *human need*. Its first part will therefore examine the constructive implications associated with the *presence* of love as *human virtue*. This will be followed by a discussion of destructive implications of love's *absence* as *human need* in the second half.

Theo's account of what love meant for him summarised some of love's plural and opposing qualities as established in Chapter 3's concept analysis. It illustrated the joy of forging and the pain of losing connection, love's healing and motivational qualities as human virtue as well as the detrimental effects of being deprived of love as a human need. Equating love with two opposing acronyms of F.E.A.R. one being "Fuck Everything And Run" (origin not known), whilst the other stood for "Face Everything And Recover" (likely originating from a popular Alcoholics Anonymous (AA) saying; see, for example, Minnesota Recovery 2009), Theo eluded to different kinds of behaviours love could elicit. On the one hand, it was connected to the meaning of fear as an impulse to "fight or flight" an emotionally painful situation, on the other hand, it represented the motivational push of fear to adopt a positive behavioural change and overcome his addiction. He further pointed towards love's irrational, "crazy" qualities as an emotion that could arise spontaneously but also towards love's virtuous quality as conscious "labour" of a moral agent. Love's connective and relational quality of furthering feelings of "belonging" also came to the forefront, only to painfully remind Theo that these had been lost upon entry into the prison environment.

Above manifestation of love in relationships also came to other interviewee's minds, and it was predominantly connected to specific people in their lives.

Being asked about which other words for love came to their minds, some respondents spontaneously thought about

> Just ... family. Family. (Phil)

> Family. Friends. Someone that you're ... close with ... You can go through anything you want, really, and you love them ... it makes you feel good. (George)

Other respondents connected love to care and related concepts:

> Just having people there that care. Security. (Frank)

> Care. Compassion. Empathy. (Peter)

> Caring for someone and sharing things. (Will)

Some of these perceptions mirrored one of the shared findings of neuroscience, psychology and sociology about love, namely that it is experienced in relation to others, and that it was represented by emotions and behaviours generally considered to promote cooperation and positive relationships. Mutual care for each other's well-being as well as the concept of sharing also emerged from interviews, echoing corresponding findings of Chapter 3. When those connecting love to an emotion were prompted to think more specifically about the kind of feeling love was and how they were feeling it, they described it, for example, as "a tingly feeling ... warm ... just nice" (Tom). For Tom, love possessed a positively animating quality, enlivening and warming his body.

Arthur likewise picked up on the point that love was connected to feelings. He qualified the type and orientation of it as an attachment and intimate identification toward *living* subjects:

> You can love your car. You're not going to have any feelings ... for your car, are you? You know what I mean? You can love all sorts. You can love a tree. I can love that cup ... but if I start having intimate feelings with that cup, um ... I'm in trouble, aren't I? [laughs] (Arthur)

Love was seen as being in an emotional bond with some*body*, not some*thing*. In Arthur's opinion, it was not achievable, let alone acceptable, when love as an intimate feeling was directed towards an inanimate object. A love of that type represented fetishism rather than real love. Although attempting to define the qualities of love in his interview, Arthur would also denote himself as an outsider when it came to personal experiences of love and intimate relationships. According to him, this was due to the long time he had spent in closed prison conditions which had led him to perceive himself as "asexual."

Whereas Arthur felt he could not contribute much detail about love in relation to personal connections, other interviewees frequently connected love to emotional bonds with other human beings. Tony, for example, described love as feeling

> really connected with somebody and ... happy and ... relaxed. It's the whole operation. It's not a single word, really, to describe ... how you're feeling for somebody. All your life works around this ... it's your central focus. (Tony)

He went as far as describing love as a central focus and purpose in his life, as being connected and focusing on another person outside of himself. His statement contained elements of creating positivity and limbic resonance, i.e. forging a connection with somebody based on attuning to each other and balancing each other's nervous systems by sharing positive feelings of happiness and relaxation. Feeling that he had been deprived from establishing any kind of this positivity with a loved one whilst in custody, led him to describe his time in prison as if someone had "chopped both [his] arms off" (Tony).

Asking respondents about their immediate associations with the word *love* served as an opener for a dialogue about the topic itself. Before delving deeper into love's representation in interpersonal relationships, I will aim at making a slow transition from the more general and superficial to the more personal and private views on love.

5.1.1 Pop-cultural symbolisms of love

Six of 16 interviewed prisoners could think of a (pop-)cultural artefact (i.e. a song, a film, a book, a poem or another work of art) that represented love for them. The fact that only a minority of respondents were able to engage with this question might be owed to the fact that many could not answer spontaneously but would have been able to, had they been provided with more time for consideration. Unfortunately, opportunities to return to individual respondents once the interview had been conducted were limited due to severe time and organisational limitations in the prison environment. Of those six respondents deriving meaning from this prompt, three picked contemporary films, two of which featured a male hero or rescuer figure:

> *Gladiator* ... See I like how they treat him ... he's a General in an army and the emperor likes him. And ... the emperor is dying, and he doesn't want his son to be the next emperor he wants the General. And then ... when the son finds out he kills his dad. And he says right, you either serve me or I'm gonna kill you. And he says, "No I'm not gonna serve you." And he tries to punish him, and he comes back, and the rest of Rome falls in love with him and not the emperor ... The moral of the story I got yeah, you can feel more love and feelings towards other people, even if they are not your family. (Bo)

The topic of love was closely linked here with the theme of loyalty and resisting oppression and punishment in favour of love. Love was expressed as a virtue by a hero withstanding "evil" and "doing the right thing." This was consequently rewarded with social admiration ("the rest of Rome falls in love with him"). However, the most important quality of love for Bo – who had been raised by foster parents and who was not in touch with any members of his family of origin anymore – was the realisation that love was not exclusively "reserved" for blood relatives. It fascinated him how his foster mother, for example, could "take someone else's children on and provide" (Bo).

Similar to Bo, Lewis also recounted the plot of a film that portrayed a love extending beyond familial bonds:

> *Man on Fire*! … Denzel Washington … It's about a guy, who rescues a little girl … from kidnappers. He does whatever it takes to get the little girl back alive. Even give his own life. So, he sacrificed his own life because he loved this little girl. He wanted to get her back home. So, I'd see that as love, yeah. Even though he wasn't a father … he was a bodyguard … I see that as good, strong love. (Lewis)

Lewis described and liked the idea of a "good, strong love," a virtuous love, a love that transcended ego-boundaries and placed the interest and well-being of another person before self-interest. To him, this seemed especially virtuous and remarkable, since the hero was not even related to the girl whom he risked his life for. Lewis himself had cut ties with most of his family due to dysfunctional relationships within it and did not feel he could rely on any of them for help or support. According to Bo and Lewis, love was not dependent or confined to a family of origin. The fact that there were people out there prepared to "go through fire" for strangers could provide an alternative source of love and protection, when family bonds were felt to be unsafe.

The film *My Blueberry Nights* spontaneously came to Will's mind. He had repeatedly watched it and recounted the following plot:

> This woman walks into a bar … it's called "Blueberry Pie," and it sells pies. This girl … leaves the keys behind, and one day she's sat down with this man and she said, "Can I have my keys back?" He brought a big bowl of keys over and she says, "What are the keys for?" … And he said "Well … you leave your keys behind for your partner. But your partner, he never comes, so, um, you could go off. But I leave the keys here, so that way, I leave the door open for … you and your partner, and then you've always got something to go back to. This café." She said "Well, why don't you throw all the keys away?" And he says, "No. I can't do that, because it means I'm shutting that door." (Will)

Considering that Will had gone through a painful separation from his wife and had not been in touch with his son since starting his sentence, the idea of "a door that was being kept open" might have appealed to him as hope for future reconciliation. When asked what he liked about the film, and why he kept watching it, Will pointed out that:

> It *meant* [emphasis in original interview[1]] something ... He cared for the customers ... He took time out to talk to them. And the customers liked him because of that ... They just sat talking till late at night. (Will)

Apart from connecting love with an "open door" of reconciliation, watching the main character of *My Blueberry Nights* display a caring and appreciative attitude towards customers made Will feel good and as if he was witnessing something meaningful. Describing this particular connection forged in a café setting between strangers[2], he equated the concept of care with taking time for meaningful conversation, a quality of love as *philia*.

Being asked to choose an artefact that symbolised love, three respondents picked a piece of music. It commonly evoked feelings or memories within them connected to love or the pain of losing someone they loved:

> It's a song called *Sara* ... It's just something I've been brought up with ... they've been around long years *Fleetwood Mac* ... you'd hear Mum and Dad playing it ... Just certain songs remind me of certain times and different things. (Tom)

Tom's associations with love, again, went back to the microsystemic family setting and something that was intrinsically connected to his primary caregivers ("you'd hear Mum and Dad playing it"). Similarly, other prisoners described how music would act as a catalyst for emotions, albeit more painful ones related to the loss of loved ones:

> There's certain songs that I can't listen to cause they immediately will make me upset. I cry ... Like ... that *Mama* from the Spice Girls [sings] "Mama, I love you." Well that was played at my nana's funeral. Whenever I hear that, it upsets me. (Frank)

In a similar vein, Bruce described how certain pieces of music would elicit strong emotional reactions connected to memories of the loss of love:

> When my mum was dying, I sang a song to her, a Michael Jackson song ... She was only 68 ... I can't sing it cause I'll cry. That song [sings] "You

---

[1] Words or expressions emphasised in interviews will be marked as italics throughout the remainder of this book.

[2] It holds symbolical meaning and will be analysed in more detail in Chapter 7.

are not alone, cause I am here with you. Though we're far apart, you're always in my heart." And she cried my Mum and said "Thanks for that Bruce" … And I said, "I can't speak now Mum." Put the phone down, went to my cell and cried my eyes out. 20 minutes later rang her back up, "You're alright mum?" That's just love, innit? (Bruce)

Singing a song to his dying mother on the prison phone to assure her that she was in his thoughts and heart expressed a love that was not dependent on face-to-face contact. Love transcended time and space and created a shared feeling of emotional support, reaffirming a previously established connection of Bruce and his mother. Love, in this sense, was a mental power. It was the belief that a person was present in the other, by keeping him or her in each other's thoughts and focusing on the other's well-being.

In Will's, Frank's and Bruce's cases, music took them back to a certain time of their lives and reminded them of emotional bonds they used to have, or which might have been lost. Those past memories were still alive in their minds. Activating them could still evoke an emotion in the present which exemplified the fact that love as a neurological, mental construct can have very tangible and moving effects.

Apart from exploring individual dimensions of love's representation through word association and pop-cultural symbolisation, the interview also enquired about prisoners' experience of love in relationships which will be the object of examination in the sections to follow.

5.2 *Love as human virtue* — The presence of love in prisoners' microsystem

I think for me there's like three loves. Three different loves. One that you'll have for your mum, and your brothers and sisters. There's one that you'll have for your children. And there's one that you'll have for … your partner. (Bo)

With this statement, Bo expressed an idea that was similar to ancient Greek moral philosophy's concept of love, dividing it into *storge* (familial love), and *eros* (romantic love). *Storge* being seen as affection, "especially between parents and their children" (Lewis 1960: 42) and *eros* as the love for a partner including a sexual component. The theme of love as *storge* predominantly emerged in response to the narrative element of the interview guideline. It encouraged participants to recount a situation when they felt loved, either in the past or recently. In six cases these narratives were related to their mothers' love.

5.2.1 Love of the mother

> [W]hen I got run over outside school. I took my bike and rode home myself, but the school had phoned my mum. And when I got home, she was on the settee crying. She thought I was seriously hurt. I just walked in … When she's seen me she was like, "Oh are you alright? I thought you were seriously hurt." That's what makes you think someone cares for you, innit? (Bo)

The fact that his foster mother was upset about the possibility that he could be seriously hurt was proof for Bo that she cared about having him in her life and would be sad if any harm came to him. The impression that his presence mattered in someone else's life was a sign of love also for Tom who described love as "being wanted. You know somebody wants you" (Tom). Love valued the existence of the individual and cared about his or her integrity. According to Bruce, this kind of love was most noticeably and most naturally displayed by mothers because "It's instinct … You knew by their eyes … Mothers know anyway" (Bruce).

A quarter of interviewees painted a picture of the naturally "good mother." She would love unconditionally and in abundance and was often portrayed as a physically weak but mentally fierce and resilient woman with "inner strength." At least four prisoners indicated that their mothers had been working in the caring profession as nurses, carers or foster parents and described them as "amazing," "selfless," "always there," "genuine," and "hard workers":

> She's just … an amazing woman my mum … I was amazed that she would … never stop … She was only a little woman, but she was strong. She was only about four foot four … and skinny, but she … had an inner strength. She had a good heart. A lot of people used to say, she's got a good heart. (Arthur)

> My mum worked hard all her life … When I tell you, a woman looking after a son … with … unconditional love, yeah, I had that in abundance. If I got locked up … she'd be there. If I needed money on a weekly basis, she was always the one. For Christmas, everything … The love and support from my Mum was just unbelievable. She blows me away, she's a very very special woman. (Frank)

Without attempting to call interviewees' experiences into question, it was noteworthy how much their descriptions portrayed an ideal type of mother. Consulting sociological studies of past and contemporary motherhood ideologies (Woodward 2003; Johnston and Swanson 2006; Takseva 2017), above excerpts can also be regarded as representations of a macrosystemic view. They embody cultural assumptions about motherhood as a natural role and identity for women "that can be taken for granted" (Woodward 2003: 18). Before proceeding with the examination of distinctive mother ideologies, however, the term ideology itself needs clarification.

Seen as a symbolisation of culturally and socially held ideas and beliefs about a certain object or concept, "the study of ideology ... encompasses in large part ... the enterprise of decoding, of identifying structures, contexts, and motives that are not readily visible" (Freeden 2003: 11). According to theories developed by Foucault (1978) and Gramsci (1971), ideologies work on a macrosystemic level and hold the power to preserve cultural and social hegemony by placing social expectations and sanctions on certain individual actions and identities. Embedded in ideologies are levels of meaning "which are at times hidden to the groups that are most affected by them and are sometimes hidden even to the very groups that produced them" (Johnston and Swanson 2006: 509).

The concept of motherhood can be regarded as such an ideology present in contemporary Western culture. According to Woodward (2003), it occupies an ambiguous place as a strongly contested as well as highly idealised female identity. Historically and culturally, some of the more "traditional Western discourses regarding motherhood and mother love can be traced from at least as far back as eighteenth-century Romanticism in Europe" (Takseva 2017: 155). Especially the image of the "good," i.e. "the ever-present, self-sacrificial, and all-providing mother" (Takseva 2017: 155) as an embodiment "of purity and virtue ... all that goes with caring for others" (Woodward 2003: 26) has been very prominent and powerful. "More recently, paid work has been added to what makes up the contemporary mother figure" (Woodward 2003: 26). The image of a mother who not only "worked hard all her life" (Frank) and who would "never stop" (Arthur), but who would also not expect anything in return for her (emotional) labour was dominant in at least three interviewees' descriptions of their mother as the epitome of unconditional love:

> [t]he only person that I believe truly loved me ... There's nothing bad behind it ... I didn't feel like I was expected to give something back ... You know, she'd be there if I needed her, she was there ... it was genuine. There was nothing fake behind it ... I knew that she meant it. (Paul)

A "good mother's" love was portrayed as pure, true, virtuous, self-sacrificing and as something that would come naturally to her, with "nothing fake behind it" (Paul). These qualities were emphasised repeatedly and vehemently, especially by Paul. In contrast to his negative perception of almost every other person in his life, Paul's mother stood out as the exception, as the only person who ever truly loved him.

The description of his mother's love included some qualities of what has been described in related literature as "intensive mothering" (Hays 1996). It represents one of the dominant motherhood ideologies in Western culture of the last century. According to Hays, "intensive mothering" is characterised as "emotionally absorbing, labor intensive" mothering that lets "children's needs take precedence over the individual needs of their mothers" (Hays 1996: 46). This approach to child-rearing has been criticised by Weingarten (1997) as not promoting love as a relationship between equals but as equating love with dependency (see Section 3.3.5). He also questioned the modelling of the "good mother" as a woman who would sacrifice her time, her money, her own well-being and factually her whole self for her children (Weingarten 1997). Johnston and Swanson furthermore alerted to the risks for intensively mothered children to "suffer from a sense of entitlement, lack of initiative, inability to establish relationships based on mutuality, and an inability to assume responsibility" (Johnston and Swanson 2006: 510).

In Paul's and Frank's interviews it became apparent that their mothers had modelled the selfless qualities of an intensively mothering figure, continuously providing for their sons economically and emotionally even as adults ("If I needed money on a weekly basis, she was always there." (Frank)), and without a sense of mutual reciprocity in their relationship ("I didn't feel like I was expected to give anything back." (Paul)). Paul and Frank also implied that their mothers had found themselves in circumstances that were highly demanding and stress-inducing, emotionally and physically. Frank's mother had become the victim of domestic violence and was struggling economically, although working in a full-time nursing job. She had fallen seriously ill before pension age. Although not much was known about Paul's mother – who had died relatively young in her late 50s – the fact that Paul had spent most of his childhood in the care system implied a possibility of familial economic or psychological hardship. However, no conclusions about their full range of mothering behaviour could be drawn from the limited amount of information provided in the interviews. It was rather this discussion's aim to depict prisoner's views on motherly love on the one hand, as well as embedding these into a critical consideration of hegemonic motherhood ideologies and their relation to the concept of love on the other hand. If motherly love was perpetuated as a synonym for self-sacrifice, then the notion of love as self-sacrifice has to be critically considered. If "the love of ... self-surrender has been praised and called the fulfilment of love ... the question is: What kind of self-surrender is it and what is it that it surrenders?" (Tillich 1954: 69).

Looking at the qualities of love as a virtue, the ideology of self-sacrificial motherly love could be questioned inasmuch as virtuous love is said to be the choice of a moral agent rather than a "natural," unlimited source of nurturing care at the cost of self-depletion. Apart from the mother's essential care and devotion to the child in its very early state of dependency, a perpetuated, unlimited "surrender of … an emaciated self is not genuine love" since "self-surrender does not give justice to the other one, because he who surrenders did not give justice to himself" (Tillich 1954: 69). In terms of motherhood ideologies, it would imply that love as a total depletion of self for another would exceed love's quality of concern for another's well-being. It would thus not represent loving from a position of moral agency and virtue, but from one of powerlessness. The topic of powerlessness will gain more visibility in the second part of this chapter that will consider the subjects of victimisation and domestic violence in relation to the absence of love.

At this point, however, we can recapitulate that more than a quarter of interviewees' narratives about people they felt close to or people they loved predominantly featured mother figures that seemed larger than life. In contrast to this, fathers were hardly mentioned, or they represented the absence rather than the presence of love. This was exemplified by Bruce who "felt loved by my mum and my nan … never felt loved by my dad." When fathers featured positively in two prisoners' accounts, however, they were portrayed as strong and protective but also as caring.

5.2.2 Love of the father

> He was a big fella. He was a miner … He was caring … Cause he supported his family … He was always working … He'd never been in trouble with the police, like me … More or less every year we'd see about four or five kids … Little boys, girls … and he used to … support them, and I used to think it was love. (Arthur)

Arthur equated the love of his father with his willingness to economically and emotionally support not only his family, but also to extend himself in *agape* towards strangers, i.e. foster children. The notion of generosity also featured in Peter's account of his father, whom he described as his role model:

> My father died when I was eight, due to an accident in the pit … My mother used to tell me off about my smoking. And I said "Ohhhhh did you use to pick on my dad like that?" "Your dad never smoked." "Oh yes he did," I said. "Cause I remember the three or four packets of Woodbine cigarettes that used to be in the cupboard." … "No that was your dad, when he was going out with his mates. He used to take a packet of fags, even though he didn't use to smoke himself. He would stand his round in the pub. When it was his turn to pass a cigarette round." And I thought for a non-smoker to do that …. [cries]. If I'd be half the man my dad was … [sobs] That is the thing, you know … to share with your friends, even though you don't do it yourself. (Peter)

The actions and demeanour of his father had installed in Peter the value of sharing his possessions with others. In his view, it was a sign of love, nobility and care to anticipate and cater for the needs and wants of those close to him. Although sharing luxuries and giving little gifts could be seen as part of affectionate communication (Mansson et al. 2017) and relationships based on love (*philia* in this case), Peter had not fared well displaying this value in his current environment. In the course of his interview, it transpired that he had lost possessions, and his generosity had been exploited by other prisoners. He described feeling vulnerable to physical and psychological exploitation by fellow prisoners but did not let this deter him from following his father's example to care and share with others.

The provision of material goods as a shared narrative in above accounts of a father's love, echoed one of the dominant socio-cultural motifs in the conception of fatherhood as breadwinning (Marsiglio et al. 2000). Although "within every historical epoch, a great deal of variability has always existed … [b]readwinning has always been a concern" (Marsiglio et al. 2000: 1175). As much as mothering ideologies are vulnerable to historical, cultural and social developments, so are those of fathering. Having been of minimal interest to social research prior to the late sixties of the last century (Drakich 1989), scholarly interest in studying fathering and its effects rose throughout the 1970s and 1980s, resulting in the production of "a more extensive … social science literature on numerous aspects of fatherhood" (Marsiglio et al. 2000: 1173) in the 1990s. Since then, conceptions of fatherhood have undergone continuous restructuring (Schmitz 2016). More recent research (Summers et al. 2006; Schmitz 2016) into fatherhood ideologies and interpretations "has shown that while men still stress the importance of the instrumental support, they provide their children, there has also been an increased emphasis on expressive and nurturing care" (Schmitz 2016: 4). Adam illustrated this development when asked about what constituted a good and loving father in his opinion:

> A Dad is somebody that's prepared to give his life … for his family. A Dad is somebody that will … when his baby comes up to him says "Daddy, Daddy can I have this bike, can I have a sweet?." A Dad is somebody who's gonna pick em up and say "My love if I had the money, I'd buy you ten bikes" … And explain to them like you ain't got the money. A Dad is somebody who don't holler at the children, don't threaten them, don't smack em. Has always got the time to pick em up and coochie coo and peek a boo, you know what I mean [laughs]? Even when they're lying in the cot … I used to lay with my arm in the cot. And I'll get up in the night and feed them. (Adam)

Adam spoke very passionately about the love of a father and expressed his "hunger to be a Dad" more than once during the interview. He perceived a good father to be someone who protected children from suffering, who was present and available to their needs. A father's love was connected to the absence of destructive behaviour ("don't holler, don't threaten, don't smack em"). The image that was painted of an ideal father was that of a provider or protector on the one hand and that of an emotionally available nurturer on the other. In this sense, Adam expressed what could be regarded as an "unconventional" opinion about the role of a father when compared to hegemonic ideologies that have been in place for a long time and only recently started changing. More and more, the themes of engagement, accessibility and responsibility (Lamb et al. 1987) as well as emotional connection with children (Schmitz 2016) are coming to the forefront in contemporary fatherhood ideologies. They counter those "tenets of hegemonic masculinity and traditional fatherhood that detach men from reproduction and parenting" (Schmitz 2016: 4). As much as those ideological changes are welcomed by contemporary social research scholars, as rarely did the emotionally connected and caring father feature in prisoners' accounts of love. The lives of a majority of interviewees had been either marked by a physically absent father, or by one whose presence was connected to (fear of) violence. As much as some prisoners' narratives of parental violence prevailed, they could nevertheless take a sudden turn, when other members of the family stepped in and showed them care and love.

5.2.3 Love of grandparents

> I did feel loved when I went to my nana's and my grandad's. So, at weekends ... when I was at theirs, I was an angel. I behaved well, but every time I was going home, I was misbehaving. Don't get me wrong, my mum loved me. But she had her own issues ... drink and stuff like that ... she just lived a chaotic life ... But it was more stable when I went to nana's, I should have lived there really ... it was structured, it was all about being and enjoying yourself. I was put first. (Theo)

Compared to a chaotic and unstable home life that seemed to bring out the worst in him, Theo recognised that not only the change of scenery, but predominantly the change in the level and quality of love he received at his grandparents' house contributed to a positive behavioural change.

Looking back at neuroscientific findings on love and attachment, Theo's grandparents seemed to represent a good source for his "limbic regulation" and stability. A mixed-methods study into the resilience and well-being of 20 children living with their grandparents (Downie et al. 2010) came to similar conclusions, with most of their participants indicating that "compared to living with their parents, they felt more valued and understood by their grandparents because of the considerable time, energy and attention that were devoted to their care" (Downie et al. 2010: 15). This and other studies' findings (Mansson et al. 2017; Brussoni and Boon 1998; Griggs et al. 2010; Kennison and Ponce-

Garcia 2012; King et al. 2000; Kornhaber and Woodward 1981; Mansson 2013; Mansson and Booth-Butterfield 2011; O'Neil and Klein 2008; Soliz 2008; Wiscott and Kopera-Frye 2000) underline the significant role grandparents can play in the lives of grandchildren. It was found that they could positively impact on grandchildren's development, values, educational success as well as positively influence their "emotional, psychological, physiological, relational, social, and spiritual well-being" (Mansson 2013: 135).

This view also points towards a macrosocial, cultural role that grandparents occupy as sources of wisdom and stability in family life (Downie et al. 2010). They are often seen as providing practical and emotional support, comfort and discipline to children in times of crisis (Dunning 2006). This was illustrated in Theo's account above and by Ryan stating that

> My grandparents ... used to step in ... when I had enough, I used to go there for sanctuary ... that's the place really where I felt that love ... It feels like they're too good for this world. They *are*! They're not like everybody else ... it still brings tears to their eyes to see me in here ... There's no badness in their hearts. ... I have so much love for them it hurts ... what they've shown me, without that I'd have been a pure bastard today. (Ryan)

In Theo's and Ryan's cases the loving intervention of a family member other than mother or father was regarded as the crucial factor that determined whether their further development would take an even more violent turn or whether it would plant the seed of constructive change and self-esteem inside them. Other studies (e.g. Maluccio et al. 1996) confirm that the presence of grandparents as positive adult role models ("They're too good for this world" (Ryan)) could be "important in fostering resilience" (Jackson and Martin 1998: 580). Grandparents often provided happiness and respite from an otherwise chaotic life:

> I remember my nana taking me to school, and we skipped to school "Nanananana" [sings]. I've seen her about every day. I miss my nana ... (Frank)

Similar to Frank's account of light-heartedness and fun, Theo and Ryan also mentioned that they had the chance to just be children at their grandparents' house, instead of stepping in as protectors and providers for siblings or their mothers. The love they felt they were shown partly related to being provided with structure and boundaries. It was also connected to little rituals of love that ensured they would feel taken care of in a physical and psychological sense. Theo, for example, recounted his experiences of feeling loved whilst spending the weekends at his grandparents' house in great and vivid detail:

> I'd be sat on the couch, she'd be sat there [points next to him]. She'd have a pot of tea on the go … I'd lie on her chest, and sit there all night … she'd tickle my back and tell me, "Right it's bedtime now" and I'd be like "Ooohh … But … I'm hungry, I'm hungry!" … so … we'd play the game, I'd stay up for an extra hour then. So, she'd make me a cheese sandwich or something like that … I'd have a drink … Hot chocolate or a Horlick's … to put me to sleep. But that was part of me getting my own way, staying up for an hour … and she'd put me in bed then … leave the door open, that was one thing. Rather than lock the door. Wrapped me up in the bed, I couldn't even move [laughs and wiggles]. She made sure I was tucked in so I wouldn't fall out. (Theo)

For Theo it was all about physical and psychological comfort: Little gestures of affectionate communication (Mansson et al. 2017) as well as physical connection like being tucked up in bed, being tickled and lying on his grandmother's chest. Similar to Harlow and Zimmermann's deprivation experiment (1958) "contact comfort" as well as leaving the door open – not locking him into his bedroom, like his parents did – were pivotal factors in creating a feeling of safety and closeness for Theo. Likewise, Downie et al. (2010) located "feeling safe and secure" as a recurrent theme in grandchildren's accounts as well as the importance of being spoilt with "love, care and attention to their basic needs" (Downie et al. 2010: 20). In Theo's opinion being raised in the stable and loving household of his grandparents could have made all the difference to his further development if continued, but then

> I got to an age in secondary school, when I started smoking, drinking and taking drugs, so … I stopped going to my nana's you know. I found that escapism somewhere else … from there then it was just a big snowball. (Theo)

When asked about the reasons why their grandparents seemed to be so much different than their parents, respondents predominantly connected it to generational differences in values and lifestyle or to a hostile dynamic between their parents, exacerbated by drug and alcohol addiction. Another source of positively associated love within the prisoners' family microsystem was found in relationships with their own or stepchildren.

5.2.4 Love for children

Asked to tell me about a situation when they felt loved, a quarter of respondents spontaneously recounted stories about children showing joy and excitement to see them, wanting to be close to them, missing their presence in their lives as well as reciprocating and mirroring their own love towards them:

> I love my son so much. I'd give him anything. And then, when he grew up, he just started giving it to me back. Brilliant … Every morning, he'd run up to me and give me a hug and a kiss … and tell me how much he loved me … And he'd always want me to read him a story … He didn't want to just go to bed. He always wanted to give me a hug … That was good. I think that was the strongest part in my life. (Will)

> [W]ith the stepchildren cuddling me and coming on visits … [Name of stepson] … when he came into [name of prison]. He's been sat down, he's been looking over the visits hall, he's seen me like a meerkat and he's been running towards me … You know, that was love. You know, my son … he upset me the other day when he said, "I miss you." [cries] (Theo)

The children's open and enthusiastic expression of love, of attachment and emotional closeness as a "sense of shared experiences, trust … and enjoyment of the relationship" (Lee et al. 1990: 433) caused strong positive emotions in their fathers and contributed to their self-esteem ("That was the strongest part in my life" (Will)). The shared physical and emotional connection between children and fathers could be seen as creating positivity as well as limbic resonance together. Consequently, the absence of the person whom positivity resonance was created with could induce sadness, palpable in Theo's tears over his son's declaration that he missed him. Even though the possibility of forging physical connections with their children might have been limited or unavailable, a psychological connection held the potential to override negative states of mind like hopelessness or depression. The love for his children had provided George, for example, with the mental power to keep pushing through his life-sentence:

> There's been dark times but having the love of all of them has got me through … Seeing my kids every day: I wake up and I got pictures of me kids on the wall, and when you don't want to get up, when you don't want to do something you look at them and you think, "It's for them." If I don't get through this, how does it impact on them? (George)

As established earlier, neurological studies have found that even just gazing at the picture of a beloved person activates regions of the brain associated with the motivation to obtain rewards (Bartels and Zeki 2000), creating positive emotions that can ultimately influence behaviour. Resorting to this positive mental power had changed George's mental state from a depressive one to a more resilient one. Putting his children's well-being before his own wish to give up and to surrender to negative affective states also echoed one of love's main qualities of transcending ego-boundaries. As a virtue, love can inspire a change in behaviour or value orientations by providing a reason to care more about another person's integrity than about immediate gains for oneself. This was also illustrated by Arthur's take on what makes a good (or bad) father:

> If you've got kids, you shouldn't be in prison. Go get a job. You know what I mean? You shouldn't steal or hurt or ... do drugs, deal drugs and that. If you've got kids, don't make them suffer. You can't say you love your kids if you're away twenty years from them. You know what I mean? Weird love that. (Arthur)

Arthur did not have children himself and clarified that he never had the conscious desire to be a father. His life had been exclusively dedicated to crime. Nevertheless, he expressed the view that love as a guiding principle or virtue should overrule other principles of personal conduct and that it could only really be practiced in physical proximity with each other ("You can't say you love your kids if you're away twenty years from them ... Weird love that" (Arthur)). A father's love required presence with and care for his children, as argued earlier.

Not only family members came to respondents' minds when they were asked to think about people they felt connected to or what love meant to them. They also frequently mentioned their partners or ex-partners in this regard. It was a different kind of love they described in these instances because "with your partner it's obviously more like lust and desire ... You wouldn't have that with your family members, would you?" (Bo).

5.2.5 Love for romantic partners

> I mean when you first meet someone, you're excited like a kid at Christmas, aren't ya? ... Oh, you get all excited, you run up the stairs, you get in the shower. Oh, gotta look nice ... You meet each other, you kiss each other, you go out for a meal, you get drunk, you have sex. You can't wait to see him again the next day. That's not love, is it? That's not love, that's like excitement, lust, and you think you love him ... But then as you progress ... and you can't be apart from each other, you're talking to each other, and you're happy. Everything is good, you're good to him, and he opens doors for you, and you open doors for him. (Bruce)

Bruce not only recounted a common storyline that romantic relationships would develop along in many contemporary Western societies. He also pointed towards factors of excitement and sexual attraction featuring in the early stages of romantic attachment. In his opinion, this could not be regarded as love, however, but rather as lust and these two were not to be confounded. When prompted to reflect on whether sex and love were the same thing, Peter likewise negated that statement, suggesting that a lot of people think that is so, but ... sex is almost animalistic, isn't it? Love is something else really ... Well, I suppose to be really in love it's like being a parent ... Whatever the other one does, you still love them. Regardless of how obnoxious they are [laughs]. (Peter)

According to Bruce and Peter, love had to stand the test of time. It would grow with continued attachment, shared communication and mutual care for the other's well-being. Peter alluded to a kind of love that would persevere anything unconditionally, thus moving it closer to the concept of earlier discussed all-forgiving motherly love. At a later point in the interview, Peter related that he had been a victim of domestic violence at the hands of his former wife. It will be interesting to return to the idea of unconditional, self-sacrificing love in a later discussion of the "dark" side of love and its role in domestic violence and abuse-scenarios. In a similar vein, the factor of mutual attachment – just as the one between child and parent – may have had a role to play in Peter's view on love as non-negotiable dedication.

This brings us back to Bruce's statement about love's consolidation over time and increased attachment between love partners. It bore a resemblance, in fact, to neurobiological findings encountered earlier. They connect romantic attachment and pair bonding to the activation of brain mechanisms that govern social bonding as well as addictive behaviour (Burkett and Young 2012). These mechanisms re-enforce reciprocal bonding behaviours of a pair, leading to the fact that "as you progress ... you can't be apart from each other" (Bruce)). Adam similarly described love as a continuous bonding experience, one that creates unity as postulated by a romantic relationship ideal:

[W]here I went, she went, I would never leave her home...it never happened ... I'd take her out with me: stealing, working, fighting, whatever ... She was always there. And they said, where you see one you see the other ... Always together ... One sneezed, the other caught a cold. (Adam)

Whereas love was connected to long-term pair-bonding for interviewees such as Bruce, Adam and Peter, others remembered love most vividly when looking back at often fleeting, yet profoundly impressive experiences: their "first love." Memories of one special woman or girl who had initiated them into the world of *eros* represented a recurring theme in three interviews:

Love is like a sexual feeling. If you feel good with that woman ... like I was when I was at school. I had a girlfriend and, uh, I thought I loved her, and she thought she loved me, and we were only fifteen ... You don't forget them things. You'll always remember the first person you ever fell in love with, whether it was love or not, when you're a kid at school ... [Name of ex-girlfriend], I got a tattoo [whispers] on me arm ... you get conditioned. You don't forget. All the other times ... as far as I'm concerned, it's either good sex or bad sex. (Arthur)

And I see this girl, and erm ... [long pause, he's searching for words] something ... something different ... it was a different feeling, I, I, I didn't know before ... Nice. It was nice, it was different ... I can only describe it as nice.

Did you ever have that again?

[Inhales] No. No ... I had something close to it ... No, I've never felt that again ... love like I had for [name of first girlfriend] No ... [long, thoughtful pause] ... oh that's that, that's that. (Adam)

These women had left a lasting impression and set the bar for all subsequent romantic relationships to feel equally new and different. Arthur's first girlfriend's mental impression had even been translated into a subcutaneous one, literally getting under his skin. Adam and Arthur recalled meeting their first love as a teenager. This experience fell into a time of transition from childhood to adulthood, marking the onset of sexual activity motivated by gender-specific hormonal changes. Especially the heightened production and release of oxytocin – neuronal signalling molecules involved in social bonding mechanisms – during puberty has been isolated by neuroscientists as one important factor in initiating "infatuation's sweet adolescent spell" (Lewis et al. 2000: 97). The onset of puberty also marked the transition from a childish way of loving (expecting love from the mother without the need to give back) to a more mature way of loving (receiving and reciprocating love). It might have been the first time their love was oriented outwardly towards giving to another person, overleaping a "wall of ... selfhood" (Lewis 1960: 131) and focusing on the interests and well-being of another. It represented a memorable event:

I've never been in love before ... I loved this girl with all my heart. 20 years later I still care and love her. And not love in that way, but I would never see harm come to her ... you never forget your first childhood sweetheart. You know, your first love. You never seem to forget that. And I haven't ... You know what, I think it's just memories. (Frank)

Falling in love for the first time was seen as a milestone in development. It had created a strong impression and still reverberated in Frank's, as well as Adam's and Arthur's memory. Lewis described love – if it was the "right" kind of love – similarly as an orientation towards the beloved that had her best interest in mind, even if it would go against one's self-interest:

So, if I'd loved her ... it weren't proper love. I wouldn't have done the things that I needed to do ... You think you love them, but it's not love, is it? Obviously, it's just in the moment. Cause ... say I'm with a girl ... I wake up in the morning and I think "What is she doing here?" So, it wouldn't be love, do you know what I mean? It's like, one day you'll love her, you think you love her, the next day, you are not ... Love means, obviously, no matter what happens, you love that person. So, you shouldn't cheat. You shouldn't ... hit 'em. You shouldn't ... try and overpower them ... You shouldn't try and tell them what they've gotta do, what they've gotta wear ... if you're in love ... you should be all about them. You should do everything for 'em. Provide them with everything they need ... If it's proper love. You'd stop everything, if you needed. And you'd have to join the rat race ... You'd have to look at nine to five. And you'd have to be there. (Lewis)

Lewis saw his duty of love in catering to the other person's needs and to focus wholeheartedly on her. Similar to Bruce and Peter he also connected "proper love" to be enduring time and challenges ("No matter what happens you love that person.") as well as forfeiting immediate self-oriented gains in exchange for adopting long-term virtuous goals ("You shouldn't cheat ... if you're in love ... you should be all about them ... Provide them with everything they need ... You'd stop everything ... and you'd have to join the rat race."). Lewis regarded love as a complete dedication to new lines of action that required discipline and a change of values and lifestyle. This ideal of love as a virtuous choice of a moral agent held the power to motivate selfless behaviour and to "do the right thing."

Up to this point, we have explored the role of dyadic interpersonal relationships in the microsystem of the individual. These represented the positive effects of love's presence in and outside the family. Although these were the most prominent figures featuring in prisoners' accounts of experiences of love, they were not the only ones. In situations when the family home was not felt to be a place of love and safety – where human beings were not perceived to be trustworthy – animals could step in to satisfy the human need for connection.

5.2.6 Love of and for pets

I used to get locked up from the age of, I don't know 4, 5, 6 ... Locked up in my bedroom at night and then they'd bugger off, go out ... Even up to the age of 10, 12. I had my telly, I even had a bucket in my bedroom, so I could use the toilet ... they'd leave the landing lights on ... and I sat with my cat, it's come to the doorway, and I'd speak to my cat and keep it company, and it would keep me company. (Theo)

Theo had experienced a lot of anxiety during recurring periods of lock-up during childhood. The awareness that he was not completely alone, but that another living being was on the other side of his bedroom door provided some relief and comfort. Theo's acutely experienced anxiety related to the separation from his parental attachment figures was a common reaction – not only for infants but also for adult human beings – to the loss of a "love object." One of the potential mental health implications – in addition to anxiety – of this loss was pointed out by Fromm (1995: 8) as a "radical withdrawal from the world" up to a point when the individual is in danger of entering a psychological state of dissociation. In Theo's case, he counteracted his fears by seeking and clinging to connection with his cat. At the time, it represented the only available source of contact to the world outside the "prison" of his bedroom.[3]

Contained within prisoners' narratives about the love they received from pets was the fact that they filled a gap left by human beings. Lewis et al., for example, relate the ability of pets to relieve human beings' anxiety, to a cerebral attachment architecture "general enough that a human being and a dog can both … exchange in limbic regulation" (2000: 98). Both are able to "read some of each other's emotional cues" (Lewis et al. 2000: 98). Further research (e.g. Brooks et al. 2018) established the important role pets can assume in providing emotional support to a person, sometimes even being viewed as "replacement family members" (Brooks et al. 2018: 5). Providing a consistent source of comfort, connection, limbic regulation and communication (as described by Theo who was "speaking" to his cat) can reduce feelings of isolation (Brooks et al. 2018). Some respondents mentioned that in times, when everybody else around them seemed to have vanished, either through separation, loss or conflict, a pet could provide emotional support and take on the role of a companion. This realisation came as a surprise to Peter during his interview:

> I'd had a dog most of my life. In fact, my other house … was called Baskerville. Cause I used to have a couple of Great Danes.
>
> *What did you like about having dogs?*
>
> The loyalty. Yeah [long pause] … I don't know, I'm getting all emotional about it. [laughs] (Peter)

Peter remembered his dogs as a source of unconditional loyalty, especially after the breakup with his wife, which left him disappointed and financially and emotionally damaged. He echoed some findings arrived at by studies on pet facilitated mental health therapies (Brickel 1986) and on social interaction between pets and their owners (Dotson and Hyatt 2008). Their findings suggest that pets are often perceived to provide more consistent and reliable

---

[3] In fact, at a later point in the interview Theo drew parallels between his childhood experiences of "imprisonment" and his current predicament as an actual prisoner. The discussion of this interplay will be taken up again in more detail at a later point of this chapter as well as in Chapter 7.

relationships than human to human (Brickel 1986). Within those relationships, "pet owners believe they not only give but receive love and affection from their animals" (Dotson and Hyatt 2008: 457). Love could therefore not only be found in interpersonal relationships, but also in relationships with pets although this form of love was mentioned only by a minority of interviewees. A majority referred to an interpersonal love as the provision of a human need directed towards or received from sources outside of themselves. Some interviewees, however, were aware of an essential love relationship only involving one person, namely themselves.

5.2.7 Self-love — A "special case"?

Although I did not explicitly ask if respondents loved themselves, I enquired into how they saw themselves as a person. It was predominantly during this interview section, when prisoners referred to positive aspects of themselves that they valued. It could involve taking care of their outward appearance as well as nurturing their basic needs, spoiling themselves occasionally, but also exercising self-discipline in favour of their own well-being as expressed by Adam and Theo:

> I buy a bag of nuts, a bag of raisins, and I tie them all together with some oats and honey and make like a nut-bar. I like this! This ... is how I express love to myself. (Adam)

> I'm showing myself love by not using drugs. (Theo)

Against the background of an environment significantly limiting his ability to eat healthily, purchasing additional nutrient-rich food items was regarded by Adam as an expression of taking care of himself as well as of individual agency. Creating healthy nut-bars catered to Adam's very own taste and provided an opportunity to attend to himself. For Theo, self-love was equated with an immediate concern for his physical and psychological well-being. Overcoming his long-standing drug addiction, he perceived as a gesture of love towards himself. Theo showed himself "self-love in acting virtuously, since the self he loves is his developed capacity for practical reasoning" (Annas 1988: 14). Choosing to "do the right thing" can be seen as an act of self-love in this context.

Arguably, Adam's and Theo's accounts of self-love displayed features of love as pointed out by psychology and moral philosophy. As a special case, however, self-love demands further differentiation. Existentialist philosopher Tillich (1954), for example, questions, whether one could meaningfully speak of self-love as a concept of its own or if it should not rather be used as "a metaphor ... in the sense of natural self-affirmation ... or selfishness" (Tillich 1954: 34). Other perspectives adopt a less exclusive view. Theological philosopher Conn (1998), for example, states his case to not see love and self-love as mutually exclusive but to rather distinguish between genuine self-love and its opposite: selfishness. According to Fromm (1995), genuine self-love can be seen as "the affirmation of one's own life, happiness, growth, freedom" and as "rooted in one's capacity to love, i.e. in care, respect, responsibility, and knowledge" (Fromm 1995: 50). This stands in opposition to the utilitarian orientation of selfishness which does not value a person for him- or herself, but for what could be gained from him or her. Adam's view on the prevailing expression of love in a prison context suggests a congruence between self-love and selfishness. In fact, he perceived the former to be expressed as the latter through personal need satisfaction stating that

> most of the love in prison is for self. Self-love ... Masturbation ... Most of the homosexual activity ... you might get yourself canteen, buy tobacco, buy a sweet. Well, that's all self-love ... And this is for preservation, this is for protection. Again: self-love. (Adam)

As above excerpt points out, Adam equated self-love with actions solely oriented towards an individual's maximum utility for himself. It does not take the other into consideration, hence can be regarded as selfish. Especially, when it comes to self-love in relation to other-love, moral philosopher Annas states that "humans come equipped both with self- love and with the ability to extend this in certain ways to others" (Annas 1988: 2). Self-love can manifest as a form of love proper but only if it is not equated with uncaring selfishness. Rather self-love extends itself as a virtuous attitude of self-respect and self-care also towards others. In that sense, self-love can only manifest itself in the treatment of external others which serves as the visualisation of its inner presence and quality. Although self-love has been discussed as actions or attitudes directed at the self, at an individual, it cannot stand fully on its own. In order to distinguish self-love from selfishness, the other has to be taken into consideration. This reaffirms a distinctly relational quality of love as established in Chapter 3.

When it came to love that expands beyond the social-ecological spheres (Bronfenbrenner 1974) of self and the microsystemic bonds of family systems or dyadic relationships with intimate partners, interviews did not deliver any data. Prisoners neither referred to any experiences or memories of love in their mesosystem (e.g. friends of the family), nor did they mention love in relation to their exosystem (e.g. social or institutional environment). Therefore, this chapter will not be able to specify or draw conclusions about these interrelations. References to prisoners' macrosystem (Bronfenbrenner 1974), i.e. the cultural and normative background to perceptions of love have been alluded to in discussing social and cultural ideologies of certain representations of love. These include the ideal types of motherly or fatherly love. Other examples could be found looking back at normative views expressed by Lewis about the quality of a "proper love" for a partner, or Bruce's summary of a typical sequence of romantic love relationships, featuring encounter, attraction, lust and long-term unity of partners which might not be a common process in other cultures or at a different time in history.

After having discussed the extension of human beings in love towards others as well as towards themselves, I will now examine in detail what effects the absence and opposites of love can have. As much as interviewees connected the presence of love as human virtue to its qualities of creating connection, cooperation, moral conduct and human resilience, as much they were aware of the detrimental effects the absence of love as human need could – and often already had – executed on their lives.

5.3 *Love as human need* — The absence of love in prisoners' microsystem

> I find that the less love people have in their life, the more brutal they are in how they treat others around them ... It's like that also for me. I could switch it off [snaps fingers] cause it hurts, you know? (Ryan)

In six interviews, a storyline similar to the above started to emerge revolving around the effects of the absence of love. These accounts mainly related to the realisation that prisoners felt they did not know what love meant or felt like, because they thought they had never experienced it. They connected this realisation to early or current deprivation experiences as mentioned by Ryan, where love had been replaced by violence. Others connected the loss of a loved person (or an animal as in Paul's case below) to the painful experience of grief. Prisoners' narratives about the loss of love sometimes featured an element of denial or repression of painful feelings accompanying these events. This was not only illustrated by Ryan "switching it off," but also by Paul who displayed a very negative attitude toward loving or caring about anyone or anything throughout his interview. He upheld this view consistently, until I decided to scratch the surface of apparent indifference:

Do you like animals?

No ... They're just expense and a mess. They just shit everywhere and eat all your shit and break all your shit. You know. They just annoy the shit out of ya.

Did you ever have animals?
[Pause] ... I've had a dog.

Mmm ... How long did you have it?

Not long, someone run it over ...

Sorry .... to hear that.

Nah. It's alright. He was alright [name of dog].

Ah [name of dog]. What kind of dog was it?

I don't know. He was a Goldie colour thing. But he was, he was ... he were [sic] shit hot man, he were a good dog. And then someone run him over [sounds low]. (Paul)

Whilst prisoners like Paul or Ryan seemed to deploy defences against remembering or feeling the pain of love's loss or deprivation, others expressed their grief and pain vividly and emotionally throughout interviews. Frank was one of two interviewees expressing an awareness that the pain of grief as well as guilt about his failure to show love for his critically ill mother, could only be felt because he inherently knew what love was:

That pain ... I feel about my mum, the guilt and the shame, and not being there for her. It's .... phew [sighs heavily] ... all that pain is based off love. It's all for love, innit? You know the pain I feel for everything and the guilt, it's based out of love. (Frank)

If no connection, no attachment, no love had been established, there would be no pain involved in the loss or absence of a love object. It therefore seemed that the absence of love was experienced as painful because the presence of love was known to be so good and so essential for human existence. Some of prisoners' most painful experiences of the absence of love were connected to a specific microsystem where love played one of the most crucial roles of all: their childhood home. Early encounters with violence, trauma and abuse within this microsystem kept haunting them:

When I was 18 months, my Dad put me in intensive care ... I always wanted to run away from a young age ... Once I remember I got a carrier bag, got me little blanket, got my teddy in it ... So, I just walked out the house and said "I'm leaving." And I was only 4 or 5. And she'd follow me obviously, watching. I just went around the back and just sat on a step. And she found that funny, that I just sat there ... You know? ... You know?

But it wasn't funny?

It's not obviously. If my kid had done that. (Theo)

Narratives like Theo's, featuring unbearable family situations marked by one or two emotionally unresponsive, addicted or violent parental figures were brought up by several interviewees. These storylines mostly emerged as a "side-story" out of asking respondents to think about a past or current situation when they felt loved or about people they loved. Struggling to recall a distinct person or experience of love, the question instead led four prisoners to recall a past devoid of love but rife with what was perceived as its opposite: violence. I decided to attach analytic importance to this somewhat limited number of accounts because they represented and illuminated the "other side of the coin," i.e. the absence of love. They furthermore represented that group of prisoners who are also represented in Table 5.1's[4] statistics of those within the male English and Welsh prison population (at the time of fieldwork) who had experienced abuse as a child (27%) and who had observed violence in the home as a child (40%). As such, they did not represent a distinct majority, but a group within the general prison population who shared above distinct features. In the following, I want to shine a light on this specific group of prisoners, their negative experiences within their microsystem as well as on the effects these could exude on their mental development and health.

5.3.1 Domestic violence, abuse and trauma as toxic stressors in childhood development

> From the age of 3, 4 I've seen a lot of domestic violence, getting woken up in the middle of the night by the police and taken to the hospital with my teddy and just in my jamas [sic]. Whilst my mum was you know [starts speaking faster] getting walking [sic] down the stairs, just seeing blood everywhere and ... I hear the arguments, so it was familiar. That's what I remember. I can remember actually, and I'll always remember, being in the refuge, child refuge. (Theo)

Theo's account of regularly witnessing violence and arguments in the family setting, especially of his mother becoming a victim of physical violence perpetrated against her by his father (and later also by his stepfather) represented not only a recurring theme in at least a quarter of interviews. It also mirrors findings of research bodies such as the World Health Organisation (WHO) on Gender-Based Violence (GBV), i.e. violence committed predominantly (but not exclusively!) by men against women. According to Fulu et al. (2013) as well as Garcia-Moreno et al. (2005), empirical evidence suggests that GBV is a world-wide occurrence. Furthermore, findings of a WHO's multi-country study (2012) revealed that Intimate Partner Violence (IPV) was the most common form of GBV (World Health Organization 2012). It can comprise "physical, sexual and emotional abuse and controlling behaviour by a current or former intimate partner or spouse" (Sikweyiya et al. 2016: 1). Going into a detailed discussion of causes and dynamics of IPV would go beyond the scope of this book. However, since its main aim is to examine the presence as well as the absence of love in prisoners' lives, the following interview excerpts will aim to convey some of the experiences they were exposed to whilst growing up and to connect them to effects that were still palpable in their present lives:

---

[4] See Bromley Briefings Factfile (2019) as reproduced in Section 5.6.

> I watched my stepdad absolutely *annihilate* my mother ... he would smash her over the head ... one day ... she made him Sunday dinner, and he wanted brown sauce. Cause there was no brown sauce, he ... [holds his speech abruptly] he put a plate over my mum's head ... He's thrown her out of windows, she got seventy odd stitches. Yeah, I watched that, and I used to run over and smother her. And I wouldn't let her go to take the beatings. The punches and the kicks, me rather than her. But then later on in the evening they'd make up, and me not being his son, and his other three kids, you know they'd all be together, and I'd be upstairs in a [sighs] ... attic where it was freezing, there was no carpets, an old battered couch ... I'd get a hiding for interfering in his business. (Ryan)

Recounting memories of their mothers being humiliated and violated by their partners still triggered distress in Theo and Ryan showing up in speech patterns and articulation. Theo, for example, started talking noticeably faster, recalling the image of his mother being "walked down the stairs, just seeing blood everywhere," and Ryan held his breath abruptly, recalling the moment his stepfather broke a plate over his mother's head. Ryan's account also illustrated that some interviewees were not only witnesses of domestic violence but could become victims of physical and emotional abuse themselves, being beaten or excluded from the family. According to findings from the *Adverse Childhood Experience Study* (Felitti et al. 1998), direct or indirect childhood experiences of violence, abuse, neglect and parental substance use such as recounted by Ryan (whose mother had also developed a drug addiction) have been classified as stressors and can lead to toxic stress responses in the developing brain of a child.

Compared to two other types of stress responses, positive and tolerable (National Scientific Council on the Developing Child 2010), toxic stress has been declared the "most dangerous form of stress response" (Shonkoff and Garner 2012: 235). Whereas positive and tolerable stress responses are marked by the presence of protective factors such as supportive adults, this factor is missing in cases where physiological toxic stress responses are activated (Shonkoff and Garner 2012; Hüther 2006). Toxic stress responses can ultimately result in neuronal dysregulation and disintegration, as asserted by Hüther (2006) previously. They have been qualified by Shonkoff and Garner (2012: 236) as "precursors of later impairments in learning and behavior as well as the roots of chronic, stress-related physical and mental illness." This kind of toxic stress, experienced in dependency relationships between young children and their parents, can alter the development of brain structures. Various neuroscientific findings likewise agree that "dysregulating levels of relational stress ... exert an enduring detrimental epigenetic impact on the developing right brain, significantly altering the individual's emotional responsiveness and stress-coping strategies later in life" (Schore 2017: 22). It also contributes to anxiety disorders and impaired memory and mood control (McEwen and Gianaros 2011). Theo was one of the prisoners who provided an insight into how toxic stress experiences in childhood had affected his later stress-coping strategies in a negative way, ranging from anxiety to self-harm and suicide attempts:

> [Friend's name] took me to hospital a few times, caught me with syringes full of bleach ... Cries for help and stuff like that. You know, overdoses ... I used to remember when I get locked in my bedroom ... I stick a panel over my head to the point of where I was going dizzy. I'd hold my breath a lot ... when I was being told off. (Theo)

> The care plan's get me out my cell, get me working. I'm behind my cell door 22 hours, all they're doing is locking me up, with my toilet and my tele behind my door. Just like I've been locked up as a youngster. I'm just living recurrent things ... And when violence is happening on the wing, I'm getting upset about it and I'm asking officers to get me a Listener. Cause with violence and that ... I'm living in fear. (Theo)

Finding himself in the same situation that had induced toxic or uncontrollable stress responses (Hüther 2006) in the past, i.e. being locked "with my toilet and my tele behind my door" and witnessing violence, now could still trigger anxiety and fear in Theo. Although he described how he had learned to ask for help ("I'm asking officers to get me a Listener"), he would sometimes resort to destructive behaviour in situations that triggered a stress response:

> I have a lot of aggression. It always goes back to there ... There was an incident last night, a woman officer was getting the truncheon out screaming, stop it, stop it! ... Sends me back there. You know, just hearing screaming and stuff like that, it does that. Any fighting, it sends me back there. But ... I've been branded a violent prisoner. I did commit violent offences, but there was instrumental use of violence, I never physically harmed somebody, it was ... psychological, it's just as bad. And I've got psychological scars, I'm aware of that now. ... There was one of my offences, when the woman started screaming, when I was doing a robbery, I stopped and ran off. I just wanted the money for drugs and stuff like that, and not been eating and stuff, you know. It's no excuse, but [inhales]. (Theo)

As related during his interview, Theo had gained some understanding and insight into his past and present behaviour through therapeutic interventions during his custodial sentence and was now more aware about the connection between his childhood experiences and current aggressive behaviour. Research into the development of aggressive behaviour problems (Dodge 2006) furthermore suggests that an early exposure to violence can lead to the development of hostile attribution bias. It is defined as the likeliness to "provide negative interpretations of the intent of another's action" (Schofield et al. 2015) and it would often be adopted "as a protective strategy growing up" (Schofield et al. 2015). Paul, for example – who described frequent experiences of abuse whilst in the care system as a child – displayed great suspicion throughout his interview towards anything "good" that might happen to him. He did not trust the declaration of positive emotions (like love) towards him, but rather expressed what could be interpreted as hostile attribution bias:

> If someone's like friendly towards me, I'm like what's behind, that's the first thing, what's behind this? They're after something … Then I'm like stand-offish … Any relationship that I've had … when that word's being mentioned, I always question it. Always. Why? What's there to love? Explain it to me why you love me? What … have I offered that could want you love me? And then I just … hear lies. (Paul)

Adverse experiences with people in his micro- and exosystem who were supposed to care about and love him had solidified Paul's belief that love or friendliness towards him had to be approached with caution and that it was "fake." "A childhood replete with suffering" seemed to be lingering in his mind "as bitter, encoded traces of pain" (Lewis et al. 2000: 131). Continuously scanning and scrutinising his environment, even a slight reminder of that suffering confirmed Paul's assumption that nothing good could happen for and to him, thus creating a "sad empirical confirmation" (Lewis et al. 2000: 131) of a seemingly self-fulfilling prophecy.

Interviewees like Paul and Theo had learned early on to expect an escalation of aggression in their environment rather than a peaceful settlement. Theo, for example, recalled that he did not feel he could choose from an array of emotional expression, but instead stated that "I didn't understand empathy. I was probably … quite angry up to the age of … 17, 18" (Theo). Such a "lack of ability in reading emotions and taking them into account" (Schofield et al. 2015: 131) as well as a developed hypersensitivity to anger can damage an individual's potential to build relationships and increase the risk of offending (Schofield et al. 2015). The topic of anger as one of the "go-to-emotions" when dealing with relational difficulties or disagreements with partners or peers was a recurring storyline in prisoners' interviews. Often it formed part of an intergenerational narrative of male violence perpetuated in a seemingly "automatic" fashion and against better judgment:

> I feel that anger … I met my stepdad quite a few years ago. I used to be a gym instructor as well. So, I was big then, I was on steroids. He thought I was gonna do him in, and we sat down, and we had this conversation, and I asked him "Why?" Why he did what he did? And he came with his honest answer as he watched that happen in his house … his dad doing this to his mum. He always felt guilty, but he couldn't change it. Erm … I have to admit

that I have assaulted my partner as well in the past. And it broke my heart that I did it. Because I had to see it all those years. (Ryan)

Although the perpetuation of anger and aggression fuelling IPV could be regarded as part of a specific masculinity ideology – which will be discussed further in Chapter 8 of this book – mirroring and modelling could also be considered as a "potential mechanism for the transmission of conduct problems" (DeKlyen et al. 1998: 5) such as physical aggression. In fact, ample evidence has been gathered verifying that observed aggression in parents can lead to similar behaviour in children (Bandura et al. 1963). As DeKlyen et al. established whilst researching interrelations between positive and negative parenting and the early onset of conduct problems:

> Parents provide the earliest and perhaps most salient models for their children by virtue of both exposure and power. If they use aggressive behaviors ... as preferred methods for solving problems or changing another's behavior ... children come to exhibit similar behaviors. (DeKlyen et al. 1998: 5)

Looking at the neurological particulars of neuroplasticity and allostasis adds an additional layer to above-described approach to behavioural conditioning of children. Since "there is constant feedback between the brain and its environment" (Ungar et al. 2013: 352), the social-ecology of childhood and especially the absence of parental love continues to matter well into adult life.

5.3.2 The absence of love from mother

> My mum didn't know how to show love. She came from such a rough background, where they hated mixed race people back then. She had worms put over her head. She had a hard life ... She loved us, but the beatings we used to get were worse off my mum. She had hands like shovels my mum, and all the anger from her from getting battered from her partner, my stepdad, that was took out on me. Which made me sit there and cry my heart out, thinking how can my mum love me, when she's doing this to me? When she's secretly taking drugs, it killed me to see that. I had that shit life of a torture. That's what it was. I got abused as well, you know, in many different ways. (Ryan)

The presence of violence and abuse signalled very clearly the absence of love to Ryan and induced major grief. He saw his life as torture and as a continuous transmission of violence and anger through caregiver attachments. These were supposed to provide him "with a sense of 'felt security' or safety" (DeKlyen et al. 1998: 7) but lacked all of these attributes. Instead, these relationships had come to represent a threat to Ryan's physical and psychological integrity. Although a healthy mother-child relationship could entail maternal ambivalence to some degree, as argued in feminist philosophy (Takseva 2017), and mothers could not always enact the role of the "good mother," there was a tipping point when the failure to safeguard the needs of a dependent child could turn into maternal abuse. This was more evident in cases of physical abuse, such as beatings but could be less overt, yet deeply disturbing, in situations of emotional or mental abuse as recalled by Theo:

> This is something that affects me. My mum had an ectopic pregnancy and then she had a miscarriage. She showed me the miscarriage in a tissue …
>
> *Why did she do that you think?*
>
> I don't know. Cause she was upset, and I was asking questions and stuff. So, when she became pregnant again, that's when I left home … I didn't feel loved or anything like that. (Theo)

Being made a confidant of his mother and being exposed to very private and highly upsetting events by her seemed overwhelming to Theo at the time and not loving at all. Consequently, when he sensed an impending danger for the disturbing event to repeat, he sought to distance himself from his mother and left home (at the age of 12, as he conveyed at a later point of the interview). Theo was not the only respondent who described a role reversal, feeling that his mother neglected to care for her children but displayed irresponsible behaviour instead. Ryan, for example, described his existence as "just a living nightmare" when referring to the trajectory his life took when his mother became involved in drug use:

> She used to do drugs, so … to stop her from going out, committing crimes, and doing stuff that I didn't want her to do … I became involved in a gang … and had to start, well I didn't have to, but … I started selling drugs … if anybody found out she was taking drugs, then the kids would be taken away, my brothers and sisters, and they needed feeding and clothing for school. So, I had to go out and do something …. My life has been just a living nightmare. With good parts. My mum was a good mum, yeah, she was a good woman, she got off drugs, but by then it was too late for me. (Ryan)

Ryan realised that an early cut-off of his childhood and the assumption of the carer and provider role for his mother and younger siblings had set the tone for a later involvement or "career" in criminal offending. Although he realised that, ultimately, he had chosen to enter into criminal offending himself, he felt there were not many alternative avenues he could have taken based on his economical, emotional and maturational state. Ryan and other interviewees saw themselves in the duty to intervene and protect their mothers and family by all means. It furthermore seemed like a means to establish closeness and "earn" their mothers' love, as Frank's vivid account of stopping domestic violence demonstrates:

> I used to watch my Dad beat my Mum up, yeah?! ... I used to hear my Dad coming home from working at night ... He put the food over my Mum's head ... and he was a bit drunk ... He used to rule the house with a rod of iron ... He started getting a bit loud and I heard my mum screaming and crying and ... I just went [pushes chair back] stood up like that [stands up] and I ... looked at him and went, "You lay one more hand on my mum, and I'm gonna smash this in your face!" And he looked at me like that, and ever since that day we never spoke ... That's why I'm so lovely close to my mum. (Frank)

Protecting their mothers often entailed standing up to their fathers or other male authority figures, thus putting themselves in the line of violence as well as taking sides. In fact, a majority of prisoners would report a closer relationship with their mothers and a more difficult, or even non-existent relationship with their fathers. The reasons for that were mainly related to perceiving their fathers as negative role models, exemplified in the following excerpt.

5.3.3 The absence of love from father

> He's just a miserable git. See his dad, my granddad ... He was a horrible, drunken, Irish man who's got pissed and batter me granny ... his dad didn't care for him. So, he doesn't know ... how to give fatherly love. He said, "I done this, when you was kids I took you to Malta." "Yeah, how did you take us to Malta Dad?" He pinched about 3000 pounds off a lad ... "Don't start saying you were doing this and doing that. Everything you got now is what my mum gave ya." (Bruce)

Apart from reiterating the narrative of intergenerational IPV and the absence of love that seemed to permeate the male line of his family, Bruce also pointed towards the failure of his father to provide and care economically for his family. In Bruce's view, this discredited his father and he depicted his mother as the "real" provider of the family. In doing so, he expressed his disrespect towards a man who could not live up to more traditional gender norms as the male provider of material resources for his family (Wyse et al. 2014). Another characteristic of a father that could be met with disrespect or even contempt was a lack of concern and care towards or interest in his family. Lewis painted an image of a father whom his son would not look up to because he could not find anything in him that he found admirable. It would prevent him from connecting with his father:

> He's bad with drugs, so I don't speak to him much ... He's got a split personality and all that, bad schizophrenic ... So, I generally don't speak

to him. When I do, it's "You need to do this, you need to do that." And I think, "You can't tell me what to do. You're at the bottom of the bottom." He got no ambition … I wouldn't look up to him. Because if he had to give a toss, he wouldn't have done what he done, and left my mum in the way she was … So, he can't … even voice his opinion to me. Because he knows I won't listen. (Lewis)

Lewis disapproved of his father leaving the family – in particular leaving his mother – in a vulnerable state. He felt appalled and angered by his lack of care and did not accept his opinions or recommendations as a parental authority figure. Frank expressed a similar disappointment about his father who was largely absent from his firstborn children's lives:

He's married now with three, four other kids … but he's not reaching out to me most of my life. I've not seen him in 20 years. He's not there for me. I was *his* little boy as well years ago! Don't need him anyway … Tried to contact him but … it's like he don't wanna know … never asked about me anyway.

Mhm … That must be hard.

No, it's not … Don't think about it. (Frank)

The insight that his side of the family did not matter to his father caused a feeling of unfairness and missing out in Frank as reflected in his exclamation "I was *his* little boy as well years ago!" Immediately after expressing his unmet need for fatherly attention, Frank minimised this wish by denying his need for connection ("Don't need him anyway."). This U-turn on vulnerability was a mechanism encountered in several accounts of prisoners' unrequited attempts for connection and will be discussed in more detail at a later point. It is now time to move on from the effects of the absence of love in the individual's past microsystem (i.e. childhood family home) to the effects that later losses of other microsystemic connections – such as breakups with romantic partners – could have on their mental and physical health.

5.3.4 The absence of love in romantic relationships

I took a load of pills and that. But that didn't work. So, I was thinking this would be an easy way. Now my cousin died in 1990 by injecting heroin. Yeah, and a load of alcohol, it killed him. He fell asleep, choked on his vomit and died. So, I thought … I can do that. That's what I was gonna do … I'd gone through a divorce, then [name of girlfriend] died, my girlfriend. I just had enough … I thought well, two people I loved left, I just had enough. (Bruce)

As established in Chapter 3's concept analysis, the loss of love could induce psychological pain and grief and a sense of despair so strong that it could lead to suicide attempts. The trauma of the loss of love-relationships experienced as the sudden cessation of human interaction (Lindemann 1944) represents a severe stressor for the human organism. The increased and prolonged release of stress hormones like cortisol as a reaction to a traumatic loss can lead to changes in brain structures and ultimately to a loss of already established connectivity. Affected individuals can experience psychological and physiological disturbances so severe that they may disrupt their daily lives, described by Will and Peter as a "breakdown":

> I had a proper breakdown ... that lasted for about two, three years, and then the result of the breakdown: you just switch off.
>
> *Mm. So, what was that breakdown related to?*
>
> Me wife, me child and me family really. (Will)
>
> [W]hen my wife went off with her boss from work, I had a total mental breakdown. (Peter)

Other prisoners described an inability to bear the trauma of a breakup and an overwhelming need to ease the pain. Frank, for example, resorted to self-medication with class-A drugs as a coping mechanism to soften the "turmoil and pain" he found himself in after breaking up with his first girlfriend:

> I lost the best thing that ever happened to me... I broke her heart... But when I had to leave ... because I was addicted to heroin and crack at that time ... I was in a lot of turmoil and pain ... I loved her that much. And heroin was the substitute that eased off the pain. (Frank)

Given the systemic concordance "between the brain regions and neurochemicals involved in both addiction and social attachment" (Burkett and Young 2012: 2), substituting one for the other – as practiced by Frank – may deliver a tentative explanation of the interplay between relational trauma and drug addiction. To do so in enough detail to explain the complete dynamic would exceed the scope of this chapter. It is important, however, to consider the use of narcotics as one potential mechanism to cope with the pain of love lost. Losing the vital bonds that provide limbic regulation can drive human beings to seek these means elsewhere. Phrased in the figurative language of Lewis et al. (2000: 212), it can lead "hungering brains to seek satisfaction from a variety of ineffectual substitutes – alcohol, heroin, cocaine" and other mood-altering agents that would obliterate their anguish for a short time, only to create an even greater desire for it afterwards. Apart from a de facto loss of close relationships, it was also possible that failed attempts to achieve reciprocity in relationships could have negative effects.

5.3.5 Unrequited and disappointed love

> Sometimes it winds me up ... Cause you ... get these feelings and you think I can't do nothing about it ... it's out of your hands, innit? ... It's hard to explain. You gotta trust the other people as well. You can have feelings and care for someone, but they might be ... ignorant and rude ... It's rejection innit? I don't want to be rejected ... It's quite embarrassing. (Bo)

Bo expressed a more passive, receptive and slightly more risky side of love, namely situations in which it was not clear whether love would be reciprocated or not. Interviewees such as Bo felt that it could put them at the mercy of others. Showing that you loved and cared for someone and exposing your feelings could make you vulnerable to the pain of rejection or being ignored. Paul recounted a similar situation of disappointment after expressing care and concern for a fellow prisoner that was not reciprocated:

> *You helped someone who wanted to commit suicide. How was that for you? Why did you help him?*

> Cause he had a baby. He had a kid, he had a girlfriend. He was only serving a small sentence. You know, he was missing his girlfriend, he was missing his new baby. He was ... depressed. And he just ... wanted it to end ... And I was there for him, and he got out ... He never even wrote a letter ... that hurt. Cause you think, I don't bother anymore, I'm helping nobody. You know, no one helps me. No one does anything for me. (Paul)

Bo's and Paul's accounts of unrequited feelings of care or love implied an element of reciprocity that, if not fulfilled could leave the giver with negative feelings of disappointment, hurt, disquiet ("Sometimes it winds me up." (Bo)) and embarrassment. It represents an incomplete exchange of earlier encountered positivity resonance, since one side fails to affirm and mirror back the positive emotion conveyed to him or her. Experiencing this feeling of incompleteness could lead the one on the receiving end to modify his perceptions of love as well as his willingness to express love in the future.

Paul's strong reaction to the lack of reciprocity he experienced when displaying care was noteworthy since he had also strongly expressed the view that true love was given freely without expecting anything in return (as provided by his mother). At the same time, he expressed his disappointment about his unrequited offerings of care. This implied the application of two differing ideals by Paul. One being that the love of a mother was perceived as unconditional and not associated with reciprocity. Love outside this bond, however, required reciprocity or else it was seen as an incomplete, pain-inducing process. As discussed previously, the ideology of the "good mother" contained the notion of love as utterly selfless giving and self-sacrifice. Otherwise, interpersonal interactions were expected to be mutually gratifying

(DeKlyen et al. 1998) or else were seen to be unsatisfactory. The discrepancy between the idealised love of the "good mother" and the "imperfect love" of and suspicion towards others emerged as a prominent theme during Paul's interview, exemplified by the following excerpt:

> I don't even know what that is. Love's manipulation. That's what love is. Love's a way to manipulate the person you're with … Like when you're with a girlfriend … I think that sometimes when you're upset and they go awww, I think it's all fake …

How can you tell that? How do you know?

> Oh I don't know … I just, I just …

You assume that?

> Yeah. Everywhere … I've been … places where it's got care in the name, yeah, there has been none. You know, there's been no care shown, there's been no love, there's been no, there's been *nothing*. (Paul)

The origins of his "negative relationship model" (DeKlyen et al. 1998) could be potentially traced back to Paul's negative experiences in the childcare system and had led to an internalisation of "hostile attributions about other people and their motives" (DeKlyen et al. 1998: 7). During his childhood, Paul had gathered and established essential emotional knowledge, extracting patterns and blueprints from his early experiences of relationships for later life (Lewis et al. 2000). Owed to the fact that an infant's brain is significantly more prone to early conditioning, the impressions "of what love *feels* [emphasis in the original] like" are indeed stored and fixed, "before any glimmerings of event memory appear" (Lewis et al. 2000: 160). Paul had learned to mistrust the declaration of love or care whilst he was growing up in care homes as a child and it still prevailed.

5.4 The absence of love in prisoners' exosystem

In Paul's and other interviews, it transpired that physical and mental abuse in care institutions had occurred on a regular basis throughout childhood. Will, for example, claimed to have filed for compensation in 16 cases of abuse in a children's care home. In Paul's case, it led him to develop a worldview dominated by suspicion and mistrust. This view became further entrenched through continuing experiences of violence and abuse in young offender institutions and ultimately in prisons. He was one of several prisoners who had (temporarily) not been raised at home. Some had been sent to children's homes, others had been raised by foster parents. Many of them described themselves as having "trust issues." They preferred to distance themselves from people around them due to adverse experiences in a care system that offered not care but maltreatment instead, as exemplified by Paul:

I don't eat vegetables. I've never eaten vegetables … cause I was forced to in one of these so called care places. And … the staff used to like really enjoy, really enjoy that time … You'd be throwing sprouts up, yeah, and then they made me eat it, eat it, getting slapped, eat it! *Eat it!* You know, and you'd have to eat spewed up sprouts. There's no duty of care, that's a load of bollocks. Health care, it's a load of bollocks, it's all bollocks. (Paul)

Paul's vehement discredit of an abusive care system chimed with similarly negative findings (Jackson and Martin 1998; Utting 1997; Berridge and Brodie 1998) corroborating that "despite a variety of initiatives … the outcomes for the majority of young people who spend any length of time in care continue to be poor" (Jackson and Martin 1998: 569). After having originally been established to deliver the Children Act of 1989 requiring "local authorities in England and Wales to look after children whose parents are unable to do so and to promote their welfare" (Jackson and Martin 1998: 570), the residential care system in England and Wales has seen a string of revelations of abuse in the past (Utting 1997; Berridge and Brodie 1998).

Further studies report an "over-representation of ex-care people among the homeless and in custodial institutions and treatment centres" (Jackson and Martin 1998: 570). Caution has to be applied however, when examining the relationship between care placement and offending pathways. It is made more complex by additional risk factors connected to childhood experiences of economic deprivation and "dysfunctional family lives including abuse and neglect" (Schofield et al. 2015: 125). Although these factors have to be taken into consideration – especially in light of previously discussed effects of abuse and toxic stress on mental and behavioural development of the child – it could be argued that the care system should not exacerbate these adverse effects but strive to achieve better outcomes for this group of children (Jackson and Martin 1998). Another institution in which these early adverse experiences could exacerbate difficulties in further development was represented by the educational system.

Due to potentially "altered brain architecture in response to toxic stress in early childhood … subsequent problems in the development of linguistic, cognitive, and social-emotional skills" (Shonkoff and Garner 2012: 236) could ensue which could make it difficult for children like Theo to keep up with educational goals:

I used to tell a lot of lies when I was young … at school. Unfortunately, society, when you're misbehaving at school and stuff and you're being disruptive, there is a reason why! No one really asked me about that. They just thought, well he's naughty, go and stick him in a room. Stick him out the way so he's not destructive, rather than looking into it … I used to struggle at school … I enjoyed learning, but when it was noisy, like that, I couldn't concentrate. So, then I play up … to get to work on my own then. (Theo)

Theo described an educational system he felt was not equipped to deal with children like him who entered it with a background of behavioural and cognitive difficulties due to early adverse experiences (Shonkoff and Garner 2012). At the same time, Theo picked up on a factor that would make learning easier for him: a quiet environment where he could focus on his schoolwork on his own. He felt that the only way he was able to work in a school environment was to forcefully extricate himself from the classroom, an environment he felt was too distracting for him. Recognising his own potential to achieve better educational outcomes under certain conditions, Theo alluded to a similar line of thought established by studies of resilience within the social-ecology of human development (Ungar et al. 2013). Findings within this field affirm that creating stable environments that offer opportunities for physical safety and psychological growth can build resilience on a neurological (Curtis and Nelson 2003) as well as a psychological level. This may consequently help to achieve better educational outcomes (Bonanno et al. 2011; Wekerle et al. 2012).

5.5 Resilience factors in social-ecological systems

The concept of resilience, as developed by Bronfenbrenner (1979), has to be understood here as (re)gaining social-ecological equilibrium. In the case of children who have experienced trauma, the study of resilience finds that the balancing of individual and environmental risk factors and protective factors increases their potential to do well later in life (Jackson and Martin 1998). Protective factors in this regard can be seen as "those dispositional attributes, environmental conditions, biological dispositions, and positive events that can act to contain the expression of deviancy or pathology" (Garmezy et al. 1984: 109). Further research into the development of resilience and the well-being of foster children and children raised by their grandparents (Downie et al. 2010; Messing 2006; Whiting and Lee 2003) establishes that the emerging sub-categories of protective factors corresponded to critical sub-categories of Maslow's hierarchy of needs. These are the "'basic physical needs', 'safety and security', 'love, care and belonging'" (Downie et al. 2010: 20). Love, in fact, matters. The concluding section of this chapter will therefore briefly revisit hitherto established qualities of love as perceived by prisoners and consider its absence and presence in relation to their incarceration experience as well as in relation to concepts of resilience and human development.

5.6 Conclusion

Although it is important to remember that prisoners' accounts of themselves were individually unique, upon closer examination, some common storylines and shared characteristics arose from their interviews. Some of these themes – as related by Ryan, Lewis, Frank, Paul, Will, Bruce and Adam – revolved around experiences of childhood abuse, witnessing domestic violence as a child, being taken into care as a child, the use of class-A drugs, suicide attempts and suffering from mental health problems such as anxiety or depression. As such they mirrored statistics published by the Prison Reform Trust (2019) on shared characteristics of the male prison population in England, summarised in the following table:

Table 5.1: Social characteristics of male adult prisoners in England. Bromley Briefings, Prison Factfile (Prison Reform Trust 2019: 20)[5]

Characteristics MALE prison population	General population
Taken into care as a child 24%	2%
Experienced abuse as a child 27%	20%
Observed violence in the home as a child 40%	14%
Regularly truant from school 59%	5.2%
Expelled or permanently excluded from school 43%	>1%
Identified as suffering from both anxiety + depression 23%	15%
Have attempted suicide 21%	6%
Have ever used Class A drugs 64%	13%

Almost every second interviewee described one or more personal experience fitting the above criteria. It illustrated the fact that members of the male prison population in England and Wales are disproportionately more likely to have

---

[5] Prison population data taken from Results from the Ministry of Justice Surveying Prisoner Crime Reduction (SPCR) survey published in:

Ministry of Justice (2012). *Prisoners' childhood and family backgrounds*. London: Ministry of Justice.

Ministry of Justice (2012). *The pre-custody employment, training and education status of newly sentenced prisoners*. London: Ministry of Justice.

Ministry of Justice (2012). *Estimating the prevalence of disability amongst prisoners*. London: Ministry of Justice.

Ministry of Justice (2010). Compendium of reoffending statistics, London: Ministry of Justice General population data taken from:

Ministry of Justice (2012). *Prisoners' childhood and family backgrounds*. London: Ministry of Justice.

Harker, L., Jütte, S., Murphy, T., Bentley, H., Miller, P., Fitch, K. (2013). *How safe are our children?* London: NSPCC

Department for Education (2013). *Pupil absence in schools in England, including pupil characteristics*. London: DfE.

Welsh Government (2013). *Absenteeism by pupil characteristics 2011/12*. Cardiff: Welsh Government.

Wiles, N. J., Zammit, S., Bebbington, P., Singleton, N., Meltzer, H., Lewis, G. (2006). Self-reported psychotic symptoms in the general population. *The British Journal of Psychiatry* (188) pp. 519-526.

Light, M., Grant, E., Hopkins, K. (2013). *Gender differences in substance misuse and mental health amongst prisoners*. London: Ministry of Justice.

experienced these than members of the general population. Being aware of these specific characteristics of the sample became especially important in the data analysis and theory inference process, as carried out in this chapter and the following.

Here, I set out to illustrate and understand the dual nature of love by painting a multidisciplinary picture of prisoners' individual perceptions of love as well as of the effects of its presence and absence throughout their lives. Prisoners' accounts implied that the presence of love could provide feelings of security, meaning, support and motivation. Its absence could induce hurt, pain, trauma and the compulsion to "switch it off" by resorting to drugs for emotional numbing, for example. Interviewees expressed individually diverse perceptions of love which turned out to be inextricably linked to past experiences with early caregivers and in other close relationships. Some of their accounts chimed in with more generalised social perceptions connected to idealised manifestations of love (e.g. the ideology of the virtuous love of "the good mother"). It pointed towards interrelations and a certain semi-permeability of different social-ecological spheres. Although a highly individualistic topic, love follows certain universal principles in human development and is highly dependent on social conventions and ideologies. This line of enquiry will be continued. In the following, I will examine the quality, meaning and trajectories of love represented in prisoners' connections to the outside world as well as the role the institution played in facilitating or limiting those.

6. The presence and absence of love in outside connections and its role in the pains of imprisonment

Ideas and feelings related to love were readily retrievable for most interviewees when asked, if there were people in their lives whom they loved. As illustrated in the previous chapter, prisoners' perceptions of love were predominantly related to people they felt attached to in their microsystem (Bronfenbrenner 1974). They described love, for example, as affection for and attachment to family members and sometimes family pets, romantic bonds with partners as well as a more general love for mankind and toward themselves. Having carved out some of the main attributes of love as a phenomenon manifesting in connection with others, it will be this chapter's task to further explore love as manifesting through relationships in prisoners' current circumstances. It will do so by inquiring which types of outside connections were upheld in interviewees' current lives and which not, for which reasons and by which means.

6.1 Types and management of outside connections

Family connections represented the most frequently mentioned outside relations. Mothers featured more prominently than fathers in prisoners' current lives. Eight prisoners named their mother as an outside connection, five interviewees were still in touch with their fathers. However, the same number of respondents had deliberately cut contact with their fathers whilst incarcerated, while no prisoner mentioned cutting contact with his mother. Of those 12 prisoners known to have children, seven mentioned they were still in touch with them. Two IPP-prisoners as well as one life-sentenced prisoner had cut contact with their children whilst incarcerated. A majority of the sample (n = 12) stated they were in touch with at least one other family member, apart from parents, siblings, partners or children such as a brother-in-law (Tony) or uncle (Frank).

Reasons for preserving connections to the family microsystem were predominantly connected to receiving and giving love as a motivational factor. George and Tony, for example, both expressed the importance of the love conveyed in family relationships for their own mental and emotional support and as a reference point in the future:

> We have a lot of family visits ... Without the support of people like [ex-partner] and my family I don't think I'd be here now ... It would be easy

for me to give up … but for them I've got to. For them and for me … I've got to make sure that when I do get out, I can lead a healthy life and I can still have my time with them. (George)

They just keep me focused, keep me calm, especially now because I'm at the end of my sentence. (Tony)

Phil appreciated the fact that phoning home on a daily basis had helped him not to become institutionalised over the last 15 years serving his life-sentence in closed conditions:

I haven't become institutionalised. My life is half outside … my head's outside. I'm always thinking "Right, I've got to do this. I've got to make that phone call tonight. You've got to sort that insurance out" … and it's just things like that. I'm always sorting things out. (Phil)

The fact that Phil could still participate in familial decision-making (by sorting out insurance, for example) represented a "social space" (Datchi 2017) to perform an important family-based role. Being able to participate in family life and to support loved ones in the best way possible had provided Phil with a purpose and a focus that prevented him from taking on a prisoner identity. He regarded this as beneficial because it kept him in touch with a "normal" outside reality.

As much as close and stable family ties were desirable and could be beneficial, not all prisoners had those to fall back on. Lewis or Ryan, for example, had cut most ties to their families because they perceived them as negative influences. They reported falling back on another type of outside relationships: friendships. They represented significant connections beyond bonds of kin and family (Meek 2008) and could be seen as part of an alternative "web of connection" (Scott and Codd 2010: 146) that consisted of relationships of equal or even more importance to familial ties. They were often seen as supportive and beneficial especially when formed within a new referential context of personal development and recovery as illustrated by Ryan:

I've also got a good friend who's a psychologist. But she's my friend … I've got a photograph in my cell … She's been a good friend over the years. I've also got friends in … Narcotics Anonymous. Got friends there, real friends.

How would you describe someone who is a real friend? What is a real friend?
She's supported me for years. You know, unconditionally … she's a psychologist … She's visited me in prison … I've seen her on the out.

She picks me up a lot of times, when I get out of prison … she's supported me a lot … A real friend. (Ryan)

Real friends[1] were seen as unwavering, loyal and providing not only unconditional mental but also practical support. Real friends were those who were attuned to the needs and aware of the struggles of those in prison. Real friends gave generously, not only of their time but also of material goods without having to be prompted to do so. In that sense, they embodied the quality of *philia*, the love of friendship, to wish and do good for the friend's sake (Annas 1988). They were the ones "who write letters and send me money when you don't even ask for it" (Lewis). As much as the support of *philia* was welcomed by Lewis, as much was it resisted by George:

> I've got old friends and people send me money. Which I hate. I hate having to rely on other people. I've always provided for myself ... Now, for people to send me stuff in, and to send me clothes in ... it's not right to me but unfortunately, I'm in that situation where I've got to take it. (George)

The fact that he was dependent on outside economic support did not sit well with George who would have liked to be more self-sufficient. In their current circumstances, prisoners had to rely on outside relationships as important means for the provision of goods such as money or clothes – albeit sometimes grudgingly as illustrated by George. He was aware that emotional and economic labour had been required on the part of those working to maintain ties with him during nine years of his life sentence. In his view, these virtuous deeds did not only reveal something about the character qualities of his supporters but also about himself as an individual. He took their "faith" and loyal support as a positive appraisal reflecting his own integrity:

> Every one of them has been fully supportive and helpful, and never, ever once doubted me. They ... make the effort to come and see me all the time ... it says a lot. It's loyalty ... I feel pride that they have that faith in me, and it makes you feel good. It makes you feel really appreciated, when you've got all these people who have stood by you, cause ... it could be easy for them to walk away. (George)

The longevity and quality of outside connections were often seen by those serving long sentences as a testimony to their own worth and value. His reasoning implied that positive affirmation conveyed through steadfast relationships could likewise influence an individual's self-image positively. In a similar vein, Giordano et al. (2007) stressed the potential of love relationships in particular to foster "concrete, positive reflected appraisals that allow the individual to see past the contours of the current self" (Giordano et al. 2007: 1615). According to their findings, these appraisals engage "self-feelings (emotions) as well as self-evaluations (cognitions)" (Giordano et al. 2007: 1615). Especially microsystemic relationships

---

[1] How these differ from "fake" friends will become clearer in Section 7.4.

fuelled by love, hold great transformational potential. Feeling that someone else was prepared to put effort into seeing him, that someone values spending time with him had a positive influence on George's self-esteem.

He was aware that his imprisonment represented a substantial hurdle to be overcome not only by him but by those still intent on relating to him. Keeping up outside connections required effort and was formalised to a certain extent. Conveying love in those relationships required even more effort. A restrictive and closed prison world immensely curtailed the amount and quality of connections. Expressions of love that were available and acceptable within prison parameters were largely dependent on institutional concessions.

6.2 Maintaining love through letters and phone calls

Being asked how they kept up connections to the outside revealed that means to do so were limited to writing and receiving letters, making phone calls from wing-based prison phones and receiving visits. Out of a sample of 16 prisoners, a majority of 13 received visits, the same amount also used letters as means of communication, and everyone in the sample (except for Arthur and Paul) resorted to prison phone calls to keep up outside connections. Their use and availability, however, were heavily policed and regulated.

At the time of fieldwork, the prison was deploying measures to comply with security standards such as opening selected private letters and monitoring correspondence as detailed in Prison Service Instruction (PSI) 04/2016[2]. This had become increasingly relevant, since sheets of Spice-coated paper started coming in via mail which the prison had to curb urgently. It can be argued, however, that love letters can still be used by prisoners and their loved ones, not only as means of communication but also as means of resistance to institutional rules (Mehta 2014). Although prisoners did not mention love letters explicitly during interviews, some kept them on display in their cells.[3]

Similar to letters, phone calls – one of the main means of communication with the outside – were also heavily curtailed. This was due to the fact that calls could only be made from wing-based public phones through an allocated pin system. The amount and length of calls solely depended on prisoners' private

---

[2] "Prison Service Instructions (PSIs) contain a number of rules, regulations and guidelines by which prisons are run. PSIs have as definite expiry date. They also introduce amendments to Prison Service Orders (PSOs). These are long term mandatory instructions which were issued until 31 July 2009. They have no expiry date and remain in force until cancelled or replaced." (Prison Reform Trust 2020 online)

[3] Unfortunately, there was no opportunity to further analyse their contents due to institutional access- and time-limitations.

funds since they could not receive external calls. Phone availability was also curtailed by the fact that the number of phones was low relative to the number of prisoners (four phones per wing housing approximately 100 prisoners). Additionally, these were only activated during dedicated time periods when prisoners were unlocked. Since this specific prison limited time out of cells severely, most prisoners (except for those working on the wings during the day) were only able to use prison phones during a daily two-hour-window. This specific time schedule often clashed with that of prisoners' contacts, such as with Theo's son who was usually still at an after-school-club when Theo was able to make phone calls. Competition and long queues for wing-based phones were often a source for intra-prisoner aggression and distress.

At the time of fieldwork costs for phone calls ranged from approximately 6p per minute for calls to a landline off-peak, to approximately 13p per minute for calls to a mobile phone. These prices stood in stark contrast to funds that were effectively available to prisoners generated through wages and private funds. It is furthermore important to consider that landlines require those outside to pay for a line rental which has become increasingly rare in the digital age. Some prisoners would get themselves into debt to pay for phone calls, if they were not able to pay for them out of their own funds. If prisoners had no funds available, families and friends would help out by sending money for phone calls and other amenities. Scott and Codd (2010) addressed this (vastly underreported) prison-specific problem, stating that "one of the most shocking aspects of the costs for families has arisen from the costs of phone calls … which exceed those available to non-prisoners" (Scott and Codd 2010: 179) by far. Campaigns to challenge these conditions were started in the past, for example, by the Prison Reform Trust (Scott and Codd 2010). However, this topic still represents a controversial issue. Prison phone calls are the only legal source of phone communication in English and Welsh prisons because the possession and use of mobile phones is punished as a criminal offence.

6.3 Prison visits — Navigating a rift between incompatible life-worlds

The provision of visits as means of connection was another source for controversy in this particular prison. These were normally scheduled for two hours, but due to high demand, prisoners and their visitors were divided into groups and allocated different starting times. This could lead to shorter than expected visits, leaving prisoners and visitors frustrated about this inconsistency:

> Some days you'll only get thirty minutes … It's not good is it? By the time you've got a coffee and sat down and had a chocolate bar and your coffee, it's time for them to go. (Oliver)

It is important to stress that above-described visit arrangements represented a specific prison at a specific point in time, strained by economic cuts, low staffing and high prisoner population levels. Under normal conditions, sentenced prisoners in England and Wales are entitled to a minimum of two one-hour visits in every four-week period with additional visits dependent on the specific prison regimes and on the prisoner's Incentives and Earned Privileges (IEP) level. Prisoners on enhanced level are entitled to more visits than prisoners on standard and basic levels (Fair and Jacobson 2016). The prison also provided family visits which were perceived by many prisoners as a great opportunity to "walk about ... play with the kids" (Oliver) and to feel more relaxed and more able to connect with children and partners. These were offered on a monthly basis to prisoners on an enhanced IEP level and aimed at strengthening and maintaining family ties. They had been implemented after a Children and Families Pathway was included in NOMS' National Reducing Re-offending Action Plan in 2005, as a framework for maintaining family relationships (Clinks Event Report 2016).

Although the prison provided practical means for connection and communication, it can be argued that these were not only hugely anachronistic (compared to the number of people in contemporary society still effectively sending handwritten letters or making landline phone calls). They also did not succeed to create "normal" experiences of real encounter. Due to heavily policed visits, it was often difficult for prisoners and their outside contacts to establish a connection, to "break through" to each other. Challenges to connect on a deeper and authentic level were mainly related to a palpable incongruity between two life-worlds. Disruptions and difficulties of connection became strikingly apparent during visits. Often a rift between inside and outside reality and identity would manifest itself in an inability to emotionally "bridge the gap," an inability to "melt the ice" as recounted by Adam:

> We got an invisible wall between us, I couldn't break through it. To survive I've had to isolate ... Putting up shields, hiding behind shields. I couldn't break through to emotionally connect with my sister and mother. That self-preservation ... you wrap yourself in this ice ball ... it's my protection. (Adam)

Not being able to break through, to effectively connect to each other was experienced by Adam as a painful and unintentional side effect of adaptation to prison life. His self-preservation strategy of putting up a psychological shield[4] in order to survive four decades of imprisonment had become a

---

[4] For insights into individual prisoners' coping mechanisms, please refer back to their Pen Pictures in Chapter 4.

hindrance for connection. Especially visits seemed to act as a magnifying glass of the pains connected to not being able to be one's authentic self. This might have been partly due to the fact that they were conducted in a highly regulated and prescribed manner. Any physical contact was prohibited (at least in closed prisons) apart from a hug and a kiss at the beginning and the end of a visit. Furthermore, prisoners and visitors usually have to sit on bolted-down seats and at tables designed to keep visitors and prisoners at a physical distance from each other. Prison Service Instructions (PSIs) also instructed prison officers to monitor visitors and prisoners as to whether they were observing the restrictions in place in the specific prison.[5]

Again, this was mainly due to concerns around security and exchange of contraband during visits. The need to uphold and deliver security in prison establishments consequently overrode the need for connection. Creating or maintaining love in relationships by means of intimate communication and privacy was therefore severely hindered. Loving encounters require privacy, time and safety to share intimate truths as prerequisite for love, as well as physical contact (such as hugs, kisses or eye-contact supporting limbic resonance). Creating those moments of love is severely curtailed through most means currently provided by the English and Welsh prison system because they are heavily regulated due to security concerns. Although time was provided by the prison system, "quality time" (Cantillon and Lynch 2017), i.e. sufficient time and privacy to build mutual trust, connection and limbic or positivity resonance – in other words love – was not. In turn, the inability to speak and share their own truth was experienced as an insincere "act," a

> [...] play where I'm acting and they're acting. Cause everyone wants to put on a brave face. You don't want to tell your family what's happening in here, cause they don't need to know. If there's shit and that going on, you don't want them to know, so you put on a brave face, and then they put on a brave face ... it's like a bit of an act where no one really wants to say how it is.

And is that difficult for you?

> Yeah. Because I like to ... speak to them. I like to interact with them ... there's been times when they stop coming up because they don't want to leave when they have to leave. My son said, "Dad I'm seeing you, but I'm not seeing you." (George)

As much as they "couldn't do without visits" (George), for some prisoners, the continuing pain of not being able to connect authentically as well as "seeing them

---

[5] Detailed instructions for delivering visits can be found in PSIs 15/2011 and 16/2011 (see bibliography).

walk away after a visit" (George) could become a strain on their mental well-being. This could result in the decision to stop trying to bridge the gap between two incongruent life-worlds altogether and to cut ties with the outside world.

6.4 Cutting outside connections for self-preservation

Some prisoners felt they would not benefit from more contact, but that they would rather become more frustrated being "constantly aware of the relationships … denied to them" (Wolff and Draine 2004):

> I get very apprehensive me, even though it's family and I'm used to seeing them. Cause I think … the less I see of them the easier it is … If you see them regularly you start missing them more … I'd rather not keep going up telephoning and not have too many visits … I don't want to know what's going on outside to be honest with you. It's all about being in here, this is where I live, innit? (Tom)

As related by Tom, the clash between two distinct realities could prove inconceivable and detrimental to prisoners' ability to adapt to, accept and navigate an inside world that required them to be different. For long-term prisoners like Tom, keeping a psychological and physical distance to his (past and future) life outside represented a crucial coping mechanism to keep unsettling thoughts and emotions at bay:

> I used to be like a touchy, feely person with my girlfriend and my kids … but in here I'm not one for hugging anymore … It's weird, it's just jail for you. It just makes you feel different.
>
> *Why is that?*
>
> Don't know. Something you can't really explain. You don't wanna get too close cause you know it's still a long way to go before you're actually getting out of jail, and … doing it for real like. That's how I look at it … trying not to get too close you know. That way you don't worry as much when you're in jail.
>
> *But you do miss the closeness?*
>
> Oh of course! Yeah. (Tom)

It was especially challenging to keep up those outside relationships requiring a physical demonstration of love (e.g. hugging, kissing) since these were severely curtailed and partly sanctioned in the prison environment. Correspondingly, interviews reflected a relatively clear absence of intimate or romantic partners (only three out of 16 respondents claimed to currently have a partner). Four prisoners explicitly mentioned separating from their partners due to their sentence. This could have partly been due to the considerable strain on partners of long-term prisoners. Holding out faithfully for an incarcerated partner's uncertain release could seem insurmountable. To decrease or eliminate fears of an imminent breakup, some prisoners, therefore, chose to withdraw from romantic relationships. Keeping up an intimate relationship could make it difficult to navigate the daily emotional tide of an already demanding prison environment:

> [H]andling a relationship in jail ... it's tough ... I've had times when it's been really, really hard. We've had our ups and downs ... I mean my Offender Manager, she says "You're still with your wife?!" and ... she's shocked ... in some ways, that made my jail a lot harder. If I'd just been single and I didn't have kids, it would have been a breeze.

> *You think you would not have missed anything?*

> No ... I think it would have been a lot easier. I used to see people who had no family, had no girlfriend, no wife, no kids. They didn't have to worry about a thing ... They just sit there and play computers and just watch some TV ... To keep a relationship together and keep everything running ... it's difficult. (Phil)

Prisoners such as Phil who managed to keep a long-term committed partnership going from inside the prison were perceived by people familiar with the effects of long-term imprisonment (in this case his Offender Manager) as a rarity. The more common expectation of long-term prisoners was one of losing relationships. Tony and Oliver, for example, had made the decision to abstain from intimate relationships for self-preservation:

> After the trial ... we finished ... it's not fair for her. It's not fair for me because you worry, and one thing you need is to keep your mind clear and without stress if you can. (Tony)

> I've had a couple of letters off a couple of ... odd girlfriends what I've had ... But I don't contact them back ... I don't really want a girlfriend ... I could end up speaking to a girl whilst I'm in prison and we could end up getting together and then she could end up messing around ... and then ... it's all in the mind, isn't it? And then when you get out and you find out something's happened ... that could turn your life around. And that could lead to me coming back to prison. I don't really wanna do that. (Oliver)

If strong negative emotions like jealousy or mistrust became too overwhelming, they could become unmanageable. Without the opportunity of privacy and sorting difficulties out as a couple, prisoners were afraid to lose control over their emotions which could reflect negatively on them.

Other prisoners chose to keep a distance from certain people in their lives for similar reasons. Their decisions, however, were not related to negative emotions experienced within the framework of romantic relationships. They were less emotionally driven but based predominantly on rational reasoning. Interviewees such as Paul and Tom – aiming to leave criminal lifestyles and drug use behind – thought that a critical re-evaluation of outside relationships was crucial, if they wanted to save their future:

> They're always trying to find something … to justify keeping me in jail. Oh, we're a bit concerned you got no family support, you've got no friends. Last time I was out, the only people I knew were like people who were taking drugs like me. And all the people who I bought the drugs off. People who I sold stuff that I stole to. So, they're the only people that I know. And I don't know them people anymore. (Paul)

> I don't speak to any of me old associates anymore or me old mates. I'm not interested anymore. Cause I look forward to getting out, I won't be going … in that old route again, you know what I mean. So, I kept more of a distance. (Tom)

The same could be true for family ties. When these were felt to be "dysfunctional, abusive, criminal and crime-supportive" (Scott and Codd 2010: 152) instead of encouraging desistance from crime, some prisoners decided to reduce or cut ties with family members. Lewis, for example, preferred to distance himself from someone who could only be a negative influence:

> They never worked a day in their life … all they were doing was drug dealing. Dad done drugs. Mum done drugs. So, it's just been crime.

> *Do you have any contact with [your father]?*

> Ah, I do, but he's bad with drugs, so I don't speak to him much. (Lewis)

His prison sentence had given Lewis time and space to reflect on negative past ties. He had decided to realign himself with people outside of his family network, people who "had something going for them" people he could "look up to" (Lewis). Cutting outside ties was beneficial for prisoners such as Lewis, Paul or Tom. For others, it represented a choice they experienced as painful, yet unavoidable, if they wanted to consider the well-being of their loved ones as well as their own.

6.5 Cutting outside connections as an act of love

Breaking up with romantic partners, for example, would be offered by long-term prisoners of the sample as a gesture of love, enabling the other to begin a new life, where theirs had ended. This was the case when Adam learned he would have to serve a life sentence:

> My wife ... at the beginning she had a two-year old ... a one-year old, and she was four months pregnant [inhales] and I begged her to take another man. It hurt me ... cause I loved her and I loved my kids. (Adam)

Although offered as a selfless act of love, it could be tentatively argued that Adam likewise profited from his decision. "Begging her to take another man" could have also been an attempt to lessen his own guilt of letting her and his children down, thus shifting responsibility to someone else to step in on his behalf. It represents an alternative interpretation of the "obvious." To Adam, however, his act was motivated by selflessness since he caused himself pain by pushing those he loved away. In a similar vein, other prisoners decided to cut ties to the outside as an emergency break to stop their family's mental anguish caused by the uncertainty of their sentence. In this case, it was Theo, an IPP-prisoner on recall, realising it was not the most constructive choice he could have made, but somehow unavoidable:

> [E]very time I'm ringing up it's about what's happened with you, when are you getting out? ... It's just frustrating. So, I ... thought, it's better for me to just totally ignore her and ... just blank them out, not contact them, not ring em ... My partner, my stepchildren, my son, my family, just everyone ... it's not good. (Theo)

Paradoxically, the very same outside ties making life inside more survivable were simultaneously able to cause additional strain on prisoners' mental health. By withdrawing as an attempt to keep his own feelings of guilt and frustration at bay and as a means of protecting his family, Theo had also lost an important source of mental and emotional support that could further his rehabilitation and sentence progression:

> I've been in this jail now for 2.5 years, I've not have no visits off [son's name]. All my sentence I had visits ... we kept ... protective factors there ... thought it was important. But because ... we now know he's got his autism ... we don't want to. (Theo)

Using the technical term "protective factors" – commonly deployed in the fields of resilience research, offender management and probation work – Theo referred to maintaining a relationship with his son as furthering his own resilience. In order to protect the psychological integrity of his son however – who had been diagnosed with autism – Theo resorted to a selfless act of love, putting another person's needs before his own. Protecting their loved ones from the negative effects and stressors of prison life was a recurring theme in several interviews. Being aware that an "unfiltered" account of their reality could shock or worry people on the outside, some prisoners would frequently censor themselves.

George, for example, would usually avoid talking to his family about anything prison-related, but he did not always succeed to cushion them from his own reality. As much as prisoners wished that outside relationships would not be influenced by the prison environment, they sometimes could not avoid a certain cross-contamination of the two life-worlds, as exemplified by George's account:

> Sometimes you'll be on the phone and there'll be shouting and screaming in the background or the bell will go off and they'll be like "What's that for?," and you'll just say, "Oh it's just a fire alarm" … I mean, they're not stupid. They know what goes on. But I just tell them it doesn't happen … I feel like I'm protecting them. (George)

Other prisoners described similar scenarios of not sharing the whole truth with their partners or family members, of holding back and self-censoring. Prison demanded emotional dishonesty and the bracketing of emotional sharing that would normally contribute to a strengthening of love relationships in outside society. Perpetuating love as intimate knowledge was often not possible in a prison environment because it could come at the price of emotional upheaval inside and outside of the walls. Especially for long-term prisoners it was a more common experience for relationships to diminish than to persist. A majority of the interview sample described this as painful and something they would have liked to avoid if they had the power to do so.

6.6 The loss of love as one of the pains of imprisonment

Asked about the presence of love in current outside connections, prisoners' narratives often alluded to the theme of the absence of love in the same breath. The fact they were separated physically – and often had been for a long time – from those they felt attached to psychologically was expressed as a painful experience. This was reflected by Tom, for example, when asked about the most difficult part of his sentence:

> I think the main one is just … missing people, family … kids growing up, grandkids and that … You miss hugging your kids … It's contact really … Just hugs and … little kisses … Smell as well, missing how your Missus smells or your kids. (Tom)

Tom referred to the very palpable effects of the loss of love, namely a lack of sensual recognition of and affective communication with those he had known intimately before his prison sentence. Additionally, not being able to participate in the passage of time with loved ones, not being able to engage in "ordinary" acts of familial love (such as pushing his grandkids in a pram) was experienced as painful estrangement by Tom and George:

> Simple things you miss to be honest with you ... take your dog for a walk or push my grandkids in a pram. (Tom)

> Being locked up isn't the worst thing. Being away from your family is the worst thing ... that time that you'll never get back. The end years for my dad ... there was times I should have been there for him ... Luckily enough, I was able to see him before he died, but he wasn't my dad then. He couldn't converse ... he wasn't the person I knew. And I just look at all that and think "these times, you'll never ever get them back again." (George)

Throughout his interview, George repeatedly expressed feelings of bitterness and resentment towards losing his own lifetime as well as family time because he saw himself as a victim of a miscarriage of justice. Appealing his case vehemently, George perceived his long sentence and the losses connected to it as deeply unjust. Other prisoners, such as Adam, occupied a different position towards the proportionality of the pains administered to him as punishment:

> All the pain, all ... the stuff I've been denied. I will never have love again. I will never have a family ... I will never experience that, and neither will the deceased man. So, what I denied him has been denied me, and ... I'm not happy with that, but it's just. I can see the justification of it. (Adam)

Bo and Arthur likewise expressed a somewhat pragmatic view towards the losses connected to serving a long sentence. They were aware that the nature of long-term imprisonment led to a weakening or vanishing of ties due to a lack of contact, to prison establishments being far away from their hometowns, and due to the nature of time having change in its tow. They did not expect people on the outside to wait and be loyal to them for decades:

> As time's gone by, people move on don't they? ... That's life ... People just move on, I don't expect them to sit around waiting. (Bo)

> [O]ver the years, things change. People ... drift. They get divorced and they lose girlfriends and they lose parents ... through death. So, it's nothing tied down ... You lose everything you value. (Arthur)

According to Crawley and Sparks (2006), losing familial attachments due to a natural ageing of family members was a common experience for older long-term prisoners such as Arthur. He had served almost three quarters of his lifespan in closed conditions and had consequently lost a majority of outside ties due to the death of relatives. Often this progression of time and the nature of change felt desperately relentless, and prisoners expressed their struggle to come to terms with their feelings and fears of (anticipated) loss:

I'm thinking: my mum's due to go, I'm the youngest in the family. How long my brother's got left on this earth I don't know ... and I'm thinking to myself, I'm not used to this ... I don't know ... how I'm gonna cope with this [choked up with tears]. (Frank)

There's always a good chance when you're doing a lot of years ... Somebody's gonna pass away. So, my mom and dad are getting a bit old you know what I mean ... You got a few years left ... anything can happen. And you're always waiting for that call or a letter or a knock on the door saying something's happened.

So that's one of your biggest concerns in here?

That's my main concern to be honest with you. (Tom)

Experiences of powerlessness in the face of disintegrating outside relationships represented a major source of emotional and mental anguish for prisoners. The inexorable loss of relationships, the loss of connection, the loss of love and "the inability to influence events beyond the prison" (Crewe 2009: 312) (re-)asserted itself as one of the most severe pains of imprisonment in long-term prisoners' accounts (see also Crewe et al. 2020).

6.7 Conclusion

Apart from examining the effects of the presence and absence of love in outside connections in long-term prisoners' current lives, this chapter also aimed to understand which types of relationships persevered or not, for which reasons and by which means. It has become apparent that the quality of outside connections – as well as most decisions related to upholding or cutting them off – was largely dictated by the prison environment and its structure. Even though the prison provided a practical framework for connection (e.g. through visits or phone calls), authentic encounters in love were often not possible. The prison's security concerns as well as a restricted regime due to low staffing levels presented the most important institutional, exosystemic factors impacting on the maintenance of love in prisoners' outside relationships.

It was a common experience for prisoners and their loved ones to feel as though they occupied different life-worlds, making it difficult, if not impossible to find common ground. This led to estrangement and an absence of love that was perceived as especially painful because it was not intended. Prisoners often felt pushed towards choices they would not have made outside of a prison context. The decision to maintain or end outside relationships was not necessarily based on an absence or presence of love in their dyadic microsystem. Sometimes love was still there, and a decision to end a relationship was made in the name of love and the wish to protect loved ones and oneself from pain. At other times it meant to sever dysfunctional ties for self-love and self-preservation.

The qualitative prison experience in relation to love in outside connections brought two dimensions of perceived powerlessness to the forefront. One of being forcefully kept *out* of and separated from outside society, the other of being kept *in* a restrictive environment that demanded adaptation. Prison required an essential reorientation in reality that permeated prisoners' identity and actions. Forging and maintaining love in outside relationships represented one arena in which this reorientation played out. It also had to be applied in navigating love in relationships within the prison.

7. The absence and presence of love in inside connections

Throughout the fieldwork and data analysis process, it became apparent that forging relationships on the inside was as complex and strategic as managing outside ties. Again, it seemed to be largely dictated by the nature of prisoners' current environment. Most interviewees were eager to point out that relationships with other prisoners had to be considered under the premise that they were somewhat forced. They were part of an involuntary adaptation to a life-world that seemed "plastic" and "artificial" (Arthur). Prisoners were aware that they had entered a prefabricated reality. They had to leave their previously known reality behind and entered a different "life-world where specific objectives and events were already found and limited their possibilities of action" (Schuetz and Luckmann 1973: 3). Decisions relating to inside associations had to cater to these environmental premises.

7.1 Functional and strategic alliances

Most prisoners of the sample perceived their inside ties to reflect a somewhat "forced" decision to make the best of an artificial situation of sharing residential spaces with strangers (Crewe 2009). This particular prison housed a large and very diverse population. Prisoners were serving sentences that varied considerably in length. They were sharing the same residential wings, with a vulnerable prisoner population housed separately. Their diversity in age, sentence-length and -stage as well as different approaches to "doing time" set the scene for internal clashes between individuals as well as between certain groups of prisoners that will become more apparent in due course. This particular inside reality played a major role in prisoners' decision-making regarding relationships. They largely resisted association with other prisoners whom they would normally not socialise with in "real" life outside, as exemplified by Peter and Phil:

> Quite a lot … would say they're my friends … there's none really that I want to see outside. Thank you very much. (Peter)

> A lot of people in jail, I wouldn't be mixing with outside. I would never have met them on tour … It's because you're on the same wing or you're next door … outside, you wouldn't talk to them in a bar or something like that for a minute. (Phil)

If there were allegiances between prisoners, they seemed to be mostly tailored around the prison's structural conditions and were seen as "social necessity"

(Crewe 2009: 304) rather than something arising naturally through congeniality. A number of participants claimed they talked to people but that they were not friends, that there was no real friendship in prison, but that relationships were predominantly forged "for preservation ... for protection" (Adam). These accounts echoed findings of earlier prison research claiming that prisoners were more likely to avoid "the complexities which could result from ... a close relationship" (Cohen and Taylor 1972: 77) rather than pursuing it. A sense of mutual care or responsibility was seen to be limited, and most prisoners were very aware of it, as the following examples demonstrate:

> The only link they have together, is what they can get off each other. Just tobacco, drugs, money ... some other form of wealth. But there's no comradeship as such. There's friends ... But if one of them died, the other one would say, can I have his lunch? (Adam)

> [I]n here he looks after me ... I look after him, get him whatever I can. So, you got to have these relationships, otherwise you can't function. (Peter)

Prison alliances could alleviate conditions of material hardship or provide physical support and safety. Especially when prisoners found themselves in vulnerable positions, were hailing from a significantly different catchment area or were physically or psychologically frail, it was paramount to forge functional connections with other prisoners:

> There's people on the wing and they would fight for me ... I could have anything I want, money, drugs, canteen, whatever I want. I walk down that landing, and I can have it ... they respect me. They know I've done a long time, and they know I am isolated. (Adam)

Adam described a form of solidarity between prisoners that served to establish and maintain intra-prisoner power structures as well as the safety of individuals. They were rarely regarded as more than strategic choices to mitigate risks emanating from other prisoners. However, not always were those allegiances marked by calculated aims to obtain protection or material goods only. Some prisoners also described connections that could be forged situationally based on one or more shared interest, a shared faith- or work-community, or shared amenities and resources (Crewe 2009; Liebling et al. 2011). These connections were seen as reasonably safe because they were temporary and did not include any obligation to be extended beyond a certain scope:

> For someone who doesn't want no trouble, that's the way you've got to go about it ... you speak to people ... you'll be friends while you're in work, you'll have a talk and you'll have a brew together and ... that's it. You'll talk about the football ... And that's how it is. (Oliver)

Most interviewees displayed similar views to Oliver and claimed that most of their interactions with other prisoners were strategically kept to a minimum. Nevertheless, some long-term prisoners acknowledged the fact that certain kinds of friendship could form.

7.2 Prison friendships — The love of *philia*

If prisoners were not drawn towards each other for mutual protective or materialistic reasons, they sometimes formed what has been coined "prison friendships" (Crewe 2009: 305). This type of friendship was still seen as a fleeting experience though due to the nature of the prison experience. This was especially true for long-term prisoners whose sentences involved being frequently transferred between prisons. They were serving only stints of time in various prisons all over England and Wales during the course of their sentences. Nevertheless, friendships could sometimes develop. They went deeper than the strategic and solely functional alliances. Prisoners involved in such "prison friendships" (Crewe 2009) saw each other as confidantes and not merely as resources to be used for personal material comfort or protection. Sometimes spatial proximity and a repeated exposure to each other was enough to plant the seed of mutual interest in each other, as described by Arthur:

> Your neighbour might be your friend … You see them every single hour of the day, and you may talk to them at night through the wall or through the pipe. And you get to know them people. And that's how … I class … a friend. (Arthur)

Once a basis of knowledge about the other has been established, *philia* can grow. Sometimes these friendships were nurtured by a sense of shared destiny or shared grievance. Peter, for example, recalled a friendship he had developed with another IPP-prisoner in this prison based on their common grievance of being "way over our tariffs" (Peter). Their relationship had developed "because we were able to open up about that to each other" (Peter) and mutually supporting the other. Tom and Bo also recalled that the shared grievance of serving a (long) prison sentence served as a basis for developing empathy and feelings of solidarity towards other prisoners but that these were specifically limited to his immediate environment, not transferable to the outside:

> You just take people's feelings on board a bit more. Out there I don't give a monkeys, you know. I'm not interested in what you're feeling I'm not interested. In here you kind of take it on board a bit.

> *Oh, why is that?*

> Well, because you know, some of the lads are in a similar position. So, you kinda know how they feel … You can kind of relate to it. (Tom)

> You make a different connection with someone in jail, than you do outside. It's … like you're in the same boat … you know where they're coming from … Outside, if you complained about something, they wouldn't understand. (Bo)

Tom was also one of a few prisoners who talked about closer, more emotionally invested prison friendships:

> Well, a friend is somebody you can confide in and tell him things, and your troubles … an extra pair of ears to listen to you innit? … Not practical things, not physical things, like emotional things … a lot of it. (Tom)

For Tom, the notion of trust and sharing of emotionally charged subjects played an important role in relations of *philia*. In his view, a friend was a confidante who could be let into his inner world. He emphasised, however, that he would only choose to get closer to someone whom he had spent a considerable amount of time with in the same prison, someone who was "doing time" with him:

> I've done six, seven years with him in jail. He's in a different jail now. I miss that contact with him … we always used to have laughs … always in each other's pockets … in B-cats you can get to know people cause you gonna be spending years with them. But in these places, it's no use getting too close, because they might only be doing short sentences … So, you distance yourself a bit. (Tom)

For Tom friendships forged in prison represented an investment of personal resources such as trust and time (see also Sloan 2016). The risk of investing these resources into someone had to be seen as worth it. One of the payoffs was a mutual feeling of emotional honesty and closeness, being able to have laughs together, being "in each other's pockets" as Tom put it. This and earlier statements of prisoners, mirror some of the main qualities of the love of friendship (*philia*). Whilst the topic of love as *philia* was mentioned sparingly, another form seemed to make an even scarcer appearance, namely *eros*.

7.3 Romantic and sexual relationships — The love of *eros*

This form of love most commonly found in microsystemic dyadic romantic relationships, the state of "being in love" (Lewis 1960) often involving a sexual element, was only mentioned by two prisoners of the sample. They spoke about having witnessed the regular occurrence of homosexual relationships between prisoners over the years. One of them provided at least some details as to how these could develop, since he had considered to start a homosexual relationship himself:

I thought about that I'm queer. And I went round and seen one bloke, and to be quite honest with you, I'm not cut out for it. It's just not there. And if it had been I would have done. So I apologised to the man. (Adam)

I've known homosexuals ... in long term jails, who are in relationships ... they're together. (Peter)

Although love as *eros* was not mentioned frequently by interviewees, when they did, they implied that erotic relationships inside prison were more common than one would assume. These could also develop between prisoners and staff, although deemed illegal. Adam, for example, made it clear that *eros* had been present during his thirty years of imprisonment stating that "I've watched prisoners fall in love with staff, I watched staff fall in love with prisoners" (Adam). Sometimes, however, these relationships were not formed on the basis of *eros*, but were mainly exploited for materialistic gains:

[A] female prison officer ... fell in love with somebody, and to look at him you wouldn't think a dog would look at him. But she loved him so much ... and he used her ... she would bring him in phones and other equipment, and drugs and that. And she got caught which is a shame really. She got caught cause he was telling everybody ... and was ... treacherous. (Adam)

Here, Adam alluded to something that was incompatible with the concept of love as selfless valuing of another person, namely using a person for selfish gains. As pointed out in the preceding sections of this chapter, prisoners were very aware of different kinds of prison connections, those that were based on short-term material or personal gain and those that were based on long-term personal valuing of and interest in a person. The next section will compare these oppositional concepts in more detail, since they seemed to illustrate the absence and presence of certain qualities of love in intra-prisoner relationships quite clearly.

7.4 Feeling used vs. feeling valued — *Sharing a cup* as framing ritual of prison friendship

What would be an example for someone you can't trust?

They're looking round your cell rather than talking to you. And they're constantly asking, can I have this, can I have that, and when you say no, they walk out in a bad mood. They've always been there for that. They've never come for you. They've come for your games or your music ... In the past, I was very stupid. I was giving all my things away. And they weren't coming back.

So, on the contrary, how can you know if someone is genuine? Or a person you can trust?

If they come in and they just want to talk to you. And ... they'll sit there and have a coffee with you. You know what I mean? And they go, "Oh that's a nice stereo" ... and that's it, really ... That means they're not there for that.

So it sounds like there's a difference between feeling used a little bit or feeling kind of ...?

[Interrupts] Yeah, it's a good word, "used." Yeah ... If you let them, they would. (Will)

Most prisoners of the interview sample had encountered similar situations to Will, and they described a similar disappointment about being taken advantage of, such as Ryan recounting his reservations towards other prisoners:

You have to be so careful! Because everybody has an agenda. It's very rare that you get people that are just living on a day to day basis, and they wanna come and have a brew and have a chat. There's always an agenda there: "By the way, you couldn't buy us coffee next week, cause I'm not on canteen?" (Ryan)

As illustrated by Ryan, prisoners were very aware that those kinds of behaviours were not connected to intentions of friendship, but that friends occupied the other end of the spectrum of self-interest, namely selfless giving. Bo illustrated this view by describing a real friend as "someone who's ... not in it to get something in return. They're off their own back ... They're not in it to get a gain" (Bo).

By equating friendship with being given time and personal attention without asking anything in return, Bo and Will also described one of love's distinct features as carved out in love's concept analysis. Their inkling that the love of friendship defied economical utility thinking, but rather presented itself as "selfless sentiment" (Illouz 2012), "caring about the other person for their own sake" (Annas 1988: 2) and "valuing" (Martin 2015: 702) of the other was in accordance with sociological and moral philosophical views on love. In a similar vein, Bo alluded to the ineffable quality of love that does not discriminate or adhere to social conventions, stating

I don't think we will fully understand love. I don't think you ever will. When I was out there, I felt love for people I thought I never would. And I felt drawn to them, that I thought I never would. Same in here. You have connections with people you think How? How have we got this connection? But there's something there.

So why did you think you would never feel love towards them?

Cause maybe what I've been brought up to like and dislike, they fell into a certain category ... we all judge a book by its cover. (Bo)

Love meant ascribing value to the person just for his or her uniqueness without really being able to rationally understand the "pull" toward them. Bo's, Ryan's and Will's above statements furthermore pointed towards a difference between manipulation for gain and love as a "free gift." In Will's and Ryan's case, this gift was given in the form of time and an interest to talk on a face-to-face basis. It was furthermore embedded within the setting of sharing a coffee or tea together. The same ritual of sharing a hot drink was described by Bo who explicitly named it as a way to show love to fellow prisoners:

Do you feel you can express love inside prison?

Yeah, I think you could. Yeah ... when you're on the landing with someone, say someone comes to my cell for a cuppa tea, that could be showing him a bit of love. (Bo)

The notion of *sharing a cup* (of tea or coffee) was a recurring theme in relation to creating a connection where the individual would feel *valued* as opposed to *used*. As a recreational setting, it supplied "the scenery and stage props for the spate of human action played out ... within ... it" (Goffman 1959: 32). Creating this specific scenery could be an indicator signalling to both parties that they were willing and ready to engage in the act of conversation on a deeper level.

Although the term commensality in its strictest meaning is mainly related to food consumption, it could also be applied to mutual drink consummation. Defined as "a gathering aimed to accomplish in a collective way some ... symbolic obligations linked to the satisfaction of a biological individual need" (Grignon 2001: 24) drink commensality held a deeper meaning. It served as social integration factor to potentially signal and tighten solidarity (Grignon 2001). As a social ritual of everyday life *sharing a cup* created a dyadic friend pairing that not only signified their respective inclusion in commensality but also defined limits and boundaries, thus physically and psychologically excluding others from this intimate gathering (Grignon 2001). *Sharing a cup* required that an invitation be extended by one party and for the other party to accept in order for the symbolic meaning of commensality to unfold. As such, it included the element of choice of a moral agent and implied voluntariness. It stands to question, however, if there would have been negative repercussions connected to declining such an invitation, thus breaking the rules of this social ritual.

Following a ritual "script," *sharing a cup* "offered an expected conversational path ... a relational purpose" (Garner 2015: 4). It represented a spatial and social setting that provided the symbolic backdrop for sharing thoughts and giving the other undivided attention. Thus, it provided the opportunity for a certain quality of love to emerge, namely positivity or limbic resonance (Fredrickson 2013; Lewis et al. 2000). Through focusing the attention on each other during a conversation over a cup of tea or coffee, the opportunity to experience moments of mutual attuning and relative safety in the company of a trusted person could arise. It also offered a chance to show interest in the other person's truth, a chance to acquire knowledge about the other which has also emerged as a quality of love during Chapter 3's concept analysis.

Sharing a cup was not only a symbolical act to initiate a conversation, but it could also function to create a somewhat homely or private atmosphere for the time being. Having a tea or a coffee together resembled a daily domestic scene played out in many homes across the world. According to Crawley, domestic or intimate settings of this kind "tend to be emotionally charged" and able to draw those involved "into emotional engagement with each other" (Crawley 2004: 415). The (re-)creation of quasi-domestic spheres (Crawley 2004) could provide a fertile ground for emotional engagement which in turn could foster the love of friendship, *philia.*

As much as these opportunities and acts were recognised by prisoners as acts of love, i.e. selfless valuing of the individual as a person in his or her own right, they were also aware that they had to tread carefully. Trusting too quickly could have consequences, and most interviewees had learned the same or a similar lesson as Will at some point in their prison sentence. Getting close to another prisoner was first and foremost seen as a risk, and time to get to know someone was the key factor in feeling able to at least mitigate that risk. If prisoners failed to do so, they could not only suffer personal disappointments and incur damage or loss of material possessions like Will ("They've never come for you. They've come for your games or your music.") or Bruce ("They come in and wanna smoke your fags while you're talking about your wife. Everyone's cunning, like a sly fox."), but in extreme cases, it could also put their physical and psychological integrity on the line.

What previous sections have not taken into consideration so far, are means of connection between prisoners and staff. These have been identified in prison research literature as one of the most important factors for prisoners' perception of prison legitimacy, safety and survivability (e.g. Liebling and Price 2001; Crawley 2004). Although staff-prisoner relationships were not explicitly chosen as a focus of this research, they nevertheless featured in prisoners' narratives about their experience of love in the prison environment.

7.5 The absence and presence of love in staff-prisoner relationships

Findings in this area tended to emerge "off the record" as additional statements made by prisoners whilst answering other interview questions. Some of these were expressed when being asked whether they thought love mattered in the prison system and were predominantly negative:

> There's ... nothing genuine. There is no love ... I don't see any love ... I don't trust anyone, they're after something. Even if it's just a member of staff talking nice to ya, they're just trying to ... unbalance you so that you ... open yourself up for them. To just take a piece of ya ... A bit of trust, and then they just stab you in the back. (Paul)

The above quote implies that Paul saw love as something genuine but perceived the prison environment and officers' caring behaviour towards him as potentially fake and a "trap" to extract compromising information from him. His suspicion prevented the building of trust which in turn prevented building more meaningful relationships with staff. It represented one of the paradoxes of staff prisoner relationships and could ultimately undermine prison legitimacy. Building on original findings by Crewe (2011) on prison officers' use of "soft power," Brunton-Smith and McCarthy likewise acknowledge this paradox. They describe how prison officers' endeavour

> to provide more meaningful forms of engagement with inmates ... can both provide a platform to enhance legitimacy, but at the same time rests on a ... potentially fragile process if the officer performs these roles in insincere forms or in ways which inmates perceive as ... deceptive. (Brunton-Smith and McCarthy 2016a: 1032)

Other prisoners expressed similar views to Paul when describing the quality of relationships between uniformed staff and prisoners. Whilst complaining about receiving an inadequate level of care, prisoners also acknowledged that this was often not due to an unwillingness or lack of concern on the side of prison staff in the first place:

> Not one member of staff has come along to me and gone "Can I have a word, you seem a bit different, you look a bit down" ... And if I'm not going for my dinner half the time, staff ain't coming down and going, "Oh how come you've not been for your food" ... Why am I sat up when the night officer comes round about 3 and 5 o'clock every morning, with my head in my hands like that? ... No empathy from staff. They don't identify people with severe problems, who are struggling. They don't identify.

And what do you think it's down to?

> Two things: Ignorance and ... government policies. Affecting how staff feel ... understaffed, more drugs ... a lot of the young new staff don't have good people communication skills. They don't know how to deal with certain individuals ... Because the training has not been adequate. (Frank)

> They're supposed to be looking after your welfare, but I think they've got other things to do that that always comes last ... I mean, if they're on association, you might have ... six staff? Seven staff? On a wing where a hundred lads are. They could not take their time to go and see one lad who's a bit poorly or feels sorry for himself ... and neglect what's going on with the others, because that's when anarchy reigns ... they haven't got the staff to do it ... And it seems to be nine times out of ten it's just: take them down the block. (George)

Cuts of financial resources within the prison system had led to cuts in staffing levels which left a depleted staff force struggling with daily demands of prison security and organisation. Forced to implement only these very basic requirements of the prison officer role also constrained staff's moral decision making. As Milliken (2018) argued in her contemplation of limits to moral agency in the caring profession, a rushed member of staff may be less likely to offer more help than practically possible.

These shortcomings in staff prisoner relationships were one factor that contributed to prisoners' predominantly negative perceptions concerning the emotional climate in the prison as well as to high levels of distress. A very limited regime had been put in place during the time of fieldwork for security reasons and due to understaffing caused by high sick-levels and a general lack of workforce due to financial cuts. Officers frequently had to be "shared" between wings so that the minimum staffing level could be guaranteed to oversee prisoners during association and unlocking periods. Prisoners were struggling to cope with unforeseeable regime and staffing changes, and the atmosphere on the wings was tense.

As Liebling (2007) found, all above factors as well as perceived personal safety levels can contribute significantly to prisoners' stress levels, and thus could be potentially undermining the legitimacy of a prison, creating an unendurable environment. George gave an inkling of how far "down" the legitimacy scale he perceived the prison to be, stating that "what matters in here is ... survival and how you get through. I don't think love matters at all" (George). When personal safety was not a given, other factors like love did not even feature in prisoners' expectations toward their environment. Paul painted a similar albeit more dismal picture of how he perceived prison to have failed its duty of care by failing to connect to and protect those who were the most vulnerable – suicidal prisoners:

> I'm thinking to myself ... why should I try and make myself healthy, yeah, what the fuck have I got to be healthy for? Why do I want to prolong this? Why why why do I wanna keep this going? ... when I could just eat shit ... and have a heart attack and fuckin end it ... You can't say ... you wanna die. Because then you're saying that you're gonna commit

suicide. Then they chuck you in that gated cell downstairs right. How is that productive for anyone who's having suicidal thoughts yeah, to have someone sat there staring at ya 24 hours a day, and other cons looking at you ... because the door is open, it's just a gated cell with plastic covering. And people come watch ya in your worst state ever ... at your lowest point, that you wanna die, yeah, and they've got you on show. How is that helpful? They don't talk to you ... At the end of the day, a man might have tried to hang himself, yeah, and yet they think it's appropriate ... to take that broken man, chuck him in a gated cell with absolutely nothing, no clothes, nothing ... can't even get any hot water himself to make himself a cuppa tea. To make himself feel a bit better. They have him in a gated cell being watched like he's in a zoo. A cage in a zoo. You know, how is that helping that man? So that man then, all he needs to do is just tell them what they want to hear. And I can tell you, next time he will feel suicidal, he ain't gonna fuckin tell em. Because they're not helping him. (Paul)

The preceding excerpt has been reproduced in its full length because it exemplifies a few important implications as to what prisoners perceived to be helpful and what they perceived to be missing in the moral and practical orientation of prison and prison staff towards its vulnerable population. Paul's main complaint related to a lack of true connection to someone in the need of care, i.e. the perceived absence of staff engagement on a personal direct level ("They don't talk to you ... They have him in a gated cell being watched like he's in a zoo." (Paul)) as well as acknowledging an individual's dignity and integrity as a person ("Take that broken man, chuck him in with absolutely nothing, no clothes ... can't even ... make himself a cuppa tea. To make himself feel a bit better." (Paul)). Not providing clothes or hot water as a basic means for comfort reflected the prison's focus on security and how they performed their duty of care, but in Paul's view, this course of action did not deliver the most crucial message needed: being seen and heard and helped without being exposed, humiliated and made feel worse. In that sense, the lack of human interaction was felt as punishment and as a deterrent for relating future suicidal feelings to staff for fear of a repetition of the same painful experience.

Without implying that the lack of engagement of prison officers with Paul's emotional needs were in any way motivated by staff's conscious decision to do so, emotionally detached staff attitudes have been found to be relatively common in prison. The prison's emphasis on the concept of "conditioning" and staff's fears to fall prey to prisoners' manipulation strategies, could often lead to curtailed emotional expression on their side (Crawley 2004). They were "expected to remain emotionally detached" (Crawley 2004: 420) and at the same time chose detachment as a strategy to avoid being conditioned. Whereas these relational strategies were fairly common for uniformed staff working on the wings, some prisoners described that relations with civilian staff were different. Oliver, for example, had found a surrogate family in the prison's chaplaincy, expressing that

> I'm connected to the church. I feel … it's Father [name] and [name]… and [name] as well … it's a special connection … where we can sit and we can talk about God and if I've got problems, like with my nan and my mum I can go and sit there and talk with [priest's name] and [priest's name]. (Oliver)

Civilian staff members of the chaplaincy not only shared his faith, but they also shared their time and provided a safe conversational space. In that sense, they displayed a more loving attitude – marked by sharing an intimate conversational space and quality time – towards prisoners than disciplinary staff might have been able (or required) to do.

7.6 Conclusion

Prisoners accounts of an acutely perceived lack of genuine human connection within staff-prisoner relationships amplified their perception of prison as an environment mainly characterised by the absence of love. It also implied an awareness and expectation on the side of prisoners' that this should not be the case if their environment was to be regarded as legitimate, fair and well-functioning. Most accounts implied that the pains of imprisonment not only comprised the absence of love and relationships from people on the outside, but also the forced connections with people on the inside, from whom there was literally no escape. Efforts to resist those inside ties deemed damaging was not only an act of partly reclaiming lost autonomy by prisoners. It also was an act of self-love exemplified by a conscious choice of a moral agent about whom to connect with and whom to keep at a distance in order to care for one's own well-being.

The prison life-world entailed certain structural and social qualities that had effects on the choices prisoners felt they had to make regarding interpersonal relationships inside. Forging prison allegiances and prison friendships appeared to be centred predominantly around pragmatic "damage-management" strategies. In a low-trust, high-uncertainty environment, knowledge about fellow prisoners was difficult to evaluate. Time seemed to be one of the few variables that could make decisions to form closer relationships inside prison less risky. If closer relationships were entered into – be it situational confidantes over a cup of coffee or tea or long-term friends doing time together – they acted as emotional support units. The love of *philia* provided the space for sharing personal truths and positivity resonance.

It will be the task of the next chapter to trace and interpret decisions of adaptation or resistance to the prison environment made by long-term prisoners in regard to emotional performances of self. These will also be examined considering individual decision criteria that were *not* related to the prison environment, because as Jewkes argued "individuals are not mere bearers of structure; they are complex amalgams of several influences ... defining their own individuality in terms of both cultural conformity and resistance" (Jewkes 2005b: 61). Individuals tend to make decisions regarding their identity and its expression based on a multifactorial set of reasons and considerations.

8. Prisoners' identity-performance in an emotionally structured life-world

Here, I shall complement a descriptive process that has been started in the previous chapter. Tracing prisoners' decision-making process around intra-prisoner relationships provided some initial information about the structural and social requirements they felt their environment exerted onto them. I will now shift the focus from decisions about *whom* to interact with onto decisions on *how* to act in relation to and around other prisoners. I will let this inquiry be informed by whether prisoners felt they could express love and other emotions easily or not and whether they thought some emotions were more acceptable to express openly in a (male) prison than others. Heralding an affective exploration process, the following sets out to uncover how the demands of prison as an emotional performance space (Crawley 2004; Crewe et al. 2014; Crewe and Laws 2015) influenced prisoners' choices about the presentation of their emotional selves. It will build on prisoners' descriptions of different versions of themselves which they decided to portray in different situations and for different reasons.

8.1 *Frontstage* emotion performance and management

> Pretence is their best friend. I see through it. I'm sick of hearing how much money somebody's meant to have, but they don't get visits, or they don't get postal orders. I'm sick of hearing peoples' crime, I'm sick of hearing about who's got this, who's got what. How hard they are. *Fed up* with it! (Frank)

Here Frank described a certain type of prisoners' self-portrayal that might generally be defined as "bravado" (e.g. Jewkes 2005a). It was achieved through talking up physical prowess to impress an audience with a "repertoire of stories" (Jewkes 2005a: 49). It was an identity display focussing especially on outside criminal offending behaviour and acquiring material wealth. Prisoners such as Peter or Tony who did not see themselves as "career criminals" found it difficult to identify with this type of behaviour:

> You find that not being of a criminal persuasion generally adds to the fact that a lot of what they're talking about goes well over my head. And you just have to smile and pretend you know what they're talking about. It's a bit like being deaf, you nod and smile ... cause it's the right thing to do. (Peter)

Peter occupied a certain outsider status within the main prisoner population and found it alien to pretend he was a "hardened criminal." It was his first prison sentence, before which he had never been in conflict with the law (according to information given by him in his interview). A stroke had left him physically frail. Nearing the age of 70 he saw himself as not fitting the criteria for joining in with the identity-performance of bravado. He could not resort to a repertoire of criminal "success stories," but nevertheless had to pretend he knew what those around him were referring to. It included an element of portraying a false self, of putting on a performance, of pretending.

The term "performance" shall be used in this chapter as defined by Goffman in his classic sociological study of *The Presentation of Self in Everyday Life* (1959). It includes "all the activity of an individual which occurs during a period marked by his continuous presence before a particular set of observers" (Goffman 1959: 22). By participating in a performance, the individual aims to influence the perception and behaviour of his audience (Goffman 1959). In Peter's case, it was his aim to be perceived as doing the "right thing." It seemed that in a "cauldron" (Ryan) of criminal offenders, one of the dominant rules was to "big up" criminal offences as a means to assert a social place and status (Goffman 1959). Some prisoners would join in, whilst others stayed on the side-lines, seeing bravado for what it was: a performance. Frank, for example, picked up on incongruences between story and reality ("I see through it ... hearing how much money somebody's meant to have, but they don't get visits or they don't get postal orders" (Frank)). It was a false front, and it served a certain purpose in this specific life-world.

Connecting the concept of *front* to the concept of *performance*, Goffman (1959: 22) defined as *front*

> that part of the individual's performance which regularly functions in a general and fixed fashion ... Front, then, is the expressive equipment of a standard kind intentionally or unwittingly employed by the individual during his performance.

It is important to emphasise the notion of "regularity" in Goffman's definition. A "general and fixed fashion" differentiates a *front* from other performances of self, such as spontaneous outbursts of emotion, for example. It resonates with the concept of "wearing a mask" which criminology scholars such as Jewkes (2005a) have come to perceive as one of the most common strategies for coping with the emotional pressures of imprisonment. According to her, "inmates feel it necessary to adopt a facade while inside" (Jewkes 2005a: 53).

Adopting a *front*, a *facade*, or a *mask* were part of a performance most interviewees of the sample claimed to deploy in order to portray themselves in a certain way in front of other prisoners, i.e. their audience. They were displaying what Goffman (1959) as well as Crewe and Laws (2015) refer to as *frontstage* behaviour. Similar to Goffman's concept of *frontstage* performance, Crawley sees emotional expressions as "parts of a play in which others are required" (Crawley 2004: 413), as emotion-work "carried out to convince a social audience that the actor is a particular kind of person" (Crawley 2004: 418). Emotion performance in front of an audience is not a one-way-entertainment but represents elements of relational emotion-work pivotal in the prison environment (Crawley 2004). The term emotion-*work* itself implies that effort is needed to construct or uphold a *front*. If and how interviewees applied effort to undertake emotion-work in an emotionally structured environment will be examined in the following.

8.1.1 Emotion expression and suppression as environmental adaptation strategies

Asked about whether he thought one could express emotions in prison, Phil pointed towards the exceptional position prison occupied as emotional space stating that

> [p]eople express their emotions more in jail than they do outside. Your emotions are higher ... In here ... everything's times by ten ... It is a depressing place at the end of the day. So, you do see more emotions in jail than you would normally outside. Plus, you live with people 24-7, so you're going to see more as well. (Phil)

In his view, an amplification of emotions "came with the territory." Exerting extreme mental pressure on a population living in very close proximity to each other, prison would act as an emotional magnifying glass ("You're going to see more" (Phil)). Declaring that he thought people expressed *more* emotions inside prison than on the outside, set Phil apart from the majority of the interview sample. When asked the same question, most prisoners would assert a view that it was not possible or even dangerous to express any emotions, as exemplified by Arthur's statement:

> If you show your feelings, in prison, you become a target ... I've been in Cat-A prisons, where the prisoners are ... all violent ... you can't show a weakness. You've got to put a mask up, a wall, to keep people at bay ... If you want to survive, it's true in prison. Only the fittest survive. If you're weak, you'll go under. (Arthur)

There were more than compelling reasons for Arthur to put up a *front* or a *mask*. He felt that his life would have been on the line, if he had given other prisoners the impression of being weak. The notion of weakness was a recurring topic in prisoners' accounts relating to the necessity to display some emotions, while keeping others hidden. The strategy of putting up a *mask* can be regarded as one example of impression management (Goffman 1959) inside prison. Putting up a *mask*, or a *front* was often described by prisoners as a form of self-censorship and emotion regulation (see also Crewe and Laws 2015). Some interviewees described certain *frontstage* situations in which they had decided to conceal specific emotions. Sometimes this could result in the drastic decision to express no emotion whatsoever, as recounted by Lewis:

> Don't wanna express nothing … If you express anger, it's gonna get you nowhere. Unless you're in danger, or you're going to have a fight, then you've got to express a bit of anger, but, in general, just walking about, just don't express nothing. Be normal, say "You're alright" and whatever … just don't show any kind of emotion.

> *Is that difficult for you?*

> No. It becomes normal … because I've done it for so long.

> *Do you think you were different before it all started?*

> I think it's all coming from my background. From my father, to be honest … I come from a background where you get a hiding for nothing … You get beat up for nothing. So, I come from a household where you get beat up for showing emotion. You cry, and you get beat up, you're happy you're getting beat up, so … I think it's come from that … Showing no emotion. You can't be happy, and you can't be sad.

> *And if you were angry?*

> If you gotta have a fight, he'd tell you to go and fight, no matter what … So, it's coming from a mad background. (Lewis)

Here, Lewis pointed towards an interplay of different factors that contributed to his emotional expression in prison. He was aware that his conditioning as a child had contributed greatly to his range of emotional expression as an adult. Anger had been encouraged by his father whereas other emotions like sadness or happiness were linked for Lewis to hurtful memories of physical abuse. He was aware that he looked back at a "mad background" (Lewis), that it was not deemed "normal" to show no emotion whatsoever. Nevertheless, he had adopted this particular "language of emotions" (Crawley 2004: 412) throughout his life and still used it as a way of carrying himself inside prison. The act of presenting an emotionally detached persona as a requirement of the prison surroundings was therefore not used by Lewis as a "false" self-representation although still being deployed strategically.

The opposite was true for Paul, an IPP-prisoner who was struggling immensely with the fact that he had served almost four times longer than his

3.5-year tariff.[1] He described consciously suppressing positive emotions. His performance was not aimed at the prisoner population though, but was supposed to manage prison officers' and Probation staff's impressions:

> I start thinking ... if I'm showing that I'm happy, then it's showing them that I'm happy with the situation I'm in ... I associate happiness with them thinking that I'm alright with this sentence. I can do more. I've got more in me. (Paul)

Paul felt that it was strategically better to not come across as proactive or to be seen as coping well. This was also given as a reason for why he had resigned from his regular job as a cleaner and also why he withdrew his application to be trained as a Listener. In his interview, he stated that he wanted to send a clear signal to the staff at this establishment that he was struggling with feeling suicidal, anxious and depressed and that he could not keep going much longer. In this regard, he was "emotionally honest," albeit selectively and with an underlying agenda. Likewise, Frank – another IPP-prisoner over his tariff and awaiting his next parole hearing after a few knock-backs – described the need to hide some of his emotions from prison and probation staff:

> [J]ust everything bothers me. But I have to hide it. If I don't hide it and react on it, then the consequences for me are just too much.

> *It must be a lot of pressure ...*

> Too much! Everybody's got a pressure valve that's gonna go. And I just know that mine is ... My parole is in a few weeks. I think I'm gonna get very emotional on this parole hearing. It might be a good thing ... Feel emotional now ... we're only scratching the surface. (Frank)

Compared to Paul's impression management strategy (Goffman 1959) of hiding positive emotions, Frank was scared to show negative emotions, to show that "just everything bothers me" (Frank). At the same time, he was aware that presenting an honest account of his emotional and psychological struggles to the Parole Board could be interpreted in his favour. It became clear during his interview that Frank's distress was not buried very deeply, but ready to show up at the right occasion ("Feel emotional now ... we're only scratching the surface"). In fact, he would have felt great release from the pressure to hide his feelings and struggles, if he could have expressed them. Frank knew it would ultimately be of greater benefit for his recovery from drug and alcohol addiction, if he could be completely honest with his Probation Officer and ask for help:

---

[1] For more details on the sample's sentence-types and background please refer to their Pen Pictures in Chapter 4.

> With Probation I'm scared to tell them the truth on certain things, because they hold it against me. So, I have to hold things back cause I can't be totally honest. They go on about it: "Oh he ... has secrets, he's in denial" ... Why would I book in with my Probation Officer or phone him up and go "Oh, last night I had a lapse ... My head's done in. This wing is full of drugs, and I ended up having a spliff last night," when I should be allowed to. Because then he could call support and all that. But I wouldn't do, because he'd beat me up over it. The parole is what I want. So, honesty can damage me ... it's finding that right person who I trust ... who understands a little bit about addiction. I will make mistakes here and there. (Frank)

Frank's impression management was influenced by his overriding wish to be released at the next parole hearing. Being an IPP-prisoner, for this to happen his risk to reoffend had to be considered low enough to not present a threat to members of outside society. Since some of his offences were related to drug use and had been violent, overcoming his drug addiction was one of the main conditions to lower his risk score. His main concern about being honest with his Probation Officer was that it might negatively influence his risk-assessment and therefore stall his progress through and out of the prison system. Although he was actively participating in a Narcotics Anonymous twelve-step recovery program at the time of the interview, Frank felt he needed more support during the transitional period from closed conditions to living in the community. As much as his strategy of self-censorship might have enabled Frank to achieve his immediate goal of being granted parole, it also prevented him "from exploring personal issues outside the boundaries of institutional power" (Crewe 2011: 517) such as achieving an understanding of and recovery from his drug and alcohol addiction.

Regarding the engagement of prisoners with agents acting on behalf of the criminal justice system, it therefore stood to reason if both sides might have not in fact been running two-way risk assessments on each other, as implied by Frank and Paul. Both interviewees described a situational adjustment of their emotional performance to create a favourable image of themselves. They felt the need to curtail self-expression and manage their emotions in order to present and preserve a front that seemed to be helpful in furthering their own agenda of sentence progression. As much as this kind of impression and emotion management seemed to be situational and tailored to prisoners' short-term goals, it could, however, affect individuals in the long-term.

8.1.2 The effects of emotion management on long-term prisoners' mental health

Flanagan, for example, acknowledged that over an extended period of time the focus on negative character traits and risk factors "might become increasingly difficult to counter ... particularly in the absence of external resources" (Flanagan 1980: 120). Theo was painfully aware of these effects and felt he could only resist them if the institutional focus was shifted onto presenting his best instead of his worst possible self:

> Unless you give me trust and responsibility, then I'm just gonna ... become a part of the environment. And I don't wanna do that. Unfortunately, your environment moulds you. No, I don't wanna be like this. Bitter ... and lose everything. I don't wanna give up ... Unfortunately, this is what you're making me feel like I need to do. I feel like I've done something I haven't done. Or perceived I wanna do something. (Theo)

As another IPP-prisoner Theo also felt the pressure to constantly work against a negative image and to be reminded that the most important part of his identity was his risk ("I feel like I've done something I haven't done. Or perceived I wanna do something" (Theo)) and not his potential. He felt an acute need to prove himself and to hold on to positive parts of his identity, although it was becoming more and more difficult for him. Prison had taken control over the display and handling of the emotional life of prisoners such as Theo, thus hugely interfering with their own value systems. By emphasising security, risk and surveillance, prison was ultimately fostering a limited self-perception and self-(re)presentation. Some interviewees expressed the distinct effort and conviction to resist these effects of imprisonment and to instead see themselves as multi-emotional human beings, as expressed by George:

> [E]very one just says I'm so relaxed and laid back. That's the way I've always been. I've always been that way. I can be the same as anybody. I can react angry if someone upsets you. I can laugh, joke and whatever ... I can react the same as everybody else. (George)

George repeatedly made the point that he had not changed during his time in prison regarding emotional traits, thus reaffirming his psychological integrity. This "ability to maintain inner sameness and continuity" (Jewkes 2005b: 60) in turn could help to maintain "a sense of ontological security" (Giddens 1992). It was important for George as well as for Theo to have a sense of who they were and what remained (apparently) unchangeable in their identity. They expressed the need to preserve positive character traits they had always thought themselves to possess ("That's the way I've always been" (George)). Not recognising themselves anymore as the person they used to be filled prisoners with unease. Noticing changes in how he perceived himself, influenced George's sense of a stable and continuous self, affecting his sense of ontological security negatively:

> I can see changes it has made. It has made me very cynical ... but I don't want it to change me totally. But I know it's going to change me. I can't get past that.

> *And how do you feel about that?*

> [long pause] Bitter. I feel very bitter ... because ... they ... made me change. And it's not change for the better, it's a change for worse. (George)

Finding themselves on the receiving end of environmental conditioning left prisoners feeling powerless. George perceived himself as a victim of environmental circumstances he would have not chosen himself. Feeling forced to suppress certain parts of their identities could contribute to negative self-perception, low self-esteem and feelings of worthlessness, all of which could create a profound pain and threat to the self. "We cannot survive when our identity is defined by or limited to our worst behaviour. Every human must be able to view the self as complex and multidimensional" (Brown 2007: 66). This was hauntingly reiterated by Paul when asked

> *How would you describe yourself as a person? What words would you use?*

> I'm, I'm ... I'm worthless me. I have no value whatsoever.

> *You see yourself like that?*

> I'm just existing, yeah, I don't feel like I'm alive, I don't feel like a person, I don't feel like a human being. (Paul)

Suppressing and bracketing feelings could have serious psychological caveats for the individual. When "feelings are deemed illegitimate ... and cannot be acknowledged" (Toch 1975: 15), identities could become fractured or even eroded. Prisoners like Paul started seeing themselves as not human and Arthur described himself as possessing a "split personality," since "you got to have a different personality when you're on the wings" (Arthur).

According to research into psychological breakdown in prisons (Toch 1975) and into psychological disorganisation (Rogers 1959), suppressing emotions represents only a short-term coping success but may develop into long-term mental health risks. Ultimately, emotions would express themselves. If then individuals could not face their emotions for what they were, it could "produce cognitive and emotional spirals in the form of compulsive acts" (Toch 1975: 15). This process could heavily backfire at an individual:

I'm sick to death you keep messing my meals up. At this point I was so frustrated, and I've been pushed and pushed and pushed. Now I won't be violent, I just take it out on myself. I'll hurt myself, I'll do things and self-harm. So, I got on the netting. Just out of frustration. That was me rather than ... assaulting the lad who does the menus ... Now I've got on the nettings a few times, cause no one's listening to me. I'm going to staff asking for help, they say "Oh speak to me later, you're getting banged up now, but when you're out for dinner, I'm in this afternoon." But they're not in this afternoon to speak to them. Next time they'll say, "I'll come and see you in a bit." You get the same excuses, same excuses. And their frustration is real ... They haven't got time, they haven't got the numbers. And it frustrates. (Theo)

Theo vividly described the process of how the continuous suppression of frustration could create an overwhelming compulsion in him to act out on it. Although he would not resort to violence against others, he would direct it against himself, violating his physical integrity to achieve a sense of psychological integrity. Theo felt there was no outlet, no one to receive his expression of frustration ("no one's listening to me"), and the emotion seemed to get amplified with every failed attempt to express himself to staff. Although Theo was aware that prison officers were pushed for time and resources, this rationalisation did not work to suppress an emotionally motivated reaction indefinitely.

Without finding ways to express, share and manage emotions adequately, prisoners sometimes experienced psychological overload, feeling confused, overwhelmed and powerless. This was expressed by Frank who felt helpless to cope with overwhelming and unfamiliar feelings of fear and grief related to impending losses of close family members:

I just feel like I'm soon gonna be on my own. If they die ... it's worrying me, cause I never had to think about certain things like who's gonna pay for my funeral? I've got no money ... Who's gonna cry at my funeral? ... These kinds of thoughts I wouldn't dream of having years ago. But I'm in a situation now ... I'm unfamiliar with. The feelings I'm not familiar ... I've got no one to share them with ... That's what does my head in ... You don't know how to deal with them because you never dealt with them before. You're thinking things ... And it's alright, if you got backup ... but my family's fallen to bits. So, I just don't know [cries]. (Frank)

Frank felt an immense strain on his mental health due to a lack of emotional outlets. It was "doing his head in" to have no one to share difficult and unfamiliar feelings with. Due to a limitation of contact with intimate confidantes on the outside, difficulties and risks involved in forming close relationships inside and an atmosphere of distrust between prisoners and staff, there was not much scope for sharing and expressing emotions relationally. It has been found however that "social sharing of emotion" (Crewe and Laws 2015: 541) especially in the form of insights into negative and trauma-related thoughts and feelings (Pennebaker 1989) can be beneficial for emotional adjustment (Crewe and Laws 2015) and enhance cognitive and emotional processing (Pennebaker 1989).

At the time of fieldwork, there were relatively few avenues for prisoners in this prison to manage and understand their emotional inner lives on a daily basis, although provisions had been put into place to help alleviate emotional struggles. Counselling services were provided by the prison's health care department, pastoral care was provided by the prison's chaplaincy team and the Samaritan Listener scheme trained and employed trusted prisoners. Nevertheless, interviewees often expressed the feeling that there were no opportunities for emotional release. When asked if there was "Any space in this place to get your emotions heard?," Frank vehemently answered, "No. No. No. Nowhere. If there is, they don't let you know" (Frank). It was difficult, however, to establish if these accounts were indeed describing the complete picture since the interview sample only consisted of 16 participants. Accounts by other prisoners who volunteered as Listeners, for example, or who had close ties with the chaplaincy, portrayed a more balanced view, implying that avenues for emotional sharing were available. Apart from the above institutional resources, prisoners such as Peter sometimes found themselves in the role of emotional confidant:

> [M]ost of them won't let their guard down ... But because I'm an old guy so to speak ... harmless, cripple, people feel more comfortable talking to me. You know, I'm not a threat. And so, people tend to open up to me a little bit. And we do have Listeners, but most of the prisoners don't trust the Listeners. Because they think they're narks or they grass ... So, it's people like myself that tend to absorb a lot of people's anger, frustration. (Peter)

Prisoners would only feel safe to open up about their innermost feelings with someone they did not perceive as a source of potential exploitation or threat of violence. If none of these avenues were available, emotional expression could sometimes be diverted "underground," if not psychologically by suppression, at least physiologically by limiting it to spaces away from the frontstage view of prisoners and staff.

8.1.3 *Backstage* emotion expression "behind the door"

Some interviewees found that the best place for expressing emotions they could not or did not want to express in front of other prisoners was "behind your door. When you're banged up" (Tom). Prisoners with a similar mindset to

Tom also preferred to lead a somewhat introverted life inside. They focused on the immediate benefits their environment could offer which they would actively use to take care of their own emotional and physical needs. Phil's and George's descriptions of their typical day exemplified this approach:

> I finish work ... go back to my cell, and I do a lot of artwork ... I socialise, but ... half the time, I just go behind the door and do my artwork or watch a bit of TV. (Phil)

> I just go in me pad ... sit down, cup of coffee, and just chill ... most of the time I'm in my pad on my own anyway. That's the way ... I prefer to do it. I do a lot of reading, I do box sets ... It's a way to unwind ... that's the way I get through. (George)

As life-sentenced prisoners, working in a somewhat structured way towards the end of their tariffs, Phil and George predominantly focused on mental stability. They saw their own company as best suited to keep them balanced, "to unwind" and to "just chill" unfazed by a chaotic prison environment. Their cells represented "safe spaces," a refuge from performance-oriented prison life on the wings. These *backstage* (Goffman 1959) spaces provided the opportunity for expressions of an authentic emotional self, not tailored towards an audience. For Goffman, *backstage* represented a place

> where one's basic, personal ontological security system is restored and where the tensions associated with sustaining the particular bodily, gestural, and verbal codes that are demanded in this setting are diffused. (Goffman 1959: 54)

For some prisoners, this space of tension diffusion was found to be their cell, their "pad," the place that offered the opportunity to unwind, to "just chill" (George). Arthur echoed this sentiment of reinstalling a sense of personal integrity – an ontological security system (Goffman 1959) – stating that "the only time ... you can be yourself is when they shut the door and you're behind the door" (Arthur).

A majority of interviewees were housed in single cells. Some of them preferred to turn them into home spaces, pursuing personal interests such as art or reading. They would create a homely atmosphere (Crawley 2004) in which to sit down with a "cup of coffee" (George), "watch a bit of TV" (Phil) to "get through" (George) their long sentences. This type of behaviour could be described as withdrawal – if not psychological at least physical – from their environment. Psychological withdrawal has been connected to potential negative effects when used as a maladaptive strategy to disengage from certain emotions (Deci and Ryan 2000). In Phil and George's case, it was used in a different sense, however. It was used as a strategy to protect their individual mental integrity, to get through the day and to relieve negative feelings ("It's a way to unwind" (George)). A physical separation from life on the wings could provide protective factors for well-being – mentally and physically – since it was there that most emotion performance work took place. Some roles seemed relatively fixed in this environment, *gender* being one of them.

8.2 Weakness and masculinity — Emotion performance as gender performance?

When it came to reasons for the suppression or expression of certain emotions, another storyline emerged, one that featured distinct social pressures demanding adaptation. It revolved around two interconnected needs: the need to not show weakness and the need to be seen as a man. In the following, I will endeavour to examine and disentangle the web of meanings connecting these two concepts. I will take a closer social-ecological look at neurological, psychological, social and ideological connotations as well as at behavioural imperatives associated with these concepts in the life-world of prison. The following interview excerpt can be regarded as an ideal illustration of the symbolical and practical interconnections and ambiguities of emotion performance as gender performance in an emotionally regulated space. It will therefore be assigned the role of stand-alone opening statement in its full length.

Do you feel it's acceptable here to show emotions?

Yeah but no, like you can't go out on the wing crying or being a baby, can you? It's a ... real man's prison, innit? It's men.

What does it mean, real man?

You can't go out on the wing crying your eyes out ... you've got to be a man, haven't you? You're in prison.

So, men don't cry?

Men do cry, but not on association, when everyone's trying to play pool ... It's that time for mixing ...

So, what would happen if you showed your emotions on association?

Nothing. Nothing would happen.

So, if other inmates see you cry, what would happen?

Nothing. They might think you're weak ... I don't know, they might, they might not ... I don't know.

Hm. What does "weak" mean?

Like ... they can just come in here and take your stuff.

Oh, ok. So, showing emotions is a sign of weakness?

No, not all the time.

When is it not?

It could be anything, couldn't it? It could be a loss ... Relationships, family, friends... anything could happen. I've never seen it on 'soc, people crying. That's what I mean.

But everybody knows that everybody else is crying? At some point?

At some point, maybe. Yeah. (Will)

This dialogue with Will picked up on a number of topics which will all feature heavily in the discussion to follow. Firstly, he pointed towards a convention already introduced, namely the division into *frontstage* and *backstage* emotional expression. It defined *frontstage* as a space that required the banning of certain emotions from public view. This time it was the expression of sadness, distress and grief through the act of crying. This could not only be considered as an act of emotional suppression but also as an environmentally dictated "language of emotions" (Crawley 2004: 412). The "speakers" of this language had to conform "to a powerful set of conventions attaching to 'proper' exhibition and expression" (Crawley 2004: 412). In this case, the proper exhibition of sadness and tears had to take place outside of association times. "When everyone's trying to play pool" (Will), the public display of "heavy" emotions seemed to contradict the emotional atmosphere required for this specific setting, i.e. easy and light-hearted.

Secondly, if this convention was not adhered to, it could result in misguided impression management hence creating the undesirable impression of being weak, of being vulnerable and defenceless to material exploitation. The ambiguity of these statements showed itself, however, when I probed around the universality of these concepts. Consequently, it emerged that Will did not perceive sadness or crying itself to be condemned completely in prison. In fact, it was treated as an appropriate and accepted expression when grieving the loss of relationships, the loss of love and connection, but it had to be done at the "right" time and in the "right" setting. Will also appreciated that there was not always a default-mechanism at play between showing emotions publicly and receiving an automatic repercussion from other prisoners. On the contrary, it was perceived as "doing the right thing" to recognise and tend to another prisoner's emotional distress, if the relation was deemed close enough. Thus, when asked if he thought there were "any places or situations in the prison where you can show love?," Will changed his response from "No, not really." to

> Yeah, you can. You can, I suppose … with certain friends and that … you can sit there and if you see them upset and chat to them. It's really like showing them that you care. (Will)

The love of friendship required the allocation of time and attention to another's well-being. It was the right thing to do in the framework of *philia*. It was therefore not always the case that a public expression of distress would automatically be interpreted as exploitable weakness.

Thirdly, Will drew a connection between a) emotional expression through crying, b) being perceived as weak and c) the concept of (not) being a "real man" in prison. When asked to further elaborate on his view on what made a real man Will explained that feeling sadness was not perceived as not part of the male emotional set-up per se. Showing it publicly, however, was seen as unmanly behaviour in prison. In a similar vein, prisoners connected the expression of love as a vulnerable emotion to the notion of weakness or softness. These views were often expressed as a response to asking participants whether they felt that love mattered or should matter in prison. Bruce, for example, had no doubt that

> [o]f course, it should matter, if you're ringing your wife up, or your girlfriend, or your kids. Of course, you show love to them, don't ya? But if lads are talking about love on the phone, and I'm on the phone next to them, they just give them that [turning around to hide what they are saying into the phone] … If someone comes next to me, it's like "Oh I can't be soft in front of him" … Most lads will do that, will turn away, whispering "I love you" … Cause if you're being all lovey dovey and you get some idiot who doesn't know what love is, who doesn't know how to show love. "Oh you big fucking soft cunt, ya!" Next thing, there's gonna be a fight. (Bruce)

According to Bruce, the public expression of love through loving words was something to hide, something to be ashamed of. It will now be the task to unpick and discuss above-presented interrelations of a) emotional expression, b) weakness, and c) masculinity with special consideration of social-ecological (i.e. individual, environmental and ideological) influences and ambiguities.

Looking at prisoners' views around the notion of weakness, it became apparent that weakness was not only associated with emotional, but also physical qualities. Ryan and other interviewees described a process by which actual physical weakness was used by other prisoners who had "nothing else to do" (Arthur). They forced weaker individuals to give up their possessions and hand them over to the physically stronger ones. If they refused to do so, they would suffer physical repercussions of violent assault. Ryan thought that this behaviour was mainly motivated by a

> fundamental self-seeking, gratification in people ... anything that puts
> somebody else down, elevates them ... people are selfish, they got a
> greedy desire, I want what he's got ... more food through servery, I want
> drugs, I want this, I want that. (Ryan)

He attributed the exploitation of weaker prisoners to the selfish and materialistic
impulses of those prisoners who were physically stronger. In this process, there
was real loss involved, the loss of material goods and the loss of physical integrity.
His decision to "get in that gym" to become physically stronger was Ryan's
immediate reaction to counter the experience of victimhood. Endeavouring to
physically draw level with his perpetrators, he could defend himself effectively. It
was also a precaution in anticipation of future exploitation or threats of violence.
As Evans and Wallace observed, fighting back and taking on the role of
perpetrator sometimes represented "the only way to ensure that one does not
become a victim" (Evans and Wallace 2008: 487) in prison. Reversing roles could
have immediate and in fact life-changing consequences because it established
boundaries and (re-)calibrated power dynamics, as experienced by Adam after
arriving in a new establishment:

> Prison is about survival ... You got a lot of men living together on the top
> of each other. The same men, day after day after day. Some of them are
> very frightened. They're the ones walking around all toughy [sic]. "Don't
> pick on me, cause I'm so hard" [imitates American accent]. You know, I
> brought one down to the ground the other day ... I've been in there for
> nine months, and for eight months he's been really gobbing me. See
> what I've done is bring him down in front of all of his mates ... I just said
> "Shut your mouth you effing minger!" And he went [imitates frightened
> shaking] ... Cause now it's on, now it's on. Now he's gotta do something.
> And I just turned around and walked away. And he said to his mate,
> don't let him walk away, and he said, "Oh shut up! He's an old man, he
> put you down" [laughs]. We're like ever since good friends. (Adam)

Above excerpts alluded to the possibility of different ways to read the use and
abuse of weakness in the prison environment. On the one hand, the physical
and material exploitation of weaker prisoners could be interpreted as a means
of self-enrichment, acquiring goods for consumption or to sell on. On the other
hand, it could also be viewed as an individual's act to enhance not only his
economic but symbolical power, as a means for self-aggrandisement, putting
others down to elevate himself (as observed by Ryan) and to establish or defend
a social position and status within a group (Goffman 1959). The latter
interpretation has also come to be frequently deployed by masculinity studies
investigating the role of gender ideologies in male behaviour. Especially the

topics of domination and power as performance of *hegemonic masculinity* featured heavily in participants' accounts of weakness and its exploitation.

8.2.1 *Hegemonic masculinity* and *hypermasculinity* — Outdated blueprints of (prison) maleness?

Masculinity studies offer a reading of the question "What makes a man?" that takes cultural, historical and social conditioning into consideration. This question has gained considerable ground throughout the last century, and "in the late 1980s and early 1990s, research on men and masculinity was being consolidated as an academic field" (Connell and Messerschmidt 2005: 833). In pursuit of understanding masculine roles, norms and values some researchers argue "that four features characterize ... dominant norms: power, ambivalence toward femininity, domination and objectification of nature and the psyche, and the avoidance of emotion" (Evans and Wallace 2008: 484). Other repeatedly emphasised ideals of masculinity are the suppression of emotions and the rigid policing of relationships with other men (Evans and Wallace 2008).

Indeed, throughout the evolution of masculinity studies efforts have been made to single out and classify different types of masculinity marked by specific values and behaviours. The concept of *hegemonic masculinity* represents one ideal and social parameter after which a "real man's" behaviour would model itself. Within the relevant literature, *hegemonic masculinity* has long been regarded as "the dominant style of masculine performance in traditional Western societies" (Evans and Wallace 2008: 485). According to masculinity researchers such as Willis (1977), Comstock (1991), or Evans and Wallace (2008) performing maleness in a certain way – particularly in front of other men – is predominately associated with access to power and (socioeconomic) status. Originally, the concept of hegemony did not include the notion of violence but was related to gaining positions of power and privilege through cultural and institutional avenues (Connell and Messerschmidt 2005). Over time it has become associated with more aggressive aspects such as "physical size, willingness and ability to fight, dominance" (Evans and Wallace 2008: 486) and enforcing superiority by means of violence or threat (Archer 1994; Bowker 1998). Modelling behaviour after a "real man's" blueprint can have negative consequences, however. It becomes especially apparent in the context of criminal violent offending or "patterns of aggression ... linked with hegemonic masculinity" (Connell and Messerschmidt 2005: 834). On the other hand, "most accounts of hegemonic masculinity do include such 'positive' actions as bringing home a wage, sustaining a sexual relationship, and being a father" (Connell and Messerschmidt 2005: 840).

Probing into prisoners' opinions on what makes a man, some ideas inherent in the concept of *hegemonic masculinity* were also expressed by Adam:

Prison has denied these men the right to be men ...

What is a man?

There's responsibilities to your family ... man goes out, he hunts his food ... he brings it back home to the cave. That's a man.

The provider?

A provider. A protector. When a woman gets a mothering instinct, she nestles. When a man gets a father's instinct, he protects. That instinct's still there ... we still got it. (Adam)

In Adam's opinion, prison denied prisoners the right to embody those traits of being a man that were represented as the more socially sanctified constituents of hegemonic masculinity (see also Sloan 2016). According to Adam, these ideas could be traced back to a biologically different set-up of men and women, preconditioning them to fulfil different roles in society following a different instinct. Due to the fact that prisoners were separated from their families – hence could not execute their roles as fathers, providers, and protectors – they were not able to be a "real man." In Adam's view, this contributed to a propensity to perpetuate patterns of criminal and violent behaviour. Prisoners had limited choices of what kind of man they wanted to be, since "aggression is the only emotion that prison allows you to display ... you have to live down with the macho, weakness thing" (Adam). The lack of family integration and relationships with female counterparts in an all-male environment therefore carried with it a specific threat to prisoners' perceptions of a male self, as pointed out by Sykes (1958: 72):

> The inmate is shut off from the world of women which by its very polarity gives the male world much of its meaning ... since a significant half of his audience is denied him, the inmate's self-image is in danger of becoming half complete, fractured, a monochrome without the hues of reality. The prisoner's looking-glass self ... is only that portion of the prisoner's personality which is recognized or appreciated by men.

Due to a curtailment of certain male roles, e.g. the father, the provider, the partner, there was "little role segregation, little opportunity for the presentation of different selves in different contexts" (Cohen and Taylor 1972: 75). Sloan (2016) likewise acknowledged, that due a lack of female presence "against whom to juxtapose one's masculine identity" (Sloan 2016: 107), "it falls to other men ... to provide the spectrum of gender against which men can position themselves" (Sloan 2016: 107). Most prisoners of my interview sample expressed not only their awareness of those socially, individually and institutionally constructed limits, but also their regret about having to adjust to an emotional corset. Ryan, for example, found it debilitating to hide what he cared about (helping other prisoners through art), and he was aware that he was not the only one doing so:

> You know it's hard for me to say to people out there, that all is what I do, is help others ... because you'd be took for a fool on the landing, you would be.

Yeah? What would people say to you?

> They'd call you a pussy.

Really? ... Why?

> Because why you're doing that? Why you're helping him? ... people like to have that macho image ...

Is that still popular?

> It still is. It still is. Even though I look and think "What are you hiding?" ... it's just an armour. (Ryan)

Ryan's account clarified that the "macho image" – a form of prison-specific *hypermasculinity* – not only required normative compliance with a behavioural code that sanctioned "soft traits" such as helpfulness, but also that this model of masculinity gained its validity and legitimisation by denigrating the female, as exemplified by the derogatory use of the term "pussy." On the other hand, the display of an exaggerated form of masculine "hardness" (Frosh et al. 2002: 12) could also be deployed as "just an armour" protecting something inside of the individual that he wanted to hide, as pointed out by Ryan.

When using the term *hypermasculinity* in relation to the expression of masculinity in male prisons, Morey and Crewe (2018: 18) provide a definition of what they termed the "hypermasculinity hypothesis" and which is based on previous criminological research:

> Hypermasculine traits are described relatively consistently as involving toughness, aggression and violence (Sykes 1958; Newton 1994; Toch 1998; de Viggiani 2012; Ricciardelli 2015), as well as homophobia and hatred of anything that appears weak, effeminate or associated with femininity (Newton 1994; Irwin and Owen 2005; Jewkes 2005a).

Considered a prison-specific phenomenon, *hypermasculinity* has been sought to be explained by the same approaches commonly deployed in prison research, focusing on the explanation of inside structures and dynamics through the deployment of importation and deprivation models. Consequently, "explanations drawing on the *deprivation* perspective contend that prisoner *hypermasculinity* is a *compensatory response* to the emasculating experience of imprisonment" (Morey and Crewe 2018: 18 [emphasis in the original]). Striving to accumulate material goods through the exploitation of fellow prisoners, some prisoners seek to "recoup masculine power and status" (Morey and Crewe 2018: 19). The importation model, on the other hand, draws the conclusion that previously learned and exposed traits of masculinity as well as "street traits" connected to acts of violence were imported from the outside (Morey and Crewe 2018).

It therefore has to be considered that prisoners' motivations to engage in acts of exploitation, threats and assaults of other prisoners could also be motivated by masculinity ideals, such as the reification of power, control and competition (Evans and Wallace 2008). Although these traits have all been mentioned by a majority of interviewees in this study in relation to emotional expression in prison, it is important to keep in mind that they were also aware that subscribing to this kind of masculinity was largely part of a *frontstage* performance (Goffman 1959). Even prisoners like Arthur who portrayed himself as someone who did "not suffer fools" – as having an image so violent that other prisoners would not even consider attacking or exploiting him – constituted that weakness was an inherent part of himself, stating that "the only time you look weak, you can be yourself is when … you're behind the door. Then you become yourself" (Arthur).

It could furthermore be disputed whether concepts such as *hypermasculinity* or *hegemonic masculinity* are factual expressions of social realities, or if their ongoing application is rather a reverberation of popular ideologies. Likewise, contemporary prison researchers such as Morey and Crewe (2018) have criticised the continued (over-)use of *hypermasculinity* to describe prisoners' male identities as portraying "a relatively reductive picture of aggression, emotional coldness and machismo" (Morey and Crewe 2018: 17). In Maycock and Hunt's recent edition of *New Perspectives on Prison Masculinities* (2018) Brown and Grant similarly argue that an academic and institutional perpetuation of "the concept of hyper-masculinity sustains the disparities and damage" (Brown and Grant 2018: 166) that may have already been present in male prisoners' pre-prison lives and which they sought to overcome. Considering alternative interpretations of male behaviour and emotional identity might gain even more foothold if assumptions such as "violence being the darker, shadow side of performing maleness" (Evans and Wallace 2008: 486) would be additionally examined from a social-ecological, multidisciplinary angle.

8.3 Alternative interpretations of (hyper-)masculine emotion expression

Findings from the field of developmental neurobiology, for example, could offer additional insights into gender differences related to processing and expressing emotions. Recent studies of early brain development in male and female children have found that parts of the male brain develop slower and are more vulnerable to external disruptions such as a lack of maternal care and bonding due to different hormonal dynamics (Schore 2017). According to Schore, this male-associated vulnerability could also leave men more vulnerable "to specific types of psychiatric disorders, especially to the externalizing psychopathologies and to deficits in the emotional and social functions of the early developing right brain" (Schore 2017: 18).

Accordingly, Holden postulates that men are more likely to express negative sentiments through externalising behaviour including "drinking, drug abuse, and violence" (Holden 2005: 1576). Similarly, Fergusson and Horwood (2003) reported findings from the *Christchurch Health and Development Study* (examining an unselected birth cohort of 1,265 children born in 1977 in Christchurch New Zealand) suggesting gender-specific strengths and vulnerabilities in adolescents related to externalising and internalising emotionally motivated behaviour. Their results conveyed the assumption that being female provided "resilience to externalizing but vulnerability to internalizing" (Fergusson and Horwood 2003: 147). When considering these findings, it is important to remember that theoretically every child's brain is vulnerable to external influences that can disturb its development in various ways. Some of these have been described previously, relating to the effects of traumatic experiences such as loss, abuse and violence in early childhood on brain development. An additional perspective can now be added to the discussion, namely that male children seem to possess a higher vulnerability connected to different behavioural outcomes that might manifest later in life.

Another main neurobiological difference between the sexes was found "in the experience-dependent patterns of the wiring of the emotion-processing limbic system" (Schore 2017: 22) implying that women and men process, regulate and express emotions differently. Although they may be exposed to the same situation, due to neurological differences men and women may be inclined to display either a different emotional reaction or a different emotion regulation strategy. Schore, for example, argued that "females under stress initially interactively regulate and males autoregulate," perceiving it as "a normal gender difference in affect regulation" (Schore 2017: 29). This additional insight into emotion regulation could also provide an alternative interpretation as to why certain emotions might be expressed *frontstage* and others *backstage* according to gender.

Indeed, it might be the case that "putting up a mask," for example, could be considered not only as proof of a culturally and socially created ideal of masculinity, but also as neurologically influenced behaviour. Likewise, the externalisation of anger as aggressiveness might be more a sign of an underdeveloped emotion regulation skill – due to earlier impediments in brain development through stress-inducing experiences – than a display of *hypermasculinity*. Some triggers in prisoners' environment might simply become emotionally too overwhelming by reigniting past trauma. Theo and Ryan, for example, described their struggle to control feelings of fear caused by their environment. Their impulsive reactions to perceived threats ran the risk of coming across as "unmotivated" aggression or violence, if they did not employ conscious emotion regulation strategies:

> Sometimes I can't even function on a psychological level ... It's that scare. I'm going back to that kid, and I don't feel secure and safe in this environment. Unfortunately, I gotta keep on living it ... I've got to be mindful, of when I go out here, I've got to ... make sure that I'm not gonna be abrasive towards any-body. Not causing anybody to be abrasive towards me ... I've got to be mindful. (Theo)

> [W]e have to admit that before anger comes fear. I don't like people getting behind me ... even today, I was talking to somebody, and somebody passed a CD over me like that, and it was this close to my head. And I had to physically get a hold of me ... because I wanted to punch his head in ... "What the fuck do you think," I felt ... You know, I've just gone like that [shows how he braced himself] and I willed it ... I said in my head, "You better get the fuck away from me!" ... I said it in my head. And the next one would have been, "Get the fuck away from behind me!" But obviously what would have come from him would've been "What?!" And the next minute we'd be fighting. I had so many fights in here. (Ryan)

Both prisoners had experienced domestic violence in their childhood homes, and both had been victims of physical and emotional abuse. Theo especially struggled with claustrophobic feelings being locked in his prison cell because he had been regularly locked in his room and abandoned by his parents all night from the age of four until twelve. Ryan had experienced regular beatings by his mother, father and stepfather at home as well as extensive bullying and violent assaults in various YOIs and prisons. He was hyper-aware of his environment and was easily startled. In examples like these the emotional expression of aggressiveness or abrasiveness was not owed to the conscious choice to display a *hypermasculinity* ideal, but to unconscious reactions to powerful emotional triggers in the environment.

Thus, it could be speculated whether aggressive and violent behaviour in male prisons, for example, was cause or effect of the *hypermasculinity hypothesis* (Morey and Crewe 2018). It could as well be interpreted as interactive amplification of behaviour displayed by a pre-conditioned majority, with few avenues of non-participation for the rest of the prison population. It is also important to keep in mind that *frontstage* and *backstage* emotion performances and emotion regulation strategies might have represented different individual choices and motivations that were not related to solely maintaining a prison-specific image of manliness. Apart from running the risk of becoming an out-dated go-to-categorisation of male behaviour in prison as criticised by Morey and Crewe (2018) or Brown and Hunt (2018), using the concept of *hypermasculinity* also might not take into consideration the diversity of individual responses to the question "What do you think is a man?" as expressed by George:

> A man can be a lot of different things. I mean, I'm completely different to a lot of other people … It's a difficult question cause there's all different types in here. (George)

In his statement, George echoed voices of masculinity researchers such as Connell and Messerschmidt (2005), or Evans and Wallace (2008) which have become more prominent recently. They draw attention to the consideration that "masculinity is not a fixed entity embedded in the body or personality traits of individuals" (Connell and Messerschmidt 2005: 836) that there is no universal pattern of masculinity, but that "different cultures, and different periods of history, construct gender differently" (Connell 2000: 10). Taking these ideas a step further and viewing masculinity as an "empty construct needing to be filled with strong ideas" (Evans and Wallace 2008: 486) could open up a space for reconsideration, or even reinterpretation of a malleable concept. After all, macrosystemic factors such as cultural values or ideologies are subject to change and reinterpretation. An attempt to do so will be made in the following sections. They aim to lead us full circle by (re-)introducing the attributes of love into the discussion of emotion expression, prison-masculinity and the creation of "emotionally honest" prison environments.

8.4 Reimagining (prison-)masculinity as emotion performance

Starting to view masculinity in a social-ecological sense – that is as individually diverse, and part of an ever-changing macrosystemic cultural and social performance – might offer an opportunity to reconsider and relax rigid gender boundaries. In Adam's opinion, this could create space for the emergence of a more wholistic view of masculinity and femininity as interrelated concepts. It would also create a safe space for love's return to the *frontstage*:

> A woman gave birth to me. It takes two gene pools to make one. So … as a man I have a certain amount of female genes, a certain amount of male genes … So yes, I have feminine traits, all men do. But we have to hide these traits under aggression. Little boys can't cry … And that sort of thing … But it is there … love is there, love is hiding. (Adam)

Adam reiterated some of the most commonly held beliefs about the emotional performance of masculinity that have been discussed previously. These included the notion of active suppression of "soft" or vulnerable feelings such as love as well as not expressing sadness or grief through tears. Instead, the expression of more "potent" emotions like anger or aggression is seen as apparently inherent in masculinity ideology. A similar conclusion was drawn by Pollack who argued "that boys are taught to repress their yearnings for love and connection and build a wall of toughness around themselves ... which leaves them isolated" (Pollack 1995: 42). Thus, not only in prison but in Western society at large men are conditioned to repress and push down "their vulnerable, empathic, caring emotions which they show from birth" (Pollack 1995: 42).

Macrosystemic views on masculinity as socially and culturally held beliefs (Freeden 2003) therefore seem to override the individual's need to express a full range of emotions. Connecting Pollack's (1995) and Adam's argumentation to findings of developmental neurobiology on the vulnerability of male brain development to a lack of parental love, would support a focus on emotional wholeness and honesty in male mental health. Frank, for example, expressed a clear openness and willingness to face his emotions and share them, but only in the right environment:

> I'm an open book me, right, to some degree. Not in here, but if I feel a connection with somebody ... I can talk to, I feel decent round ... I wouldn't feel no way about opening up, been crying [during the interview] and what not. As long as it's with the right people ... who are learning something from me, but also .... not judging me. (Frank)

Frank described a setting that was conducive to opening up (Pennebaker 1989) and sharing those emotions which were usually not acceptable (i.e. sadness and tears) to be expressed openly. It had to fulfil the conditions of feeling a "connection with somebody" (Frank), mutual learning about the other and a non-judgmental attitude toward the one who was sharing emotions. Sharing the full range of emotions could provide men with an opportunity for a more expansive and comprehensive "recreation of different versions of ... masculinity" emanating "from spaces where men set their own priorities and practices of manhood and masculinity" (Brown and Grant 2018: 166). In her study on *Emotion and Performance* in prisons, Crawley (2004) had also arrived at the conclusion that "emotional interchanges are more likely ... in contexts in which there are high levels of intimacy, shared knowledge of context and a ... 'dialogue'" (Crawley 2004: 413). Sharing intimate knowledge, the creation of a sensory and mental connection and the notion of equals engaged in dialogue rather than in judgment or assessment of the other were all preconditions of love (see Chapter 3). Some of these conditions were already being created in the prison.

8.5 Opportunities for an "emotionally honest" prison environment incorporating the benchmarks of love

To avoid a misrepresentation of the current prison system, it is essential to take the developments into account which have already taken place focussing on "the legitimization of feelings and emotional expression" (Evans and Wallace 2008: 503). For example, parenting classes, counselling, Enhanced Thinking Skills (ETS), or courses delivered by charities that encourage more constructive and less violent strategies for emotion regulation are now ranking on the rehabilitation agenda of most English and Welsh prisons. Prisoners' accounts such as Ryan's and Theo's of how they would purposefully regulate their learned violent behaviour in a stressful situation bear witness to the success of individual and institutional efforts. Oliver and George likewise acknowledged a change in their emotion performance and how being inside had changed them as a person:

> I'd say, I've changed … I'll be a different person when I get out than what I was outside the last time. Because I didn't care … about doing what I'd done … it was a man and a lady came in … and they've been burgled. Now, before… it wouldn't have bothered me but when they told the story, they were lovely old people. And, it teared me up a bit, you know what I mean?… Because it wasn't nice. With … what they said and what they experienced and that made me think about it. You know? For someone to feel like that … it broke my heart. (Oliver)

> I'm very much a closed book. I keep stuff inside. I wouldn't talk about them … Whereas … now I do … talk about things … perhaps I realise now you need someone to talk to take the burden from you. (George)

Oliver had taken part in a course on Restorative Justice arranged by the prison, but apart from this "officially" encouraged engagement with emotions, prisoners also recounted examples of individually motivated efforts. Some of them had found a channel for expressing love and other publicly "unacceptable" emotions like sadness, grief or anxiety through artistic endeavours such as painting or writing poems. It could provide a form of therapeutic outlet for feelings that could not be processed otherwise, as explained by Frank:

> I've been drawing faces, you'd think, what's going on in his head. Cause I'm drawing some crazy looking faces. Screaming ones … and I don't know, I don't know where they come from. (Frank)

These emotional expressions were still largely part of prisoners' private *backstage* persona. Expressing a range of more "vulnerable" feelings, especially love, was still seen as largely unattainable *frontstage*. A majority of participants put this down to a seeming incompatibility of a negative, disjunct and restrictive prison environment and the presence of love which requires vulnerability, trust and closeness to others. Love did not feature in these accounts because it was mainly regarded as an outside resource and links to the outside were scarce, as expressed by Oliver and Tom, for example:

> *Do you think that love matters ... in this prison?*
>
> Yes, for family. (Oliver)
>
> *Do you think love should matter more?*
> Yes, I suppose ... But you got to rely on people outside being the same as you ... If people outside, your friends or your family, they're not willing to show you any love, it doesn't mean nothing in jail does it? (Tom)

Some prisoners also expressed a preoccupation with personal safety, with surviving of and progressing through their sentence, so love would only feature as an afterthought. This was as exemplified by Tom and Tony, stating:

> No, it doesn't matter, nooo! ... Not in here. Doesn't mean nothing, nothing here. Nothing! (Tom)
>
> Nah. There's nothing to love in here. Like I say, it's such a negative place ... you can't really, nah. (Tony)

They expressed a very clear conviction that love was more or less unthinkable as an occurrence or constituent in their environment. Tony's statement represented the view of a majority of interviewees, namely that prison in itself was negative and love was something positive. Therefore, the two excluded or repelled each other.

As much as prisoners felt they had to rely on sources of love on the outside, they also felt that if given the opportunity to think about including love in the prison environment, they could imagine it taking on a more prominent role. However, only a minority was able to conduct this "thought experiment" practically. Relying on love as ethical or moral guideline was one of their main arguments. They stressed the importance of love as a structuring principle of intra-prisoner relationships. As such it could set the tone and create a certain atmosphere in the prison. Ryan, Will or Arthur, for example, expressed the view that it was important to remind people of their capacity to love, in order to raise awareness of self and others:

> [To] realise what they're doing. That when they walk past somebody and call them a name ... That might be the final straw for that person that might go and commit suicide ... I think that ... love is important because without that you'd be unable to say to somebody, well, you love your mum, don't you? They obviously do in most cases ... So how would you feel, if somebody went and robbed your mum's purse? Do you know what I mean? (Ryan)

Do you think love should matter in here?

Yeah definitely, yeah ... If everyone's going around, not nice people, it wouldn't be a nice place, would it? ... If everyone's not showing any appreciation towards each other, then it can be a problem. (Will)

There would be a bit care more, wouldn't it, I don't know. ... People would probably get on a bit better ... Instead of just trying to rob each other and whatever else. (Arthur)

These excerpts illustrated some of love's features that could be related back to its quality as a human virtue. As such, it could help to curb the compulsion of violent interactions between human beings, and in its place, encourage empathy and self-transcendence in favour of the other's well-being. Looking at the root causes of his and other prisoners' violent behaviour we can resort back to Ryan's earlier conclusion that "the less love people have in their life, the more brutal they are in how they treat others around them" (Ryan). For Ryan, the estrangement from love could result in brutality and an estrangement from himself. Asked whether he thought love mattered, he was very clear that it indeed mattered greatly "because without that, can we call ourselves human?" (Ryan). He saw love as an essential quality and attribute of the human species. The same view was expressed by Bo who saw the absence of love as the absence of (human) life or aliveness in others around them:

Do you feel that love matters in here?

I think so, yeah. If you look at someone who is possibly not loved, they walk round like a Zombie ... You can see if someone's not got as much outside than some other people. I think you'd see it in them. I think everyone wants to be loved don't they?

You said they walk around like Zombies – how do you mean that?

There's like no life in them ... Or they've got nothing to get up for ... You can see that in some people. (Bo)

As an essential human need, love is a nutrient of human psychological health and growth. When it is lacking it can have grave consequences for an individual's psychological health and development. Bo, in fact, described those whom he perceived to not have access to any source of love as Zombies – the living dead, blood- and life-less. Zombies do not show signs of human life inside them nor a marked participation or interest in their environment. These prisoners might as well be dead, since life had lost one of its basic motivators and "they've got nothing to get up for" (Bo). Other prisoners expressed a similar view about love as inherently human. Peter, for example, described it as an organising principle of human societies, stating that "we all hang around in packs still and look after each other" (Peter). He touched on the qualities of love which can enhance human community and organisation as a form of "social glue."

Other prisoners described individual rather than social benefits they enjoyed in return for showing love through helping others. It let them experience themselves in a different context where it was possible to display caring and positive emotions and attitudes. These prisoners particularly enjoyed helping others to do well, to grow and to change emotionally and behaviourally. They described it as a reciprocal process in which one side provided time and expertise to further the other side's development. In return, the helping side experienced their own value, their own potential and their own validation as a human being. This was exemplified by Adam who was working as a volunteer representative for a charity dedicated to setting prisoners up with job opportunities pre- and post-release:

And how does it make you feel, your work?

Quite good, quite good [smiles], human, even warm inside [smiles]. I get up in the morning, and if there is somebody I can help, I feel good … It's not very often, that you can justify your existence. And you're continuously looking for reasons to get up in the mornings … me being able to help break this chain being in and out of prison for other men, it gives me a purpose in life. If you take away all purpose and all reason for life, then the end of that is death …. And this is a reason, a purpose, something for me to do today. (Adam)

For Adam, his involvement in helping others through his work had taken on an existential role. Without a purpose to "justify your existence" (Adam) life would lose meaning and could descend into a downward negative spiral with death at its very end. This resonated with some basic principles outlined in Frankl's (1985) existentialist psychology approach in which he asserts the importance of finding and using meaning for self-transcendence and mental well-being, even if other avenues to do so are blocked. According to Frankl (1985), meaning is more likely to be found through creative activities and attitudes towards others fuelled by self-transcendence rather than actions fuelled by self-interest.

These creative activities could be represented, for example, by creating a poem or portrait for another prisoner who in turn would gift it to a loved one outside. Providing these "services" came with a non-economical but rather emotional gain as pointed out by Tom. What he enjoyed most about drawing portraits for other prisoners was being praised for it. He found it "nice to be appreciated" (Tom). Appreciation was a highly valued "currency" for Tom since he felt that "you don't get much of it in here" (Tom). Ryan likewise expressed that helping others held more value for him than being involved in self-interested activities like committing crime or taking drugs. He had found personal meaning in helping other prisoners to express their emotions through creating drawings with and for them. He encouraged them to address difficult feelings and to connect with loved ones on the outside through visual expression on paper:

> One minute it's about a piece of art, but the next minute they're pouring their heart out to you. That has value because I can directly see that that's helped that person ... It is hard to have that realisation, yeah I've just helped that person ... in here provides you with ... the opportunity to not have to commit crime ... Some people choose to run around, smoke Spice, take drugs. You know, I choose to try and sort my head out a bit. I don't want gratitude for what I'm doing. As long as I have that bit of realisation in my head that's helped that person. (Ryan)

Having a focus on helping others and on positive emotional experiences could broaden horizons. Prisoners such as Ryan and Adam had found an opportunity to foster self-confidence and what might be called self-love. Developmental psychologist Peck (2006), for example, described the extension of one's self in service to others as an act of love not only towards others but simultaneously towards the provider himself. He asserted that "to be dedicated to human ... development is to be dedicated to the race of which we are a part, and this therefore means dedication to our own development as well" (Peck 2006: 70). Transcending their ego-boundaries by extending themselves to other prisoners beyond mere self-interest ("I don't want gratitude for what I'm doing" (Ryan)) had provided Adam and Ryan with an opportunity to practice love as *agape*, as a human virtue, as the choice of a moral agent. Incorporating the concept of human virtue as human means to establish personhood into the set-up and purpose of prison could, in fact, offer a turning towards the realisation of human potential instead of emphasising human deficit.

From a psychological point of view, introducing the provision of love as human need provision may enhance prisoners' mental well-being. For prisoners such as Paul, for example, who did not see himself as human but rather as worthless, an emphasis on a mindset of love might (re-)open a perspective of valuing himself. Apart from individual benefits, focusing on love as the will to abandon immediate self-interest in favour of the communal good might contribute to social coherence by strengthening social ties and potentially dissolving social division within the prison population. How these theoretical and idealistic considerations could be translated into realistic and feasible practice will be critically discussed in the final Chapter 9 of this book.

8.6 Conclusion

This chapter set out to explore some of the interrelations between the prison environment and the expression and perception of prisoners' emotional selves. However, it is important to point out at this stage that the conclusions drawn in this and other chapters have to be considered in light of influencing factors that might have coloured them one way and not another. Firstly, most respondents were part of a specific age bracket (between 29 and 70 years) and had served considerable lengths of time in prison (between 7 and 40 years). Thus, they were supposedly more likely to have reached a stage of maturity and insight leading them towards seeing through most of the performances going on around them as well as being "sick of it" (Frank). It could be speculated that had the interview sample consisted of younger participants, views regarding bravado and other *frontstage* performances might have differed. Secondly, due to research methods only deploying semi-structured interviews but not participant observation, it was not possible to bolster interview accounts about emotional performances with corresponding observations in the environment. Hence prisoners' accounts of their life-world were taken at face value, and theoretical inferences were scrutinised along the way by comparing them with research findings of similarly oriented classic and contemporary prison research.

Most findings support those of earlier studies about factors influencing prisoners' situationally adapted emotional performance. Potent emotions like anger or aggressiveness were largely displayed *frontstage* (Goffman 1959), whereas vulnerable emotions like sadness or grief were mostly released behind closed doors or *backstage* (Goffman 1959). Participants' descriptions of emotion management strategies were also partly related to an effort to conform to *hegemonic* and *hypermasculinity* ideologies which shunned weakness and rewarded toughness. Scrutinising and comparing these ideologies with prisoners' rationale for displaying or acting out emotions like aggression or anger led to the insight that these were not solely motivated by the pressure or will to display an image of *(hyper-)masculinity* but could also be owed to individual psychological and neurological conditioning. Nevertheless, many prisoners of the sample acknowledged that their behaviour and emotion management was still affected by certain expectations and pressures connected to a "code of manliness" they felt bound to.

Being asked to imagine a setting in which authentic emotional expression would be possible, prisoners equipped it with certain qualities of love. In their opinion, creating a prison environment around these benchmarks would be more conducive to emotionally honest self-expression and facilitate a more realistic appraisal by prisoners of personal attributes. The concluding chapter of this book will tie in with this line of thought and consider how an inclusion of love's parameters in the set-up of prison may factually look like.

9. After all, does love matter? — Findings, recommendations and implications

> The whole trouble lies in that people think that there are conditions excluding the necessity of love in their intercourse with man, but such conditions do not exist ... Mutual love is the basic law of human life. True, man cannot compel himself to love, as he can compel himself to work, but it does not follow from this that in his dealings with men he can leave love out of consideration, especially if he wants something from them. (Tolstoy 2011: 421)

Tolstoy's view of love as "the basic law of human life" and as a motivating factor to inspire cooperation from other people "if he wants something from them" echoes this book's explorational endeavour to understand the role of love as a human need and human virtue. It built on the supposition that love is important – in fact crucial – enough to human life and well-being to be included in the academic conversation about the effects of long-term imprisonment.

This concluding chapter will therefore revisit and summarise my findings in relation to my research aims and my contribution to the existing body of knowledge on the role of love in human development as well as the effects and pains of long-term imprisonment. Subsequently, these insights will be used to formulate a critical theory, scrutinising the human costs of love's absence and its related pains in long-term imprisonment. Aiming to inspire practical impact, I will furthermore assess potential future ways to design long-term imprisonment and a prison experience that promotes social-ecological resilience rather than pain by including the qualities of love. Finally, I am going to use the opportunity to sketch out a starting point for a discussion of potential directions for love-, prison- and social research that incorporate a wholistic social-ecological perspective in their disciplinary approach.

9.1 Summary of main findings

The initial bafflement about the perceived absence of the topic of love in an English high-security prison presented itself as a prompt to delve deeper into the lived experience of long-term prisoners and to address a gap in the prison research literature. It was one of the aims of this book to bring the hitherto largely unaddressed undercurrent of long-term prisoners' pains and emotions connected to the absence and presence of love to the forefront of academic discussion. As a preparatory step, however, it was necessary to inquire into the concrete meaning of the abstract concept of love, if it was to be operationalised for empirical research purposes.

This book therefore presents itself as a hybrid of two approaches toward the qualitative exploration of love: Firstly, it seeks to explore how and which of this concept's qualities play an essential role in human life. Secondly, it endeavours to illuminate love's role in specific circumstances, namely in the lives of a small sample of male long-term prisoners in a particular English prison at a particular point in time. It seeks to reveal the effects of love's absence and presence as experienced in the absence and presence of human connection and relationship. The original contribution of this book lies in the synthesis of the above two approaches through their application within a social-ecological framework as well as in addressing love as a standalone topic of prison research. What, then, has this theoretical and empirical exploration of love taught us?

9.1.1 The role of love in human development, behaviour and well-being

One of the most prominent themes to emerge – not only from the theoretical exploration of love in Chapter 3's multidisciplinary concept analysis, but also during empirical data analysis conducted in Chapters 5, 6, 7 and 8 – is that, although a seemingly abstract concept, love's absence as well as presence can have real and tangible consequences. It appears as a dual principle, as a coin with two sides, influencing human existence and well-being either through its absence or its presence.

Findings in neuroscience define love as connective and protective element in the neurobiological predisposition of human beings. As major inter-relational factor love greatly influences human development and human behaviour. Through intimate identification and limbic resonance with another, love broadens our neuronal horizon and enables learning about the other. Love as a sentiment and behavioural addiction can furthermore motivate human action.

Psychological approaches – regarding love predominantly as attachment and as nutrient in early and lifelong human development – point towards the importance of close relationships in human need satisfaction. In its "ideal" form of attachment, love acts as protective factor against dysfunctional psychological coping strategies and in favour of human resilience and growth.

Sociological analysis of the meaning and expression of love brings to the forefront its malleable quality as a concept that structures social and individual relationships. As a mental construct – an idea that can potentially develop into ideology – it is amenable to changes in historical, cultural and political developments in any given society. Its frameworks and rules are vulnerable to reinterpretation, as the example of the rise (and foreshadowed fall) of romantic love illustrates.

Lastly, moral philosophy's ideas provide an understanding of love's role in "the bigger picture." Moral philosophical enquiry illustrates how values and beliefs around love are connected to ethically motivated social and individual life- and identity-choices. As a virtue love is said to promote selfless behaviour and valuing of the other as well as self-transcendence to further another's well-being.

Implementing these theoretical findings in the development of empirical research and data analysis has ultimately led to a better understanding of long-term prisoners' experiences in relation to the absence and presence of love. Tracing love throughout the interview sample's various social-ecological systems, delivered an insight into the effects of love deprivation as well as love provision on development, behaviour and well-being for this specific group.

When it comes to the validity and generalisability of this book's findings, it is important to remember that an interpretation of empirical findings here is based on a small number of 16 semi-structured interviews. These were furthermore conducted under very specific circumstances. A shorter fieldwork phase than hoped for as well as organisational constraints within the specific prison environment have likely impacted on the quality of the data. Although interviews were designed to delve into deeper levels of feelings and perceptions around love, a lack of opportunity to build rapport and trust between researcher and interviewees might have produced accounts that did not go as deeply as hoped for. If this study had been conducted at a different – less stressful – time and incorporated a larger sample, findings might have differed. Frequently checking data analysis against love's operationalised framework, however, aimed to create consistency in findings. Therefore, findings may nevertheless be able to yield insights that can be applied on a more general level. The following section endeavours to summarise main findings and the degrees to which these can be transferred onto a more general level of the human experience of love.

9.1.2 The role of love in the lives of long-term prisoners

Interview questions inquiring into prisoners' perceptions of love and its role in their lives brought to the fore this concept's many objects and practices. It became apparent that love can play different roles, it can be expressed in different ways and relate to different objects of affection. Participants described different kinds of love (e.g. the love for family vs. the love for friends) that were related to variable effects on their well-being. Individually varying perceptions of the quality of love turned out to be inextricably linked to participants' past experiences with early caregivers and in other close relationships. Some interviewees valued the love of friends or of an animal higher than the love of a romantic partner, for example, due to adverse experiences with the latter. These empirical findings reaffirmed the malleability of perceptions of love dependent on the quality of relationships as established by psychology, for example.

Applying these views of love to participants' experiences of long-term imprisonment, utmost attention was paid as to whether an interrelation between the absence of love as one of the pains of long-term imprisonment could be empirically verified. Throughout the course of data analysis, it became apparent that this was the case. Prisoners felt the absence of love to be one of the most stressful and pain-inducing factors pervading their long-term prison experience and life in general.

The loss of close relationships with outside family members and partners presented a source for emotional pain, including grief and distress. This could prompt prisoners to deploy dysfunctional coping mechanisms such as withdrawal and numbing through drug use as self-medication or externalising emotional pain through aggressive and impulsive behaviour towards other prisoners and prison staff. Other findings implied that the effort to uphold close loving outside relationships could place strain on the mental well-being of long-term prisoners and their loved ones. This realisation would sometimes result in the intentional severing of outside ties as an act of love towards either party involved.

A relative absence of love was felt by prisoners also within the prison environment itself. Participants' (almost) unanimously expressed impression of their current life-world was one devoid of opportunities to experience or express love along with other more vulnerable emotions such as sadness or weakness. A commonly deployed defence against these vulnerable emotions was the concept of overemphasised (hyper)-masculinity. These findings chime with themes that have been well established in previous academic work of prison researchers and the prison effects literature (e.g. Richards 1978; Flanagan 1980; Sampson and Laub 1993; Giordano et al. 2002; Brunton-Smith and McCarthy 2016b; Crewe and Laws 2015; Morey and Crewe 2018; Crewe et al. 2020).

This book ultimately wants to use these findings as a stepping-stone to take the inquiry into the effects and pains of imprisonment one step further. It thus inquired into the views of long-term prisoners about whether they thought love mattered in the prison system and if indeed it *should* matter. Findings imply that prisoners would like love to be considered for incorporation into their environment. They echo the theoretical implications of the concept analysis set out in Chapter 3, namely that love as a dual concept continues to play an essential role in prisoners' and more generally human lives. They advocate for certain qualities of love, such as knowing the other intimately, a concern for the other's well-being and overcoming selfish interest, to feature in the prison environment. Long-term prisoners' wish for love to (re-)appear in their lives – especially if they had experienced love deprivation in the past – was expressed clearly. Love continues to matter for prisoners, influencing their outlook on life and how they view other people and themselves. Based on these findings, I will critically (re-)consider the effects of the pains of love deprivation as a "legitimate" part of the long-term prison experience.

9.2 Contributing to a critical theory of the pains and effects of long-term imprisonment

Apart from creating practical impact, this book also endeavours to add to a critical theory of the moral legitimacy of prison regarding the absence and presence of love. In doing so, it follows a path that critical scholars such as Garland (1990), Drake (2012) or Sparks and Bottoms (1995) have already tread by addressing moral issues in criminology. As such it aims to close a gap in the prison research literature that Drake highlighted, when arguing that "moral issues … are an area that still lacks significant critical attention and debate" (Drake 2012: 165). This book seeks to deliver this critical contribution by focusing on the interplay of the prison environment's affective qualities and penological ideologies in relation to its legitimacy.

It has been suggested by scholars such as Garland (1990), Drake (2012) and others that it has been and still is relatively common to condone human costs of the pains of imprisonment – such as mental and physiological health issues – in favour of punishment. These ("invisible") individual and social costs and harms are still largely tolerated today by society in favour of pursuing "other objectives such as retribution, incapacitation, and exclusion" (Garland 1990: 289).

Liebling et al. (2005) likewise acknowledged it might still be the case that these pains may be underestimated due to a missing scale of human suffering. This line of argument gains even more weight considering that the effects of imprisonment will eventually transcend the incarcerated individual's scope of action. They may potentially manifest in long-term prisoners' future interaction with outside society as social maladjustments and problems of relatedness and identity. Being exposed to an environment that stifles "the capacity to build or sustain social connections, can make coping with the demands of everyday life extremely difficult" as argued by Liebling and Maruna (2005: 16). Psychological and emotional adaptations to long-term imprisonment can lead to hypervigilance, the denial of intimacy, withdrawal, self-isolation, the suppression of emotion, avoidance of communication and a distrust of the world (Haney 2003).

Especially regarding long-term imprisonment, it has been found that these adaptations can become "deeply internalised so that, even though surrounding conditions may change, many of the once-functional but ultimately counterproductive patterns remain" (Haney 2003: 39). Whereas research from the 1970s and 1980s (Richards 1978; Coker and Martin 1983; Sapsford 1978, 1983) suggested that long-term prisoners coped and resettled well after an initial period of disorientation and restlessness upon release (Liebling and Maruna 2005) more recent studies contradict these assumptions. Contemporary prison researchers such as Maruna and Liebling extensively discuss the effects of imprisonment in juxtaposition with the "deep freeze" paradigm in their edited volume on *The Effects of Imprisonment Revisited* (2005). Contributions of Jamieson and Grounds (2005), Haney (2005), Irwin and Owen (2005) and King (2005) critically question the idea that prisoners' identities are essentially impervious to the effects of imprisonment (see also Zamble and Porporino 1988), just waiting to be "reactivated" upon release. Liebling and Maruna (2005) take this to be an over-estimation of human resilience and as a "dangerously taken-for-granted assumption in contemporary thinking about prison effects" (Liebling and Maruna 2005: 3). Similarly, other studies conclude that it is indeed more plausible that long years of imprisonment alter a person in profound and enduring ways (Crewe et al. 2020). Grounds (2004) similarly argues that enduring personality change may be the result of prolonged imprisonment and neuroscientific findings on neuronal plasticity and adaptability may further undergird this argument.

As Liebling and Maruna suggest, these long-lasting pains of imprisonment "have not been measured or taken seriously enough by those interested in the question of prison effects" (Liebling and Maruna 2005: 3). They point out that "the first justification for researching prison effects is to lessen the pains suffered by prisoners" (Liebling and Maruna 2005: 21). They furthermore refer to the work of Zamble and Porporino who argue that "in order to be sound and reasonable, the design and operation of prisons should be based not on any particular theory or ideology, but on some fundamental understanding of how imprisonment affects individuals" (Zamble and Porporino 1988: 2). It might, in fact, still be the case that "the public, and many of those who work in and manage prisons, may underestimate how painful the prison experience is" (Liebling et al. 2005: 224).

In a similar vein, the frequency of self-directed violence and harm calls the ability for prisons to deliver a sufficient duty of care into question. It also constitutes a challenge to the legitimacy of prison as Liebling had already warned in 2007, affirming that "if prisons are to be more rather than less legitimate, they should not be places, that prisoners cannot endure" (Liebling 2007: 443). This book therefore not only addresses a gap in prison effects literature related to love, but also continues the work of scholars such as Drake or Liebling by asking "to what extent experiences of imprisonment fulfil the supposed or official purposes of prisons as a social institution" (Drake 2012: 77) and to what extent these are linked to broader moral and social issues?

Addressing these moral and social issues has been a main motivator and driver of my work in general and this book in particular. I aimed to make these personal normative, ideological and philosophical orientations as transparent as possible from the outset. As such, this book clearly argues in favour of curtailing institutional, political and economic investment into a punitive prison environment. Taking findings of Crewe et al. (2020) on the effects of long-term imprisonment into account, it still is (and perhaps becoming even more) important to consider the corroborating effects on the individual of sustained exposure to pains and other negative environmental influences. Given the fact that the prison system in England and Wales finds itself (still) in an alarming state of rising human costs such as suicide, self-harm and violent assaults (e.g. Bulman 2018) this book's appeal to (re)consider love as human need and human virtue in its set-up suggests nothing less than a paradigm shift.

Practical recommendations and theoretical implications will thus emanate from a critical theory paradigm, promoting a "'zemiological' or social harms perspective" (Yar 2012: 56). Ultimately, this contribution formulates a critical challenge to "forms of harm that emerge from dominant patterns of social, economic ... and cultural practices" (Yar 2012: 56) and instead vouches for "the broader pursuit of social justice" (Yar 2012: 56). The institutional deprivation of human needs and virtues such as love could even represent a case of social injustice, since it curtails a person's moral agency. It may lead to an individual's resistance to a perceived injustice towards his or her person. As argued by Tillich in his contemplations on the interrelation of *Love, Power, and Justice* (1954):

> The "thou" demands by his very existence to be acknowledged ... as an "ego" for himself. This is the claim which is implied in his being. Man can refuse to listen to the intrinsic claim of the other one. He can disregard his demand for justice. He can remove or use him. He can try to transform him into a manageable object, a thing, a tool. But in doing so he meets the resistance of him who has the claim to be acknowledged as an ego. (Tillich 1954: 78)

Tillich's statement points towards the same type of legitimacy that Sparks and Bottoms (1995) as well as Tolstoy (2011) were alluding to. It contains the attribute of love as the recognition of a person for his or her intrinsic value and humanity rather than classifying his or her way of being a priori as in need of improvement and reformation. It includes the recognition of both, human needs and human virtues, of defeat and victory, of failure and success. Similarly, moral philosopher Smith cautions us to not forget that "human life is not a simple story of smooth and happy fulfilment of moral imperatives" (Smith 2003: 29), but that it includes struggles and resistance to those imperatives as well. Hence adopting a wholistic view of incarcerated individuals as human bearers of contradiction, suffering from exclusion (from society, from love, from moral agency) but also representing a potential threat to those they have been excluded from would invite a social-ecological perspective that considers individual, micro-, meso-, exo- and macrosystemic harm patterns. A social-ecological perspective (Bronfenbrenner 1974) could also identify potential means to create resilience and reparation of harm within parameters of security, safety and practical feasibility. Only if patterns of deprivation and harm can be identified on all levels of human development, will it be possible to cater towards a multi-level ramification. Prison as an institution only represents one level of intervention and can only operate within its own limits.

"Of course," as Toch reminds us, a "prison setting has to try to survive, but the real point of the endeavour must be to demonstrate that it can effectively contribute to the common good" (Toch 2006: 8). He connects the purpose of prison not only to the direct interaction with and provision for those exposed to it but also locates it in an exo- and macrosystemic context of creating social capital and contributing to the common good. If "the common good" was translated into keeping human costs of suffering to a minimum, and creating prosperity in individuals and society at large, it would also imply that the role of state institutions such as prison would have to be adjusted around these claims. Applying this argument of critical theory onto the life-world of long-term prisoners, necessarily leads to questions of practicality which will be addressed in the following.

9.3 Reducing pain and enhancing resilience in the long-term prison experience

Looking at the adverse effects of love deprivation in participants' social-ecological systems, it becomes apparent that those can indeed be seen as health risks. Being exposed to the absence of love in its extreme forms of violence, abuse and trauma exerts severe stress on the human organism and can lead to long-term mental and physiological health implications. Having accentuated and carved out the same factors as main stressors for long-term prisoners of the sample in their current prison experience, it remains to ask how a stressful and depriving environment like prison could be designed to not be a place, prisoners cannot endure (Liebling 2007)?

Looking at love's previously discussed role as potential resilience factor counteracting deprivation effects not only in prisoners' microsystemic but also exosystemic environments, suggests that reconsidering the set-up and purpose of prison from a social-ecological health and resilience perspective could yield some benefits. Developing interventions seeking to reduce stress and adversity in human social-ecological systems and to promote resilience instead could not only benefit the individual but generate returns for society at large (Shonkoff and Garner 2012). Social and economic costs of toxic stress over the lifespan do not stop at the individual's microsystem but ripple out into relations outside of his or her inner circle. As this book has discussed, love deprivation and witnessing domestic violence, for example, can induce a cycle of intergenerational violence affecting whole families, establishing patterns of violent behaviour, leading to incarceration and potentially causing trauma for victims outside of the domestic circle. Ultimately, the effects of toxic stress, induced by love deprivation, can transcend the microsystemic psychological realm and manifest as social and economic costs. The following recommendations consequently emanate from asking the following question: What could be achieved if prison operated under a resilience and health-based scheme instead of (mostly) following an incapacitation approach geared predominantly towards offenders' exile from society?

9.4 Including the qualities of love in the long-term prison experience

Developing practical suggestions for an implementation of the qualities of love in long-term imprisonment will proceed from the basic assumption – derived from empirical data analysis – that the experience of disconnection from love found in outside microsystemic relationships is indeed experienced as most painful by prisoners of the sample. It also departs from the assumption that love relationships of a certain quality (i.e. non-abusive and inspired by love as mutual concern for the other's well-being) exert benefits and can act as a resilience factor in incarcerated individuals' lives. These assumptions will be taken as the basis for considering potential avenues for love-provision in the long-term prison experience in the English penal system.

9.4.1 Love-provision through microsystemic outside connections

Reviewing opportunities for love and connection available to English long-term prisoners and their outside relationships suggests that the provision of quality contact is currently limited due to practical considerations of security and a lack of institutional (staff and time) resources. Looking outside of the English jurisdiction, however, it becomes clear that other countries have decided to take a different approach to the provision of privacy and family contact.

One example is the provision of conjugal or private visits which are not permitted in England and Wales but which are a regular practice in other European countries and in certain US-states. As pointed out by Scott and Codd, conjugal visits provided in private facilities "allow for a kind of relaxed intimacy which is not possible under the constant surveillance of officers in the visits room" (Scott and Codd 2010: 153). Portugal, for example, provides the opportunity for prisoners and their families to make use of extended family visits every three months (subject to risk assessment) which are seen as particularly important for long-term prisoners. The Department of Corrections runs Family Reunion Programs in the US-states of New York and California. These are overnight visits taking place in mobile homes within prison perimeters (Fair and Jacobson 2016).

Special emphasis on maintaining bonds between incarcerated parents and their children is part of several prison regimes in New York, for example, where an initiative has introduced "tele-visiting" for children not able to visit their parents in person (Fair and Jacobson 2016). Northern Ireland has taken this arrangement as an inspiration to establish their own virtual video visiting system. It has meanwhile been established in all Northern Ireland prison establishments. It supports "face-to-face visits by giving those in custody the chance to 'visit' the home environment and see their family and loved ones in their environment" (Fair and Jacobson 2016: 8). Strengthening family and other relational ties qualitatively could be furthered in these ways without compromising security. Creating opportunities for love by means of physical as well as psychological closeness (e.g. intimate physical encounters, reading, cooking or sharing other family activities together) may facilitate intimate knowledge about the other. Aspects of emotional attachment such as "showing an active interest in one another" (Ungar et al. 2013: 352) in turn could foster the resilience of families and prisoners.

Especially in an environmental context of significant adversity such as prison, fostering resilience through relationships may enable prisoners as well as their family members to access "psychological, social, cultural, and physical resources that sustain their well-being" (Ungar 2013: 225). As much as these outside resources could foster resilience, they could nevertheless also be riddled with uncertainty, especially for long-term prisoners. Seeing outside relationships vanish over decades of incarceration often seems unavoidable despite best institutional efforts. Apart from penal reforms focused on a reduction of sentence lengths and a swift processing of long-term prisoners "stuck" in the prison system, there are currently not many ways to avoid this effect. The question therefore remains what else could be done in the English prison system to reduce the pains of long-term imprisonment related to the absence of love? A more immediate approach towards the inclusion of love's parameters could focus on changes within the environment itself.

9.4.2 Love-provision through microsystemic connections inside prison

A recent and fitting example which could be directly used to rethink the set-up and purpose of long-term imprisonment can be found in the relatively newly established Psychologically Informed Planned Environments (PIPEs). They form a key part of the offender Personality Disorder (PD) strategy introduced by the Department of Health (DH) and NOMS in 2011 for England and Wales. These contained environments operate as separate units or wings within "conventional" prison establishments and are run as a pilot scheme in a small number of prisons and approved premises throughout England. Departing from the idea of "advantaged environments" (Ungar et al. 2013) PIPEs fit with this approach. They are specifically designed as "enabling environments" that aim to facilitate the development of those who live there and "actively recognise the importance and quality of relationships and interactions" (Turley et al. 2013: 2). In this context, they reflect some of the previously discussed and advocated features of a stance towards imprisonment that incorporates a social-ecological as well as a relational and health perspective. According to NOMS and DH (2011), PIPEs' core focus lies on the quality of staff prisoner and intra-prisoner relationships as well as on providing specific psychological training to its staff.

Not only does this imply the importance of relationships per se, but it also underlines the importance of a well-resourced and psychologically trained custodial staff force. This resource is currently mostly underused (and even undermined) through staffing cuts motivated by economic austerity measures. In his considerations of a future for humane imprisonment, Toch (2006) likewise stresses the (often missed) opportunity to integrate and value staff as a crucial factor in offender treatment. Especially considering their practical experience on "the front-line of prisons on a 24/7 basis" (Toch 2006: 8) prison officers could make their way back to the centre of attention as a valued resource for creating meaningful relationships. This inclusion and valuing of prison officers is actively practiced in PIPE units. Prisoners report that they feel it supports their development and progress as well as a positive atmosphere on the wing. This is sought to be achieved by "staff looking to understand offenders' challenging behaviour and address underlying meaning and issues; an emphasis on respectful communication … staff spending time with prisoners … informally … and accommodating their ideas and suggestions" (Turley et al. 2013: 3).

Keywords such as *understanding, communication, spending time together informally* and acknowledging prisoners' individual ideas and contributions all relate to the vocabulary of love as determined previously. More specifically, these relate to the concepts of (inter-)personal *valuing* and *intimate knowledge* about the other. When it comes to the qualities of the relationships between staff and prisoners in PIPE units, prisoners are particularly positive about these "where staff were open, honest, non-judgmental and shared their own experiences" (Turley et al. 2013: 4). Again, the parameters of love such as a mutual sharing of personal truths as a prerequisite for *philia* were appreciated as positive and enhancing features, as well as ultimately enabling staff to challenge prisoners about problematic behaviour (Turley et al. 2013). Simultaneously Turley et al. (2013) reported improved relationships between prisoners, a recognition when others needed support, as well as less bullying (Turley et al. 2013). It is important to be aware, however, that the success of this model depends heavily on staff resources as well as on staff "buying into" PIPE's philosophy and values. Channelling more economic and training resources towards custodial staff could therefore address systemic issues lying at the root of conflictual relationships and environments (Hamric et al. 2015).

Going back to the creation of enabling or advantaged prison environments, Toch (2006) describes such environments as settings that ideally "should be able to consistently support the personal development of its residents" (Toch 2006: 8), thus also reiterating a key orientation of PIPE units. Gilligan (2015) delivers a similar recommendation for prison reform. He advocates the introduction of "a new system based on a new paradigm for preventing violence, based on applying psychoanalytic principles ... rather than ... inflicting pain ... in order to achieve 'retributive justice'" (Gilligan 2015: 146). The theoretical and practical structure of such an alternative prison experience in relation to the inclusion of love's qualities through therapeutic relationships will now be discussed in more detail.

9.4.3 Love-provision in microsystemic therapeutic encounters

In his *Modest Proposal to Universalize the Insanity Defense and Replace Prisons and Punishment with Treatment and Education*, Gilligan (2015: 147) advocates for "a human development center" with enabling features similar to the PIPE model or those underlying Therapeutic Communities introduced earlier. He argues for a recognition of the suffering of those who caused suffering to others. In Gilligan's view "physical, emotional and cognitive abuse and deprivation" (Gilligan 2015: 147) experiences in the past may prevent some prisoners from "achieving the degree of healthy, life-sustaining development ... that are prerequisites for the ability to respect, care for and love others" (Gilligan 2015: 147). This book's analysis paints a similar picture, namely that those who had suffered love's absence in the form of deprivation, domestic violence and abuse in earlier life, now represent a significant proportion of the male English prison population. The painfully experienced absence of love featured as a prominent storyline in prisoners' interviews. So did the wish to escape and change these trajectories of lack and deprivation, the wish to experience the presence of love. Trauma as the sudden disconnection of human attachment had been frequent in prisoners' lives occurring prior to and inside prison. Therefore, scholars such as Kupers argue that special attention should be paid to these factors and that "given the omnipresence of trauma in prisoners' lives, education about and treatment ... needs to be readily available" (Kupers 2006: 15).

Seeing trauma as human disconnection and the absence of love, the presence of love can act as a (re-)connector of ruptured ties. Findings in psychology and neuroscience document an empirical, tangible manifestation of this theoretical claim. Psychologist Peck, for example, relates successful outcomes in psychotherapy not to anything insubstantial such as "magical words, techniques or postures but rather to human involvement and struggle ... the willingness of the therapist to extend him- or herself for the purpose of nurturing the patient's growth" (Peck 2006). These qualities of love can be retrieved in Chapter 3's concept analysis and are likewise taken up by Peck (2006: 161) who asserts that "the essential ingredient of successful deep and meaningful psychotherapy is love." In their extensive neuroscientific examination of love, Lewis et al. (2000) come to a similar conclusion. Findings delivered by imaging technologies imply "that psychotherapy alters the living brain" (Lewis et al. 2000: 168) through therapeutic somatic relatedness. Describing the process, goals and effectiveness of psychotherapy Lewis et al. reiterate some of the qualities of love that have reappeared throughout this book. They state that knowing someone was the first goal of therapy. The second goal centres on balancing or "modulating emotionality ... by relatedness" (Lewis et al. 2000: 176). Thirdly, they perceive therapy's most ambitious aim to lie in "revising the neural code that directs an emotional life" (Lewis et al. 2000: 176).

The themes of intimate knowledge and the power to change an individual's outlook and behaviour have emerged as two of the main qualities of love in Chapter 3's concept analysis. The latter alludes to the neuroplasticity of the human brain as a prerequisite for change. The power of love as psychotherapy lies in the neurological fact that the limbic region of mammalian brains can be restructured by attuning to the limbic brain of another (Lewis et al. 2000; Hüther 2006). "When a limbic connection has established a neural pattern, it takes a limbic connection to revise it" (Lewis et al. 2000: 177). In other words: only love can change what love (or attachment and rupture, human connection and disconnection) has created. In turn, prisoners who find themselves on the receiving end of the negative effects of early love deprivation – toxic stress, abuse and violence – would likely benefit from individual psychotherapy to ameliorate these effects, thus working towards mental and physical well-being. However, as an act of self-love of a moral agent, I would like to suggest that entering into psychotherapy has to be voluntary, not generically administered as an institutional moral rehabilitation imperative or as "coercive caring" (Bottoms 1980: 20). How the above theoretical discussion might ultimately be translated into practical implementation will be outlined in the following.

9.4.4 Summary of practice recommendations

I would like to take the above theoretical propositions as the final building block to reinforce my recommendations for redesigning the long-term prison experience. I would like to argue in favour of an incorporation of the qualities of love, i.e. human connection, intimate knowledge, valuing of the person, human virtue and moral agency into a social-ecological framework for designing and evaluating institutional practice and legitimacy. Practical suggestions will therefore aim to include these theoretical parameters. They depart from earlier discussed national and international best-practice examples and converge in the following recommendations:

1) Preserving microsystemic outside relationships by creating opportunities for high-quality interaction between long-term prisoners and their families and partners, for example, by providing conjugal or extended visits arrangements catering for privacy and intimacy.

2) Providing resilience factors through strengthening prisoners' bonds with children and family members through meaningful ways of free – or at least affordable – communication (e.g. tele-visiting, affordable or free phone calls).

3) Lowering toxic stress and deprivation levels inside prison by creating "advantaged environments" or "enabling environments" similar to PIPE units, adopting a health- and resilience-centred approach. This could include the provision of psychologically informed staff training, as well as investing in a well-resourced staff force.

4) Enhancing staff-prisoner and intra-prisoner relationships through the creation of "spaces for encounter" in a physical and symbolical way. These could depart from PIPE's example of sharing informal time and information (within security parameters) over, for example, a cup of tea or coffee in physical spaces designed specifically to enhance feelings of safety and intimacy.

5) Catering to prisoners' wishes to perform love as human virtue as moral agents. This could result in providing opportunities for being emotionally honest and acknowledging individual strengths and weaknesses. One avenue towards the realisation of this goal could be through the provision of (confidential) therapeutic encounters. Inspiration and best practice examples can be taken from Therapeutic Communities such as HMP Grendon and PIPE units.

6) Another avenue for catering to love as human virtue could be informed by individual prisoners themselves. Taking inspiration from those prisoners of the sample engaged in voluntary charity or personal support work, resilience could be enhanced by providing prisoners (who wish to embark on this endeavour) with the opportunity to create an alternative identity through their preferred way of "showing love" to fellow prisoners or to a good cause. Furthermore, these acts of love should be recognised in prisoners' risk assessments and sentence progression reports.

7) Related to the above-mentioned risk assessments, this book would like to suggest the following thought experiment: Considering love as intimate knowledge and the negative consequences of emotional suppression, I would like to suggest an amended way of risk assessments that acknowledge the "truth" of an individual. These assessments would likely

act as "safe spaces" for sharing stories of relapse or "risky behaviour" as well as success stories of (self-)loving behaviour. It could be used to create a multi-dimensional, wholistic profile of offenders that value the person as a whole.

Taking these recommendations for reform of the long-term (but also general) prison experience on board could yield several benefits. From a social-ecological perspective, it could contribute to individual, social and institutional enhancement of (mental) health, human capital and human growth. It could furthermore support a decrease of the human costs of violence, mental and physical illness, trauma and pain. These changes could come at a cost, however: A careful weighing up of security issues as well as the recognition of crime victims' needs is necessary, when considering these implementations. It would also require an economic investment in human resources which would have to be carefully considered against effective economic budgets. I would nevertheless like to encourage a critical political and public discussion of the ratio between economic costs and human costs. What this could look like for future academic scholarship will be outlined in the final discussion of this book.

9.5 Conclusion and outlook — Love's role in prison research as human science

By adopting a social-ecological wholistic view of the individual in relation to his or her environment, this book aims to contribute an additional perspective to the prison effects literature. Although Toch (1992) already deployed an ecological framework studying long-term prisoners' adaptation strategies, this study hopes to develop this framework further. Especially love's qualities as a virtue, motivating power and resilience factor in human development can be taken as a starting point to consider potential changes in the set-up and purpose of the long-term prison experience. Whilst considering the risks of leaving love *out* of consideration (Tolstoy 2011), a new perspective opens up that includes love *in* the conversation. Looking at prisons through an affective lens may contribute to a change in cultural and political perceptions and values towards a more wholistic view of the offender as an emotional human being and of prison as moral practice in relation to that. This approach follows what Drake (2012) has pointed out as one of the responsibilities of criminologists as commentators on social problems and dominant ideologies, namely to challenge and to question with a view to improve the current state of human affairs.

In taking up the critical discussion and challenging afresh the idea of a state, culture or society that does not seem to consider human needs (such as love) satisfaction as one of its guiding principles, this book also hopes to contribute to a broadening of scientific interest and dialogue. As such, it not only argues for an expansion of a criminological research focus towards the affective dimensions of its subject. It also vouches for an extension of research realms in the social and political sciences. These partially still "neglect love relations, concentrating instead on the political relations of the state, the economic relations of the market, and the cultural relations" (Cantillon and Lynch 2017: 172) as governing forces of social and human life. It is hence an additional motivation of mine to inspire alternative thought processes and to re-evaluate love as a guiding principle for those human relations which have previously been allocated to the realm of economic, political and utility thinking.

Some of this work has already been done. Important examples can be found in the oeuvre of feminist scholars such as Gilligan (1982; 1995), Tronto (1987; 1993), Okin (1989), Nussbaum (1995), Sevenhuijsen (1998), Kittay (1999), hooks (2000) or Fineman (2004) who take the concepts of care and love out of the privatised sphere. They draw "attention to the salience of care and love as public goods, and ... identify the importance of caring as a human capability meeting a basic human need" (Cantillon and Lynch 2017: 171). In this sense, feminism denominates love as a political matter necessitating that the state creates infrastructures for love labour to produce "the nurturing capital that enables people to flourish" (Cantillon and Lynch 2017: 178). Feminist scholars in fact advocate for public policies "to be directed by norms of love" (Cantillon and Lynch 2017: 169). Love research could therefore play a bigger role as social and human science expanding research agendas towards relationships outside of the private microsystemic realm (e.g. families or romantic relationships) to include exo- and macrosystemic relationships between individuals and institutions as well as within society itself.

Multidisciplinary research co-operations could be created that examine love as a parameter for exosystemic and macrosystemic matters of social justice or public health. Thus, social-ecological benefits could be achieved by creating more wholistic and more sustainable human environments that stimulate human growth and development. Social-ecological spheres do not exist isolated from each other but can exert ripple effects all the way from macrosystemic and exosystemic levels through to the neuro-biological set-up of human beings (and vice versa). Neuroscientific research into brain plasticity and adaptability has shown, for example, that interrelations exist between the emotional climate and culture a state or a society promotes and the microsystemic relations that are conducted under those premises. These in turn have effects on the internal state of individuals, either contributing to mental well-being and balance or to toxic stress and mental imbalance. This is predominantly due to the way the human brain has developed in the course of evolution. As explained by Lewis et al. (2000), the dependency on others for limbic resonance "chains mammals to a certain emotional climate" (Lewis et al. 2000: 197). A climate that provides opportunities for love is necessary for mental and emotional health, which "some cultures encourage ... others do not" (Lewis et al. 2000: 197). From a social-ecological perspective, it matters how love as human need is provided throughout all systems the individual is exposed to. These systems are interdependent and interactional. It is thus important to think holistically and to keep in mind that "humanity's limbic ties make any social structure a web of interdependencies" (Lewis et al. 2000: 204).

After all, the social-ecological approach is also suited to follow what is deemed as the ultimate purpose of critical theory: producing an inter- and multidisciplinary critical social theory "aiming to diagnose perils and potentials of the present" (Zurn 2015: 15). As an overarching aim, this book hopes to contribute to social change. It adopts critical theorist Honneth's (1995) view of social analysis as a means for identifying pathologies and within them opportunities for change. In the same vein, my research commits itself to using its empirical findings to formulate a social critique of the status quo based on normative standards and a moral standpoint (Honneth 1995). I am of the conviction that this study's focus ultimately has to expand beyond an endeavour to achieve specialist academic insight but instead to also aim at contributing to a critical theory, oriented towards creating impact for the greater good.

Superimposing this approach onto the field of prison research and, more specifically, the set-up and purpose of the long-term prison experience, however, appears by no means a straightforward task. As this book has argued, academic knowledge about the harms and deprivations of the prison environment reaches back more than half a century. Yet it seems that the same problems and harms persist. A few questions arising from this research therefore would likely have to address the matter of *omission*: What are we (as a society but also individual agents) deciding to ignore when it comes to the human costs of imprisonment, and why do we continue to do so? What are we not prepared to give up or to give to create more just institutions and ultimately more just societies? Which work needs to be done that we have convinced ourselves is impossible or unacceptable to even consider, let alone to start? Is it, for example, possible to consider the absence and presence of love not only as individual failure and responsibility of mother and father but as a social one, and what benefits could this have? These and other questions could be addressed in the future by criminological as well as multidisciplinary scholars.

What my exploration of the role of love in the lives of long-term prisoners would like to ultimately encourage, is a continued inquiry into opportunities for reform we have not explored yet (or which might have sunken into oblivion). It should be regarded as a critical thinking exercise. Especially when it comes to questioning implicit agreements within social and political systems about the moral, social and cultural architecture of state institutions, it is important to keep academic attention "onto such issues of power, authority and complex rationalities, which allows us to ask difficult questions" (Cote and Nightingale 2012: 485).

Addendum

In light of current global developments, it is important to keep in mind that all fieldwork, data analysis and recommendations relate to a pre-Covid19 world. Since then, a lot of changes have been implemented (sometimes forced) on our relationships. The same holds true for prisoners' relationships with the outside. Visits have been suspended and prison regimes have been drastically changed to accommodate social distancing regulations, trying to prevent an exponential spread of the virus. Hence, it is fair to say that recommendations in this book would only be able to come to fruition in a post-Covid19 regime, whenever this may be…

Bibliography

Albertse, L. (2007). *Gang Members' Experiences of Victimization and Perpetration of Rape in Prison.* University of the Western Cape Faculty of Community and Health Sciences. [online] Available at: https://core.ac.uk/download/pdf/58913217.pdf [Accessed 01/07/2020]

Alcoholics Anonymous Minnesota (2009) *Phrases, Acronyms and Clichés of A.A.* [online] Available at: http://www.minnesotarecovery.info/literature/phrases.htm [Accessed 10/02/2020]

Annas, J. (1988). Self-Love in Aristotle. *Southern Journal of Philosophy,* 27, pp. 1-18.

Ansbro, M. (2008). Using Attachment Theory with Offenders. *Probation Journal-The Journal of Community and Criminal Justice,* 55(3), pp. 231–244.

Archer, J. (1994). *Male Violence.* London: Routledge.

Armstrong, J. (2002). *Conditions of Love - The Philosophy of Intimacy.* London: Penguin Books.

Arnold, H. (2005). The Effects of Prison Work. In A. Liebling and S. Maruna (eds.), *The Effects of Imprisonment.* Cullompton: Willan Publishing, pp. 391-420.

Badiou, A. (2009). *In Praise of Love.* New York: The New Press.

Baker, S. E. and Edwards, R. (2012). How Many Qualitative Interviews is Enough? Expert Voices and Early Career Reflections on Sampling and Cases in Qualitative Research. Southampton: National Centre for Research Methods.

Bandura, A., Ross, D. and Ross, S. A. (1963). Imitation of Film-Mediated Aggressive Models. *Journal of Abnormal and Social Psychology, 66,* pp. 3-11.

Bartels, A. and Zeki, S. (2000). The Neural Basis of Romantic Love. *Neurological Report,* 11(1), pp. 1-6.

Becker, H. (1967). Whose Side Are We On? *Social Problems,* 14(3), pp. 234-247.

Bennett, J., Crewe, B. and Wahidin, A. (eds.) (2008). *Understanding Prison Staff.* Cullompton: Willan Publishing

Bennett, J. (2015). The working lives of prison managers: Global change, local cultures and individual agency in the late modern prison. Basingstoke: Palgrave MacMillan.

Bennett, J. and Shuker, R. (2017). The potential of prison-based democratic therapeutic communities, International Journal of Prisoner Health, 13(1), pp. 19-24.

Berridge, D. and Brodie, I. (1998). *Children's Homes Revisited.* London, PA: Jessica Kingsley.

Beyens, K., Kennes, P., Snacken, S. and Tournel, H. (2015). The Craft of Doing Qualitative Research in Prisons. *International Journal for Crime, Justice and Social Democracy,* 4(1), pp. 66-78.

Blackash, R. (2015). Expressions of Male-to-Male Intimacy in a UK Prison (and What we Might Learn From Them). *Journal of Prisoners on Prisons, 24*(1), pp. 55–64.

Bloor, M. J. (2011). Addressing Social Problems Through Qualitative Research. In: D. Silverman (ed.), *Qualitative Research.* London: SAGE Publications Ltd., pp. 305-324.

Bohman, J. (2005). *Critical Theory. Stanford Encyclopaedia of Philosophy.* [online] Available at: https://plato.stanford.edu/entries/critical-theory/#3 [Accessed 10/06/2020].

Bonanno, G.A., Westphal, M. and Mancini, A.D. (2011). Resilience to Loss and Potential Trauma. *Annual Review of Clinical Psychology,* 7, pp. 511–535.

Boswell, G. (1998). Research-minded Practice with Young Offenders who Commit Grave Crimes. *Probation Journal,* 45, pp: 202–97.

Bottoms, A. E. (1980). An Introduction to The Coming Crisis. In: A. E. Bottoms and R. H. Preston (eds.), *The Coming Penal Crisis: A Criminological and Theological Exploration.* Edinburgh: Scottish Academic Press.

Bowker, L. (1998). *Masculinities and Violence.* Thousand Oaks, CA: SAGE Publications.

Bowlby, J. (1973). *Attachment and Loss. Vol. II: Separation: Anxiety and Anger.* London: Hogarth Press.

Brickel, C. M. (1986). Pet Facilitated Therapies: A Review of the Literature and Clinical Implementation Considerations. *Clinical Gerontology,* 5, pp. 309–332.

British Society of Criminology (BSC). (2006). *Code of Ethics PDF.* [online] Available at: http://www.britsoccrim.org/docs/CodeofEthics.pdf [Accessed 15/08/2018]

Broekaert, E., Vanderplasschen, W., Temmerman, I., Ottenberg, D.J. and Kaplan, C. (2000) Retrospective study of similarities and relations between American drug-free and European therapeutic communities for children and adults. *Journal of Psychoactive Drugs,* 32, pp. 407-417.

Bronfenbrenner, U. (1974). Developmental Research, Public Policy, and the Ecology of Childhood. *Child Development,* 45, pp. 1–5.

Bronfenbrenner, U. (1976). The Experimental Ecology of Education. *Teachers College Record,* 78, pp. 157–204.

Bronfenbrenner, U. (1977). The Ecology of Human Development in Retrospect and Prospect. In: H. McGurk (ed.), *Ecological Factors in Human Development.* Amsterdam: North Holland, pp. 275–286.

Bronfenbrenner, U. (1979). *The Ecology of Human Development: Experiments by Nature and Design.* Cambridge, MA: Harvard University Press.

Brooks, H. L., Rushton, K., Lovell, K., Bee, P., Walker, L., Grant, L. and Rogers, A. (2018). The Power of Support from Companion Animals for People Living with Mental Health Problems: A Systematic Review and Narrative Synthesis of the Evidence. *BMC Psychiatry,* 18(31), pp. 1-12.

Brown, B. (2007). *I Thought it was just me (but it isn't).* New York: Gotham Books.

Brown G. and Grant P. (2018). Hear Our Voices: We're More than the Hyper-Masculine Label—Reasonings of Black Men Participating in a Faith-Based Prison Programme. In: Maycock M. and Hunt K. (eds.), *New Perspectives on Prison Masculinities.* London: Palgrave Macmillan.

Brunton-Smith, I. and McCarthy, D. J. (2016a). Prison Legitimacy and Procedural Fairness: A Multilevel Examination of Prisoners in England and Wales. *Justice Quarterly,* 33(6), pp. 1029-1054.

Brunton-Smith, I. and McCarthy, D. J. (2016b) The Effects of Prisoner Attachment to Family on Re-entry Outcomes: A Longitudinal Assessment, *The British Journal of Criminology,* 57(2), pp. 463–482.

Brussoni, M. J. and Boon, S. (1998). Grandparental Impact in Young Adults' Relationships with their Closest Grandparents: The Role of Relationship Strength and Emotional Closeness. *International Journal of Aging and Human Development*, 46, pp. 267–288.

Buber, M. (1970). *I and Thou*. New York: Scribner's.

Bulman, M. (2018). *Violence and Self-Injury in Prisons hit Highest Levels on Record, Figures Show*. The Independent. [online] Available at:https://www.independent.co.uk/news/uk/home-news/prison-violence-self-injury-uk-highest-level-record-inmates-figures-hmp-liverpool-nottingham-a8177286.html [Accessed 02/09/2018]

Burkett, J. P. and Young, L. J. (2012). The Behavioral, Anatomical and Pharmacological Parallels Between Social Attachment, Love and Addiction. *Psychopharmacology*, 224(1), pp. 1–26.

Cantillon, S. and Lynch, K. (2017). Affective Equality: Love Matters. *Hypatia*, 32(1), pp. 169-186.

Christie, N. (1981). *Limits to Pain*. Oxford: Martin Robertson.

Clemmer, D. (1940). *The prison community*. New York, NY: Holt, Rinehart and Winston.

Clinks Event Report (2016). Supporting Positive Relationships Between Prisoners and their Families.Clinks [online] Available at: http://www.clinks.org/sites/default/files/basic/files-downloads/event_report__supporting_positive_relationships_between_prisoners_and_their_families.pdf [Accessed 02/09/2018]

Coffey, A. and Atkinson, P. (1996). *Making Sense of Qualitative Data*. London: Sage Publications.

Cohen, S. and Taylor, L. (1972). Psychological Survival. The Experience of Long Term Imprisonment. Middlesex: Penguin Books.

Coker, J. and Martin, J. P. (1983) *Licensed to Live*. Oxford: Blackwell.

Comfort, M. (2008). *Doing Time Together: Love and Family in the Shadow of the Prison*. Chicago: University of Chicago Press.

Comstock, G. (1991). *Violence Against Lesbians and Gay Men*. New York: Columbia University Press.

Condry, R. (2007). Families shamed: the consequences of crime for relatives of serious offenders. Crime ethnography series. Cullompton: Willan Publishing.

Conn, W. E. (1998). Self-Transcendence, the True Self, and Self-Love. *Pastoral Psychology*, 46(5), pp. 323-332.

Connell, R. W. (2000). *The Men and the Boys*. Cambridge: Polity Press.

Connell, R. W. and Messerschmidt, J. W. (2005). Hegemonic Masculinity. Rethinking the Concept. *Gender and Society*, 19(6), pp. 829-859.

Cote, M., Nightingale, A. J. (2012). Resilience Thinking Meets Social Theory: Situating Social Change in Socio-Ecological Systems (SES) Research. *Progress in Human Geography*, 36(4), pp. 475–489.

Crawley, E. (2004). *Doing Prison Work: The Public and Private Lives of Prison Officers*. Cullompton: Willan Publishing.

Crawley, E. and Sparks, R. (2006). Is There Life after Imprisonment? How Elderly Men Talk about Imprisonment and Release. *Criminology and Criminal Justice*, 6, pp. 63–82.

Crewe, B. (2009). The Prisoner Society. Power, Adaptation and Social Life in an English Prison. Oxford: Oxford University Press.

Crewe, B. (2011). Depth, Weight, Tightness: Revisiting the Pains of Imprisonment. *Punishment & Society*, 13(5), pp. 509–529.

Crewe, B., and Bennett, J. (eds.) (2012). *The Prisoner*. Abingdon: Routledge.

Crewe, B. (2014). Not Looking Hard Enough: Masculinity, Emotion, and Prison Research. *Qualitative Inquiry*, 20(4), pp. 392–403.

Crewe, B., Warr, J., Bennett, P. and Smith A. (2014). The emotional geography of prison life. *Theoretical Criminology*, 18(1), pp. 56–74.

Crewe, B. and Laws, B. (2015). Emotion Regulation Among Male Prisoners. *Theoretical Criminology*, 20(4), pp. 529-547.

Crewe, B., Hulley, S. and Wright, S. (2020). *Life Imprisonment from Young Adulthood Adaptation, Identity and Time*. Basingstoke: Palgrave Macmillan.

Crotty, M. (1998). Foundations of Social Research: Meaning and Perspective in the Research Process. London: Sage Publications.

Csikszentmihalyi, M. (1980). Love and the Dynamics of Personal Growth. In: K. S. Pope (ed.), *On Love and Loving - Psychological Perspectives on the Nature and Experience of Romantic Love*. San Francisco: Jossey Bass Publishers, pp. 306-326.

Curtis, W.J. and Nelson, C.A. (2003). Toward Building a Better Brain: Neurobehavioral Outcomes, Mechanisms, and Processes of Environmental Enrichment. In: S. S. Luthar (ed.), *Resilience and Vulnerability: Adaptation in the Context of Childhood Adversities*. Cambridge, UK: Cambridge University Press, pp. 463–488.

Datchi, C. (2017). Masculinities, Fatherhood, and Desistance from Crime: Moderating and Mediating Processes Involved in Men's Criminal Conduct. *Journal of Men's Studies*, 25(1), pp. 44–69.

DCSF and MoJ (2007). *Children of Offenders Review*. London: Department for Children, Schools and Families and Ministry of Justice.

Deci, E. L. and Ryan, R. M. (2000). The 'what' and 'why' of Goal Pursuits: Human Needs and the Self-Determination of Behavior. *Psychological Inquiry*, 11, pp. 227–268.

DeKlyen, M., Speltz, M. L. and Greenberg, M. T. (1998). Fathering and Early Onset Conduct Problems: Positive and Negative Parenting, Father-Son Attachment, and the Marital Context. *Clinical Child and Family Psychology Review*, 1(1), pp. 3-21.

De Leon, G. (2000). *The Therapeutic Community. Theory, Model and Method*. New York: Springer Publishing Company.

Department for Education (2013). *Pupil absence in schools in England, including pupil characteristics*. [online] Available at: https://www.gov.uk/government/collections/statistics-pupil-absence [Accessed 24/10/2020]

De Viggiani, N. (2012). Trying to be Something you are not: Masculine Performance Within a Prison Setting. *Men and Masculinities*, 15(3), pp. 271-291.

De Zulueta, F. (1993). *From Pain to Violence. The Traumatic Roots of Destructiveness*. London: Whurr Publishers.

Dixon-Gordon, K., Harrison, N. and Roesch, R. (2012). Non-suicidal self-injury within offender populations: a systematic review. *International Journal of Forensic Mental Health*, 11(1), pp. 33-50.

Dodge, K. A. (2006). Translational Science in Action: Hostile Attributional Style and the Development of Aggressive Behavior Problems. *Developmental Psychopathology*, 18(3), pp. 791–814.

Donaldson, S. (2001). A million jockers, punks and queens, In: D. Sabo, T.A. Kupers and W. London (eds.), *Prison Masculinities*. Philadelphia: Temple University Press, pp. 118-126.

Dotson, M. J., Hyatt, E. M. (2008). Understanding Dog–Human Companionship. *Journal of Business Research*, 61, pp. 457–466.

Downie, J. M., Hay, D. A., Horner, B. J., Wichmann, H. and Hislop, A. L. (2010). Children Living with Their Grandparents: Resilience and Wellbeing. *International Journal for Social Welfare*, 19, pp. 8–22.

Drake, D. and Crewe, B. (2008). Deprivations/Pains of Imprisonment. In: Y. Jewkes and J. Bennett (eds.), *Dictionary of Prisons and Punishment*. Cullompton: Willan Publishing.

Drake, D., (2012). *Prisons, Punishment and the Pursuit of Security*. Basingstoke: Palgrave Macmillan.

Drake, D., Darke, S. and Earle, R. (2015). Sociology of Prison Life: Recent Perspectives from the United Kingdom. In: J. Wright (ed.), *International Encyclopaedia of Social and Behavioural Sciences* (2nd ed.), pp. 924-929.

Drakich, J., (1989). In Search of the Better Parent: The Social Construction of Ideologies of Fatherhood, *Canadian Journal of Women and the Law*, 3, pp. 69-87.

Dunning, A. (2006). Grandparents - An Intergenerational Resource for Families. *Journal of Intergenerational Relationships*, 4(1), pp. 127-135.

Earle, R. (2014) Insider and Out: Making Sense of a Prison Experience and a Research Experience. *Qualitative Inquiry*, 20(4), pp. 429–438.

Edinete, M. R. and Tudge, J. (2013). Urie Bronfenbrenner's Theory of Human Development: Its Evolution from Ecology to Bioecology. *Journal of Family Theory & Review*, 5, pp. 243–258.

Einat, T. and Chen, G. (2012). What's love got to do with it? Sex in a female maximum security prison. *The Prison Journal*, 92(4), pp. 484-505.

Einstein, A., Nathan, O. and Norden, H. (1960). *Einstein on Peace*. New York: Simon and Schuster.

Eriksson, K. (1990). *Pro Caritate. En lägesbestämning av caritativ vard (Caritative Caring. A Positional Analysis)*. Vasa: Department of Caring Science, Abo Akademi University.

Eriksson, K., Raholm, M. and Thorkildsen, K. (2013). The Substance of Love When Encountering Suffering: An Interpretative Research Synthesis with an Abductive Approach. *Scandinavian Journal of Caring Sciences*, 27, pp. 449–459.

Evans, T. and Wallace, P. (2008). A Prison within a Prison? The Masculinity Narratives of Male Prisoners. *Men and Masculinities*, 10(4), pp. 484-507.

Fair, H. and Jacobson J. (2016). Family Connections: a review of learning from the Winston Churchill Memorial Trust Prison Reform Fellowships – Part II. London: Institute for Criminal Policy Research, Birkbeck, University of London.

Farrington, D.P. (1997). Human Development and Criminal Careers. In: M. Maguire, R. Morgan and R. Reiner (eds.), *The Oxford Handbook of Criminology*. Oxford: Clarendon Press, pp. 361 408.

Felitti, V. J., Anda, R. F. and Nordenberg, D. (1998). Relationship of Childhood Abuse and Household Dysfunction to Many of the Leading Causes of Death in Adults. The Adverse Childhood Experiences (ACE) Study. *American Journal for Preventive Medicine*, 14(4), pp. 245–258.

Fergusson, D. M. and Horwood, L. J. (2003). Resilience to Childhood Adversity: Results of a 21-year Study. In: S.S. Luthar (ed.), *Resilience and Vulnerability: Adaptation in the Context of Childhood Adversities*.Cambridge, UK: Cambridge University Press, pp. 130–155.

Fineman, M. (2004). *The Autonomy Myth: A Theory of Dependency.* New York: The Free Press.

Flanagan, T.J. (1980). The Pains of long- term Imprisonment: A Comparison of British and American Perspectives. *British Journal of Criminology*, 20(2), pp. 148-160.

Foucault, M. (1978). *The History of Sexuality, Vol. 1.* New York: Pantheon.

Frankl, V. E. (1985). *Man's Search for Meaning.* New York: Simon & Schuster Inc.

Fredrickson, B. (2013). *Love 2.0.* New York: Hudson Street Press.

Freeden, M. (2003). *Ideology: A Very Short Introduction.* Oxford: Oxford University Press.

Fromm, E. (1995). *The Art of Loving.* London: Thorsons, Harper Collins Publishers.

Frosh, S., Phoenix, A. and Pattman, R. (2002). *Young Masculinities.* Basingstoke: Palgrave.

Fulu, E., Warner, X. and Meidema, S. (2013).Why do Some Men Use Violence Against Women and how can we Prevent it? Quantitative Findings from the United Nations Multi-Country Study on Men and Violence in Asia and the Pacific. Partners for Prevention. [online] Available at: http://www.partners4prevention.org/about-prevention/research/men-and-violence-study [Accessed 02/09/2018]

Gadd, D., Karstedt, S. and Messner, S.F. (eds.) (2012). *The SAGE Handbook of Criminological Research Methods.* London: SAGE Publications.

Garcia-Moreno, C., Jansen, H. A. F. M., Ellsberg, M. (2005). WHO Multi-Country Study on Women's Health and Domestic Violence Against Women: Initial Results on Prevalence, Health Outcomes and Women's Responses. Geneva, Switzerland:World Health Organization [online] Available at: http://www.who.int/reproductive health/publications/violence/24159358X/en/ [Accessed 02/09/2018].

Garland, D. (1990). *Punishment and Modern Society - A study in Social Theory.* Oxford: Clarendon Press.

Garmezy, N., Masten, A. S. and Tellegen, A. (1984). The Study of Stress and Competence in Children: A Building Block for Developmental Psychopathology. *Child Development*, 55(1), pp. 97-111.

Garner, B. (2015). Interpersonal Coffee Drinking, Communication Rituals. *International Journal of Marketing and Business Communication*, 4(4), pp. 1-12.

Gauke, D. (2018). *Prisons Reform Speech – GOV.UK. Ministry of Justice.* [online] Available at: https://www.gov.uk/government/speeches/prisons-reform-speech [Accessed: 02/01/2020]

Gerhardt, S. (2004). *Why Love Matters. How Affection Shapes a Baby's Brain.* East Sussex: Brunner-Routledge.

Giddens, A. (1979). Central Problems in Social Theory: Action, Structure, and Contradiction in Social Analysis. Berkeley, CA: University of California Press.

Giddens, A. (1992). *The Transformation of Intimacy.* Cambridge: Polity Press.

Gilligan, C. (1982). *In a Different Voice. Psychological Theory and Women's Development.* Cambridge: Harvard University Press.

Gilligan, C. (1995). Hearing the Difference: Theorizing Connection. *Hypatia,* 10(2), pp. 120–27.

Gilligan, J. (2015). A Modest Proposal to Universalize the Insanity Defense and Replace Prisons and Punishment with Treatment and Education. *International Journal of Applied Psychoanalytic Studies,* 12(2), pp. 134–152.

Giordano, P., Cernkovich, S. and Rudolph, J. (2002). Gender, Crime, and Desistance: Toward a Theory of Cognitive Transformation. *American Journal of Sociology,* 107(4), pp. 990–1064.

Giordano, P., Schroeder, R. and Cernkovich, S. (2007). Emotions and Crime over the Life Course: A Neo-Meadian Perspective on Criminal Continuity and Change. *American Journal of Sociology,* 112(6), pp. 1603-1661.

Gladiator. (2000). Ridley Scott. dir. USA: Scott Free Productions, Red Wagon Entertainment.

Goffman, E. (1959). *The Presentation of Self in Everyday Life.* New York: Double Day.

Goffman, E. (1961). Asylums: Essays on the Social Situation of Mental Patients and Other Inmates. London: Aldine Transaction.

Gramsci, A. (1971). In: Q. Hoare and G. Newell-Smith (eds.), *Selections from the Prison Notebooks of Antonio Gramsci.* New York: International Publishers.

Griggs, J., Tan, J. P., Buchanan, A., Attar-Schwartz, S. and Flouri, E. (2010). They've Always Been There for me: Grandparental Involvement and Child Well-Being. *Children and Society,* 24, pp. 200–214.

Grignon, C. (2001). Commensality and Social Morphology: An Essay of Typology. In: P. Scholliers (ed.), *Food, Drink and Identity. Cooking, Eating and Drinking in Europe Since the Middle Ages.* Oxford: Berg, pp. 23-36.

Grossi, R. (2018). Love as a Disadvantage in Law. *Journal of Law and Society* 45(2), pp. 205-225.

Grounds, A. (1996). Psychiatric Morbidity amongst Long-Term Prisoners and Their Families. Unpublished manuscript. Cambridge: Institute of Criminology.

Grounds, A. (2004). Understanding the effects of wrongful imprisonment. In: M. Tonry (ed.) Crime and Justice: A Review of Research, Volume 32. Chicago, IL: University of Chicago Press, pp. 1-58.

Guessous, F., Hooper, N. and Moorthy, U. (2001). Religion in Prisons 1999 and 2000 (England and Wales). London: Home Office. [online] Available at: https://webarchive.nationalarchives.gov.uk/20101208203730/http://rds.ho meoffice.gov.uk/rds/pdfs/hosb1501.pdf [Accessed 15/06/2020]

Hairston, C. F. (1991). Family Ties During Imprisonment: Important to Whom and for What. *Journal of Sociology and Social Welfare,* 18, pp. 87–104.

Hamric, A. B., Arras, J. D. and Mohrmann, M. E. (2015). Must we be Courageous? *Hastings Center Report,* 45(3), pp. 33–40.

Haney, C. (2003). The Psychological Impact of Incarceration: Implications for Post-Prison Adjustment. In: J. Travis and M. Waul (eds.), *Prisoners Once Removed: The Impact of Incarceration and Reentry on Children, Families, and Communities.* Washington DC: Urban Institute Press, pp. 33–66.

Haney, C. (2005). The contextual revolution in psychology and the question of prison effects. In: A. Liebling and S. Maruna (eds.), *The Effects of Imprisonment.* Cullompton: Willan, pp. 66-93.

Harker, L., Jütte, S., Murphy, T., Bentley, H., Miller, P., Fitch, K. (2013). *How safe are our children?* London: NSPCC

Harlow, H. F. and Zimmermann, R. R. (1958). The Development of Affective Responsiveness in Infant Monkeys. *Proceedings of the American Philosophical Society*, 102, pp. 501-509.

Harrison, T. and Clarke, D. (1992). The Northfield Experiments. *British Journal of Psychiatry*, 160, pp. 698-708.

Hays, S. (1996). *The Cultural Contradictions of Motherhood.* New Haven, CT: Yale University Press.

Helm, B. W. (2010). *Love, Friendship and the Self. Intimacy, Identification, and the Social Nature of Persons.* Oxford: Oxford University Press.

Herman, B. H. and Panksepp, J. (1978). Effects of Morphine and Naloxone on Separation Distress and Approach Attachment: Evidence for Opiate Mediation of Social Affect. *Pharmacology, Biochemistry and Behavior*, 9(2), pp. 213-220.

Hiller, M.L., Knight, K. and Simpson, D. (1999). Prison-based substance abuse treatment, residential aftercare and recidivism. *Addiction*, 94, pp. 833-842.

Hirsch, J. S. and Wardlow, H. (2006). *Modern Loves. The Anthropology of Romantic Courtship and Companionate Marriage.* Michigan: University of Michigan Press.

HM Government (2011). *No Health Without Mental Health: A Cross-Government Mental Health Outcomes Strategy for People of All Ages.* Mental Health and Disability Department of Health [online]. Available at: https://www.gov.uk/government/uploads/system/uploads/attachment_data/file/213761/dh_124058.pdf [Accessed: 21/09/2017]

HMPPS (2011). *Prison Service Instruction (PSI) 15/2011: Management and Security at Visits.* [online] Available at: https://www.justice.gov.uk/offenders/psis/prison-service-instructions-2011 [Accessed 02/09/2018]

HMPPS (2011). *Prison Service Instruction (PSI) 16/2011: Providing Visits and Services to Visitors.* [online] Available at: https://www.justice.gov.uk/offenders/psis/prison-service-instructions-2011 [Accessed 02/09/2018]

HMPPS (2016). *Prison Service Instruction (PSI) 04/2016: The Interception of Communications in Prisons and Security Measures.* [online] Available at: https://www.justice.gov.uk/downloads/offenders/psipso/psi-2016/PSI-04-2016-The-Interception-of-Communications-in-Prisons-and-Security-Measures.doc [Accessed 02/09/2018]

Holden, C. (2005). Sex and the Suffering Brain. *Science*, 308, pp. 1574–1577.

Honneth, A. (1987). Critical Theory. In: A. Giddens and J. H. Turner (eds), *Social Theory Today.* Stanford: Stanford University Press, pp. 347-382.

Honneth, A. (1995). The Struggle for Recognition – The Moral Grammar of Social Conflicts. Cambridge: Polity Press.

Hooks, B. (2000). *All About Love.* New York: William Morrow & Co.

Horkheimer, M. (1972). *Critical Theory.* New York: Seabury Press.

Howard League for Penal Reform (2013). *The Howard League – Consensual sex among men in prison.* [online] Available at: https://howardleague.org/publications/consensual-sex-among-men-in-prison/ [Accessed 02/07/2020]

Howard League for Penal Reform (2020) *The Howard League – Justice and Fairness in Prisons* [online] Available at: https://howardleague.org/our-campaigns/transform-prisons/justice-and-fairness-in-prisons/ [Accessed 01/06/2020]

Hüther, G. (2006). *The Compassionate Brain - How Empathy Creates Intelligence.* Boston Massachusetts: Shambala Publications Inc.

Illouz, E. (2012). *Why Love Hurts.* Cambridge: Polity Press.

Irwin, J., and Cressey, D. R. (1962). Thieves, convicts and the inmate culture. *Social Problems,* 10, pp. 142-155.

Irwin, J., and Owen, B. (2005). Harm and the Contemporary Prison. In: A. Liebling and S. Maruna (eds.), *The Effects of Imprisonment.* Cullompton: Willan Publishing.

Jackson, M. (1995) You are not alone. Robert Kelly. *HIStory.* [Single]. Los Angeles: Epic.

Jackson, S. and Martin, P. Y. (1998). Surviving the Care System: Education and Resilience. *Journal of Adolescence,* 21, pp. 569–583.

Jacobs, J. (1977). *Stateville: The penitentiary in mass society.* Chicago, IL: The University of Chicago Press.

Jamieson, R. and Grounds, A. (2005). Release and adjustment: perspectives from studies of wrongly convicted and politically motivated prisoners. In: A. Liebling and S. Maruna (eds.), *The Effects of Imprisonment.* Cullompton: Willan Publishing, pp. 1-32.

Jardine, C. (2018). Constructing and Maintaining Family in the Context of Imprisonment, *The British Journal of Criminology,* 58(1), pp. 114–131.

Jewkes, Y. (2005a). Men Behind Bars: 'Doing' Masculinity as an Adaptation to Imprisonment. *Men and Masculinities,* 8(1), pp. 44-63.

Jewkes, Y. (2005b). Loss, Liminality and the Life Sentence: Managing Identity Through a Disrupted Lifecourse. In: A. Liebling and S. Maruna (eds.), *The Effects of Imprisonment.* Cullompton: Willan, pp. 366–388.

Jewkes, Y. (2018). Just design: Healthy prisons and the architecture of hope. *Australian and New Zealand Journal of Criminology,* 51(3), pp. 319-338.

Johnston, D. D. and Swanson, D. H. (2006). Constructing the 'Good Mother': The Experience of Mothering Ideologies by Work Status. *Sex Roles,* 54(7), pp. 509-519.

Johnson, R., and McGunigall-Smith, S. (2008). Life Without Parole, America's Other Death Penalty: Notes on Life Under Sentence of Death by Incarceration. *Prison Journal,* 88(2), pp. 328–346.

Jones, M. (1952). Social Psychiatry. A Study of Therapeutic Communities. London: Tavistock Publications.

Jones, M. (1968). Beyond the Therapeutic Community. Social Learning and Social Psychiatry. New Haven, Connecticut: Yale University Press.

Jones, M. (1982). *The Process of Change.* Boston: Routlegde and Kegan Paul.

Jones, S. (2000). *Understanding Violent Crime.* Philadelphia: Open University Press.

Kaufmann, J. (2012). *Love Online.* Cambridge: Polity Press.

Kennard, D. (1998). *An Introduction to Therapeutic Communities*. London: Jessica Kingsley Publishers.

Kennison, S. M. and Ponce-Garcia, E. (2012). The Role of Childhood Relationships with Older Adults in Reducing Risk-Taking by Young Adults. *Journal of Intergenerational Relationships*, 10, pp. 22–33.

Kierkegaard, S. (2009). *Works of Love*. New York: Harper Perennial.

King, V., Elder, G. H. and Conger, R. D. (2000). Church, Family, and Friends. In: G. H. Elder and R. D. Conger (eds.), *Children of the Land: Adversity and Success in Rural America*. Chicago, IL: University of Chicago Press, pp. 151-159.

King, R. (2005). The effects of supermax custody. In: A. Liebling and S. Maruna (eds.), *The Effects of Imprisonment*. Cullompton: Willan, pp. 118-145.

King, R. and Liebling, A. (2008). Doing Research in Prison. In: R. King and E. Wincup (eds.), *Doing Research on Crime and Justice*. Oxford: Oxford University Press, pp. 431-455.

King, R. and Wincup, E. (2008). The process of criminological research. In: King, R. and Wincup, E. (eds.), *Doing Research on Crime and Justice*. Oxford: Oxford University Press, pp. 13- 44.

Kittay, E. F. (1999). *Love's Labor*. New York: Routledge.

Kornhaber, A. and Woodward, K. L. (1981). *Grandparents / Grandchildren: The Vital Connection*. Garden City, NY: Doubleday.

Kraut, R. (2008). Plato on Love. In: G. Fine (ed.), *The Oxford Handbook of Plato*. Oxford: Oxford University Press, pp. 286-310.

Kupers, T. A. (2006). How to Create Madness in Prison. In: D. Jones (ed.), *Humane Prisons*. Oxford: Radcliffe Publishing, pp. 47-59.

Lamb, M. E., Pleck, J. H., Charnov, E. L. and Levine, J. A. (1987). A Biosocial Perspective on Paternal Behavior and Involvement. In: J. B. Lancaster, J. Altmann, A. S. Rossi and L. R. Sherrod (eds.), *Parenting Across the Lifespan: Biosocial Dimensions*. New York: Aldine de Gruyter, pp. 111–142.

Laub, J. H., Nagin, D. S. and Sampson, R. J. (1998), Trajectories of Change in Criminal Offending: Good Marriages and the Desistance Process. *American Sociological Review*, 63, pp. 225–38.

Lee, T. R., Mancini, J. A. and Maxwell, J. W. (1990). Sibling Relationships in Adulthood: Contact Patterns and Motivations. *Journal of Marriage and the Family*, 52, pp. 431–440.

Lewis, C. S. (1960). *The Four Loves*. London: Geoffrey Bles.

Lewis, T., Amini, F. and Lannon, R. (2000). *A General Theory of Love*. New York: Vintage Books.

Liebling, A. (1992). *Suicides in Prison*. London: Routledge.

Liebling, A. (1999). Prison Suicide and Prisoner Coping. *Crime and Justice, 26*, pp. 283-359.

Liebling, A. (2001). Whose Side are we on? Theory, Practice and Allegiances in Prison research. *British Journal of Criminology*, 41, pp. 472-484.

Liebling, A., Price, D. and Shefer, G. (2001). *The Prison Officer*. Leyhill: Prison Service and Waterside Press.

Liebling, A. and Arnold, H. (2004). *Prisons and their Moral Performance: A Study of Values, Quality and Prison Life*. Oxford: Oxford University Press.

Liebling, A., Durie, L., Stiles, A. and Tait, S. (2005). Revisiting Prison Suicide: The Role of Fairness and Distress. In: A. Liebling and S. Maruna (eds.), *The Effects of Imprisonment.* Cullompton: Willan Publishing.

Liebling, A. and Maruna, S. (2005). Introduction: The effects of imprisonment revisited. In: A. Liebling and S. Maruna (eds.), *The Effects of Imprisonment.* Cullompton: Willan, pp. 1-32.

Liebling, A. (2007). Prison Suicide and its Prevention. In: Y. Jewkes (ed.), *Handbook on Prisons.* Cullompton: Willan Publishing, pp. 423-446.

Liebling, A., Arnold, H. and Straub, C. (2011). *An Exploration of Staff-Prisoner Relationships at HMP Whitemoor: 12 years on.* Home Office [online] Available at: http://www.justice.gov.uk/publications/research-and-analysis/moj/an-exploration-of-staff-prisoner-relationships-at-hmp-whitemoor-12-years-on [Accessed 06/05/2015]

Liebling, A. (2014). Moral and Philosophical Problems of Long-Term Imprisonment. *Studies in Christian Ethics,* 27(3), pp. 258–273.

Light, M., Grant, E., Hopkins, K. (2013). Gender differences in substance misuse and mental health amongst prisoners. London: Ministry of Justice.

Light, R. and Campbell, B. (2007). Prisoners' Families: Still Forgotten Victims? *Journal of Social Welfare and Family Law,* 28(3-4), pp. 297-308.

Lincoln, Y. S. and Guba, E. G. (1985). *Naturalistic Inquiry.* Newbury Park, CA: Sage Publications.

Lindemann, E. (1944). Symptomatology and Management of Acute Grief. *American Journal of Psychiatry,* 101(2), pp. 141-148.

Lindemann, H. (2014) *Holding and Letting Go. The Social Practice of Personal Identities.* Oxford: Oxford University Press.

Lipton, D.S. (1998). Therapeutic community treatment programming in corrections. *Psychology Crime & Law,* 4, pp. 213-263.

Lloyd, C. (1990). Suicide and Self-Injury in prison: A literature review. Home Office Research Study 115. HMSO BOOKS: London

Loader, I., Karstedt, S. and Strang, H. (eds.) (2011). *Emotions, Crime and Justice.* London: SAGE Publications.

Lopez-Cantero, P. (2020) *Your love story is a narrative that gets written in tandem – Aeon Ideas* [online] Available at: https://aeon.co/ideas/your-love-story-is-a-narrative-that-gets-written-in-tandem [Accessed 01/06/2020]

Lopoo, L. M. and Western, B. (2005). Incarceration and the Formation of Stability in Marital Unions. *Journal of Marriage and Family,* 67, pp. 721–734.

Luhmann, N. (2012). *Introduction to Systems Theory.* Cambridge: Polity Press.

Lurigio, A.J. (2000). Drug treatment availability and effectiveness. Studies of the general and criminal justice populations. *Criminal Justice and Behavior,* 27, pp. 495-528.

Lynch, J. P. and Sabol, W. (2001). *Prisoner Reentry in Perspective.* Washington DC: The Urban Institute.

Mackenzie, S., Rubin, E. and Gómez, C. (2016). *Prison is one place you don't want your sexuality. Champ pénal/Penal field XIII* [online] Available at: http://journals.openedition.org/champpenal/9364 [Accessed: 01/07/2020]

Maeve, K. (1999). The social construction of love and sexuality in a women's prison, *Advances in Nursing Science*, 21(3), pp. 46–65.

Maluccio, A., Abamczyk, L. and Thomlison, B. (1996). Family Reunification of Children in out-of-home Care: Research Perspectives. *Children and Youth Services Review*, 18, pp. 4–5.

Man on Fire. (2004). Tony Scott. dir. USA: Regency Enterprises, Scott Free Productions.

Mansson, D. H. and Booth-Butterfield, M. (2011). Grandparents' Expressions of Affection for their Grandchildren: Examining Grandchildren's Relational Attitudes and Behaviors. *Southern Communication Journal*, 76, pp. 424–442.

Mansson, D. H. (2013). College Students' Mental Health and their Received Affection from their Grandparents. *Communication Research Reports*, 30, pp. 157–168.

Mansson, D. H., Floyd, K. and Soliz, J. (2017). Affectionate Communication is Associated with Emotional and Relational Resources in the Grandparent-Grandchild Relationship, *Journal of Intergenerational Relationships*, 15(2), pp. 85-103.

Marsiglio, W., Amato, P. Day, R. D. and Lamb M. E. (2000). Scholarship on Fatherhood in the 1990s and Beyond. *Journal of Marriage and Family*, 62, pp. 1173-1191.

Martin, A. M. (2015). Love, Incorporated. *Ethical Theory and Moral Practice*, 18, pp. 691–702.

Maruna, S. (2004). What's love got to do with it? *Safer Society - Nacro*, 22, pp. 12-14.

Maslow, A. H. (1987). *Motivation and Personality.* London: Harper Collins Publishers.

Maycock M. and Hunt K. (eds.) (2018). *New Perspectives on Prison Masculinities.* London: Palgrave Macmillan.

McEwen, B. S. and Gianaros, P. J. (2011). Stress- and Allostasis-Induced Brain Plasticity. *Annual Review of Medicine*, 62, pp. 431–445.

Meek, R. (2008). Experiences of Younger Siblings of Young Men in Prison, *Children and Society*, 22, pp. 265-77.

Mehta, R. (2014). So Many Ways to Love You/Self. *International Feminist Journal of Politics*, 16(2), pp. 181-198.

Messing, J. T. (2006). From the Child's Perspective: A Qualitative Analysis of Kinship Care Placements. *Children and Youth Services Review*, 28, pp. 1415–1434.

Milligan, T. (2011). *Love.* Durham: Acumen Publishing.

Milliken, A. (2018). Refining Moral Agency: Insights from Moral Psychology and Moral Philosophy. *Nursing Philosophy*, 19(1), pp. 1-6.

Mills, C.W. (2000). *The Sociological Imagination.* New York: Oxford University Press.

Mills, A. and Codd, H. (2008). Prisoners' families and offender management: Mobilizing social capital, *Probation Journal*, 55(1), pp. 9-24.

Ministry of Justice (2010). Compendium of reoffending statistics, London: Ministry of Justice.

Ministry of Justice (2012). The pre-custody employment, training and education status of newly sentenced prisoners. London: Ministry of Justice.

Ministry of Justice (2012). *Estimating the prevalence of disability amongst prisoners.* London: Ministry of Justice.

Ministry of Justice (2012). *Prisoners' childhood and family backgrounds.* London: Ministry of Justice.

Ministry of Justice (2018). *Safety in Custody Statistics Quarterly January 2018.* London: Ministry of Justice.

Ministry of Justice (2020). Offender Management Statistics Bulletin, England and Wales. [online] Available at: https://assets.publishing.service.gov.uk/government/uploads/system/uploads/attachment_data/file/861889/Offender_Management_Statistics_Quarterly_Q3_2019.pdf [Accessed 24/10/2020].

Morey, M. and Crewe, B. (2018). Work, Intimacy and Prisoner Masculinities. In: M. Maycock and K. Hunt (eds.), *New Perspectives on Prison Masculinities.* London: Palgrave Macmillan.

Murray, J. (2005). The effects of imprisonment on families and children, In: A. Liebling and S. Maruna (eds.), *The effects of Imprisonment.* Cullompton: Willan Publishing, pp. 442-462.

My Blueberry Nights. (2007). Wong Kar-Wai. dir. USA: Block 2 Pictures, Studio Canal, Jet Tone Films.

Naser, R. L. and La Vigne, N. G. (2006). Family Support in the Prisoner Reentry Process: Expectations and Realities. *Journal of Offender Rehabilitation,* 43, pp. 93–106.

National Offender Management Service (NOMS) (2005). The National Reducing Re-Offending Action Plan: A cross-government outline plan for reducing re-offending. NOMS [online] Available at: https://www.ihop.org.uk/ci/fattach/get/51/0/filename/Reducing+Reoffending+Delivery+Plan+2009.pdf [Accessed 02/09/2018]

National Scientific Council on the Developing Child (2011). *Excessive Stress Disrupts the Architecture of the Developing Brain: Working Paper #3.* Center on the Developing Child, Harvard University. [online] Available at: https://developingchild.harvard.edu/wp-content/uploads/2005/05/Stress_Disrupts_Architecture_Developing_Brain-1.pdf [Accessed 02/09/2018].

Neef, M. (1991). *Human Scale Development: Conception, Application and Further Reflections.* New York: The Apex Press.

Neher, A. (1991). Maslow's Theory of Motivation - A Critique. *Journal of Humanistic*

Nelson, S. (2004). The Search for the Good in Nursing? The Burden of Ethical Expertise. *Nursing Philosophy,* 5(1), pp. 12–22.

Newbold, G., Ian Ross, J., Jones, R. S., Richards, S. C., and Lenza, M. (2014). Prison Research from the Inside: The Role of Convict Autoethnography. *Qualitative Inquiry, 20*(4), pp. 439–448.

Newton, C. (1994). Gender Theory and Prison Sociology: Using Theories of Masculinities to Interpret the Sociology of Prisons for Men. *The Howard Journal,* 33(3), pp. 193-202.

Nicks, S. (1979). Sara. Fleetwood Mac. *Tusk.* [Single]. Los Angeles: Warner Bros. Records Inc.

Niven, S. and Stewart, D. (2005). *Resettlement Outcomes on Release from Prison in 2003.* Home Office Research Findings 248. [online] Available at: http://webarchive.nationalarchives.gov.uk/20110218143221/http://rds.homeoffice.gov.uk/rds/pdfs05/r248.pdf [Accessed 02/09/2018].

Nussbaum, M. (1995). Emotions and Women's Capabilities. In: M. Nussbaum and J. Glover (eds.), *Women, Culture and Development: A Study of Human Capabilities.* Oxford: Oxford University Press.

Okin, S. M. (1989). *Justice, Gender, and the Family.* New York: Basic Books.

O'Neil, N. B. and Klein, S. (2008). *Grandparents and Grandchildren: Do Grandparents Socialize their Grandchildren about Attitudes Surrounding Love and Marriage?* Paper presented at the annual meeting of the National Communication Association, San Diego, CA.

Palmer, R. (1986) Addicted to Love. Robert Palmer. *Riptide.* [Single] London: Island.

Parkes, C. M. (2006). *Love and Loss.* London: Routledge.

Parsons, T. (1951). *The Social System.* New York: The Free Press.

Paterline, B. A. and Petersen, D. M. (1999). Structural and Social Psychological Determinants of Prisonization. *Journal of Criminal Justice,* 27, pp. 427-441.

Peck, S. (2006). *The Road Less Travelled.* London: Arrow Books.

Pennebaker, J. W. (1989). Confession, Inhibition, and Disease. *Advances in Experimental Social Psychology,* 22, pp. 211–244.

Perlman, F. T. (1999). Love and its Objects: On the Contributions of Psychoanalysis of Martin S. Bergmann. *Psychoanalytic Review,* 86(6), pp. 1-35.

Peterson, C. and Seligman, M. E. P. (2004). *Character Strengths and Virtues: A Handbook and Classification.* Oxford: Oxford University Press.

PLATO (1998) *Symposium.* In: Rowe, C. J. (ed.), Warminster, England: Aris & Phillips Ltd.

Plutchik, R. (1994). *The Psychology and Biology of Emotion.* New York: Harper Collins.

Pollack, W. (1995). Deconstructing Dis-Identification: Rethinking Psychoanalytic Concepts of Male Development. *Psychoanalysis and Psychotherapy,* 12(1), pp. 30-45.

Pope, L. (2018). *Self-harm by adult men in prison: A rapid evidence assessment (REA). HMPPS. Ministry of Justice Analytical Series.* [online] Available at: https://assets.publishing.service.gov.uk/government/uploads/system/uplo ads/attachment_data/file/739521/self-harm-adult-men-prison-2018.pdf [Accessed 02/07/2020]

Prison Reform Trust (2019). *Bromley Briefings Prison Factfile. Autumn 2019.* Prison Reform Trust [online] Available at: http://www.prisonreformtrust.org.uk/Portals/ 0/Documents/Bromley%20Briefings/Winter%202019%20Factfile%20web.pdf [Accessed 24/10/2020]

Prison Reform Trust (2020). Prison Rules. Prison Reform Trust [online] Available at: http://www.prisonreformtrust.org.uk/ForPrisonersFamilies/Prisonrules#:~:text =Prison%20Service%20Orders%20(PSOs)%20are,issued%20until%2031%20July %202009.&text=Prison%20Service%20Instructions%20(PSIs)%20contain,also% 20introduce%20amendments%20to%20PSOs. [Accessed 24/10/2020]

Rawlings, B. (1999). Therapeutic communities in prisons. *Policy and Politics,* 27, pp. 97- 111.

Restive, S. P. (1977). An Evolutionary Sociology of Love. *International Journal of Sociology of the Family,* 7, pp. 233-245.

Ricciardelli, R. (2015). Establishing and Asserting Masculinities in Canadian Penitentiaries. *Journal of Gender Studies*, 24(2), pp. 170-191.

Richards, B. (1978). The Experience of long-term Imprisonment: An Exploratory Investigation. *British Journal of Criminology*, 18(2), pp. 162-169.

Robbins, B. D. (2013). *Dietrich von Hildebrandes Phenomenology of Love: Contributions to a Hermeneutics of Love.* [online] Available at: http://www.say brook.edu/blog/2013/01/15/01-15-13/ [Accessed 09/02/2020]

Rocque, M., Bierie, D. M., Posick, C. and MacKenzie, D. L. (2013). Unraveling Change: Social Bonds and Recidivism among Released Offenders. *Victims and Offenders*, 8, pp. 209–30.

Rogers, C. (1959). A Theory of Therapy, Personality and Interpersonal Relationships as Developed in the Client-Centered Framework. In: S. Koch (ed.), *Psychology: A study of a science. Vol. 3: Formulations of the person and the social context.* New York: McGraw Hill, pp. 185-252.

Roy, K. M. and Dyson, O. L. (2005). Gatekeeping in Context: Babymama Drama and the Involvement of Incarcerated Fathers. *Fathering*, 3, pp. 289-310.

Rubin, Z. (1973). *Liking and Loving. An Invitation to Social Psychology.* New York: Holt, Rinehart and Winston.

Ruskin, J. (1985). Unto this Last and Other Writings by John Ruskin. London: Penguin Books.

Rykkje, L., Eriksson, K. and Raholm, M. and (2015). Love in Connectedness: A Theoretical Study. *SAGE Open*, 5(1), pp. 1-11.

Sampson, R. J. and Laub, J. H. (1993). *Crime in the Making: Pathways and Turning Points through Life.* Harvard: Harvard University Press.

Sapsford, R. (1978) Life sentence prisoners: psychological changes during sentence, *British Journal of Criminology*, 18 (2), pp. 128-145.

Sapsford, R. (1983) *Life Sentence Prisoners.* Milton Keynes: Open University Press.

Schinkel, M. (2014). Being Imprisoned: Punishment, Adaptation and Desistance. Palgrave Macmillan.

Schmitz, R. M. (2016). Constructing Men as Fathers: A Content Analysis of Formulations of Fatherhood in Parenting Magazines. *Journal of Men's Studies*, 24(1) pp. 3–23.

Schofield, G., Biggart, L., Ward, E. and Larsson, B. (2015). Looked After Children and Offending: An Exploration of Risk, Resilience and the Role of Social Cognition. *Children and Youth Services Review*, 51, pp. 125–133.

Schore, A. (2017). All our Sons: The Develomental Neurobiology and Neuroendocrinology of Boys at Risk. *Infant Mental Health Journal*, 38(1), pp. 15-52.

Schroeder, T., Roskies, A. L. and Nichols, S. (2010). Moral Motivation. In: J. M. Doris (ed.), *The Moral Psychology Handbook.* Oxford, UK: Oxford University Press, pp. 72–110.

Schuetz, A. and Luckmann, T. (1973). *The Structures of the Life-World.* Evanston: Northwestern University Press.

Scott, D. and Codd, H. (2010). *Controversial Issues in Prisons.* Maidenhead: McGraw-Hill, Open University Press.

Scott, D. (2015). Walking amongst the Graves of the Living: Reflections about Doing Prison Research from an Abolitionist Perspective, In: D.H. Drake, R.

Earle and J. Sloan (eds.), *The Palgrave Handbook of Prison Ethnography*. London: Palgrave Macmillan, pp.40-58.

Seale, C. (1999). *The Quality of Qualitative Research*. London: Sage Publications.

Sevenhuijsen, S. (1998). *Citizenship and the Ethics of Care: Feminist Considerations on Justice, Morality and Politics*. London: Routledge.

Shonkoff, J. P. and Garner, A. S. (2012). The Lifelong Effects of Early Childhood Adversity and Toxic Stress, *PEDIATRICS*, 129(1), pp. 232-246.

Sikweyiya, Y, Nduna, M., Khuzwayo, N., Mthombeni, A. and Mashamba-Thompson, T. P. (2016). Gender-Based Violence and Absent Fathers: A Scoping Review Protocol. BMJ Open, 6(6), pp. 1-6.

Sloan, J. (2016). Masculinities and the Adult Male Prison Experience. London: Palgrave Macmillan.

Smith, C. (2003). *Moral, Believing Animals. Human Personhood and Culture*. Oxford: Oxford University Press.

Smith, C. (2010). *What is a Person?* Chicago: The University of Chicago Press.

Smith, C. and Wincup, E. (2000). Breaking in: Researching Criminal Justice Institutions for Women. In: King, R. and Wincup, E. (eds.), *Doing Research on Crime and Justice*. Oxford: Oxford University Press, pp. 331- 349.

Smith, P.S. (2014). When the Innocent are Punished. Palgrave Studies in Prisons and Penology. London: Palgrave Macmillan.

Snow, L. (2002). Prisoners' motives for self-injury and attempted suicide. *The British Journal of Forensic Practice*, 4(4), pp. 18-29.

Soliz, J. (2008). Intergenerational Support and the Role of Grandparents in Post-Divorce Families: Retrospective Accounts of Young Adult Grandchildren. *Qualitative Research Reports in Communication*, 9, pp. 72–80.

Spalek, B. and El-Hassan, S. (2007). Muslim Converts in Prison. *The Howard Journal of Criminal Justice*, 46, pp. 99-114.

Sparks, J. R. and Bottoms, A. E. (1995). Legitimacy and Order in Prisons. *The British Journal of Sociology*, 46(1), pp. 45-62.

Sparks, R. (2007) The Politics of Imprisonment. In: Y. Jewkes (ed.) *Handbook on Prisons*. Cullompton: Willan Publishing, pp. 73-94.

Spice Girls. (1997). *Mama*. Matt Rowe, Richard Stannard, Spice Girls. *Spice*. [Single]. UK: Virgin.

Stevens, A. (2011) A 'Very Decent Nick': Ethical Treatment in Prison Based Democratic Therapeutic Communities, *Journal of Forensic Psychology Practice*, 11(2-3), pp. 124-150.

Stevens, A. (2012). 'I am the person now I was always meant to be': Identity reconstruction and narrative reframing in therapeutic community prisons. *Criminology & Criminal Justice*, 12, pp. 527-547.

Stevens, A. (2016). *Sex in prison Experiences of former prisoners. A report for the Howard League's Commission on Sex in Prison*. [online] Available at: https://howardleague.org/wp-content/uploads/2016/03/Sex-in-prison-web.pdf [Accessed 06/06/2020]

Summers, J. A., Boller, K., Schiffman, R. F. and Raikes, H. H. (2006). The Meaning of 'Good Fatherhood': Low-Income Fathers' Social Constructions of their Roles. *Parenting*, 6, pp. 145-165.

Suttie, D. (1935). *The Origins of Love and Hate.* London: Free Association Books.

Sykes., G. (1958). *The Society of Captives: A Study of a Maximum-Security Prison.* Princeton: Princeton University Press.

Takseva, T. (2017). Mother Love, Maternal Ambivalence, and the Possibility of Empowered Mothering. *Hypatia,* 32(1), pp. 152-168.

Taylor, P., and Williams, S. (2014). Sentencing reform and prisoner mental health. *Prison Service Journal,* 211, pp. 43-49.

Taylor, S. J. (1991). Leaving the Field: Research, Relationships, and Responsibilities. In: W. B. Shaffir and R. A. Stebbins (eds.), *Experiencing Fieldwork: An inside View of Qualitative Research.* London: Sage Publications, pp. 238-247.

Tillich, P. (1954). *Love, Power, and Justice.* Oxford, England: Oxford University Press.

Toch, H. (1975). *Men in Crisis. Human Breakdowns in Prison.* London: Aldine Transaction.

Toch, H. (1982). Studying and Reducing Stress. In: R. Johnson and H. Toch (eds.), *The Pains of Imprisonment.* Beverly Hills: Sage Publications, pp. 25-44.

Toch, H. (1992). *Living in Prison. The Ecology of Survival.* Washington DC: American Psychological Association.

Toch, H. (1998). Hypermasculinity and Prison Violence. In: L. Bowker (ed.), *Masculinities and Violence.* London: SAGE Publications.

Toch, H. (2006). Is there a Future for Humane Imprisonment? In: D. Jones (ed.), *Humane Prisons.* Oxford: Radcliffe Publishing, pp. 1-10.

Tolstoy, L. (2011). *The Awakening: The Resurrection.* Auckland: The Floating Press.

Travis, J. (2005). *But They All Come Back: Facing the Challenges of Prisoner Reentry.* Washington DC: The Urban Institute Press.

Tronto, J. (1987). Beyond Gender Difference to a Theory of Care. *Signs,* 12(4), pp. 644–663.

Tronto, J. (1993). *Moral Boundaries: A Political Argument for an Ethic of Care.* New York: Routledge.

Turley, C., Payne, C. and Webster, S. (2013). *Enabling Features of Psychologically Informed Planned Environments.* NatCen Social Research, Ministry of Justice Analytical Series.

Ungar, M., Ghazinour, M. and Richter, J. (2013). Annual Research Review: What is Resilience within the Social Ecology of Human Development? *Journal of Child Psychology and Psychiatry,* 54(4), pp, 348–366.

Utting, W. (1997). *People Like Us.* London: Stationery Office.

Vandevelde, S., Broekaert, E., Yates, R., and Kooyman, M. (2004). The Development of the Therapeutic Community in Correctional Establishments: A Comparative Retrospective Account of the 'DEMOCRATIC' Maxwell Jones TC and the Hierarchical Concept-Based TC in Prison. *International Journal of Social Psychiatry, 50*(1), pp. 66–79.

Visher, C. A. and Travis, J. (2003). Transitions from Prison to Community: Understanding Individual Pathways. *Annual Review of Sociology,* 29, pp. 89–113.

Walker, L. O. and Avant, K. C. (1994). *Strategies for Theory Construction in Nursing.* New Jersey: Pearson Prentice Hall.

Warr, J. (2012). Afterword. In: Crewe, B. and Bennett, J. (eds.), *The Prisoner.* Abingdon: Routledge, pp. 142-148.

Watts, J. H. (2008). Emotion, Empathy and Exit: Reflections on Doing Ethnographic Qualitative Research on Sensitive Topics. *Medical Sociology*, 32), pp. 3-14.

Weingarten, K. (1997). The Mother's Voice: Strengthening Intimacy in Families. New York: Guilford.

Wekerle, C., Waechter, R. and Chung, R. (2012). Contexts of Vulnerability and Resilience: Childhood Maltreatment, Cognitive Functioning and Close Relationships. In: M. Ungar (ed.), *The Social Ecology of Resilience: A Handbook of Theory and Practice*. New York, NY: Springer, pp. 187–198.

Welsh Government (2013). *Absenteeism by pupil characteristics 2011/12*. Cardiff: Welsh Government.

Whiting, J. B. and Lee, R. E. (2003). Voices from the System: A Qualitative Study of Foster Children's Stories. *Family Relations*, 52, pp. 288–295.

Wiehn, P. J. (1982). Mentally Ill Offenders: Prison's First Casualties. In: R. Johnson and H. Toch (eds.), *The Pains of Imprisonment*. Beverly Hills: Sage Publications, pp. 221-241.

Wiles, N. J., Zammit, S., Bebbington, P., Singleton, N., Meltzer, H., Lewis, G. (2006). Self-reported psychotic symptoms in the general population. *The British Journal of Psychiatry* (188) pp. 519-526.

Williams, D. D. (1968). *The Spirit and the Forms of Love*. Welwyn, Herts: James Nisbet and Company.

Willis, P. (1977). *Learning to Labour*. Aldershot: Gower.

Wilson, J. (1963). *Thinking with Concepts*. Cambridge: Cambridge University Press.

Wiscott, R. and Kopera-Frye, K. (2000). Sharing the Culture: Adult Grandchildren's Perceptions of Intergenerational Relations. *International Journal of Aging and Human Development*, 51, pp. 199–215.

Wolff, N. and Draine, J. (2004). Dynamics of Social Capital of Prisoners and Community Re-Entry: Ties That Bind? *Journal of Correctional Health Care*, 10(3), 457-90.

Woodward, K. (2003). Representations of Motherhood. In: S. Early and G. Letherby (eds.), *Gender, Identity and Reproduction. Social Perspectives*. Basingstoke: Palgrave Macmillan Basingstoke, pp. 18-33.

World Health Organisation WHO (2012). Understanding and Addressing Violence Against Women: Intimate Partner Violence. Geneva: World Health Organization [online] Available at: http://www.who.int/reproductivehealth/topics/violence/vaw_series/en/ [Accessed 02/09/2018].

Wyse, J. B., Harding, D. J. and Morenoff, J. D. (2014). Romantic Relationships and Criminal Desistance: Pathways and Processes. *Sociological Forum*, 29(2), pp. 365–385.

Yar, M. (2012). Critical Criminology, Critical Theory and Social Harm. In: S. Hall and S. Winlow (eds.), *New Directions in Criminological Theory*. London: Routledge, pp. 52-65.

Zamble, E. and Porporino, E. J. (1988). *Coping, Behaviour and Adaptation in Prison Inmates*. New York: Springer-Verlag.

Zurn, C. F. (2015). *Axel Honneth – A Critical Theory of the Social*. Cambridge, UK: Polity Press.

Index

Lightning Source UK Ltd.
Milton Keynes UK
UKHW022221110522
402858UK00010B/512/J